17TH LANCERS.

THE

REGIMENTAL RECORDS

OF THE

BRITISH ARMY

A Historical Résumé Chronologically Arranged

OF

TITLES, CAMPAIGNS, HONOURS, UNIFORMS,

FACINGS, BADGES, NICKNAMES, ETC.

BY

JOHN S. FARMER.

ILLUSTRATIONS
BY
RICHARD SIMKIN

CRÉCY BOOKS

First published by Grant Richards, 1901
Reprint edition published by Crécy, 1984

Crécy Books
an imprint of
CATHEDRAL PUBLISHING LTD.
96 Queens Road, Clifton, Bristol BS8 1NS

ISBN 0 947554 03 3

British Library Cataloguing in Publication Data

Farmer, J. S.
The regimental records of the British Army
1660–1901.
1. Great Britain. *Army*—History
I. Title
355.3'1'0941   UA649

ISBN 0–947554–03–3

Printed in Great Britain by
REDWOOD BURN LTD.
Trowbridge, Wiltshire

CONTENTS.

ILLUSTRATIONS.

THE CAVALRY.

The First Life Guards.

TITLES.

1660–85. The 1st, or His Majesty's Own Troop of Guards.
1685–1788. The 1st Troop of Life Guards of Horse.
1788 (from). The 1st Life Guards.

PRINCIPAL CAMPAIGNS, BATTLES, &c.

* "Honours" on the Colours.

1673. Maestricht.	1693. Neer Landen.	1815. Netherlands.
1690. Boyne.	*1743. Dettingen.	*1882. Egypt.
1692–97. Flanders.	*1812–14. Peninsula.	*1882. Tel-el-Kebir.
1692. Steenkirk.	*1815. Waterloo.	1884–5. Khartoum.

UNIFORM.—Scarlet (from 1660). Facings, Blue (probably from 1660, certainly from 1679). Plume, White.

REGIMENTAL BADGE.—"The Royal Arms."

NICKNAMES.—"The Cheeses :" when re-modelled in 1788 the veterans declined to serve, alleging that the regiments of Life Guards then consisted of cheesemongers, not gentlemen ; also "The Piccadilly Butchers" (having been called out to quell the Piccadilly Riots in 1810); also "Tin Bellies" (from the cuirasses); also "The Patent Safeties."

NOTES.—Raised in Holland by Charles II., when in exile, and composed mainly of (80) Cavaliers who had fought in the Civil War under Charles I. The 3rd and 4th (Scots) Troops of Life Guards, added at the Union, but disbanded in 1746, saw much service in Flanders (1742–47). The 1st Life Guards wore cuirasses from its formation to 1698, and resumed them in 1821.

The Second Life Guards.

THE ROYAL ARMS.

TITLES.

1660–70. The 3rd, or The Duke of Albemarle's Troop of Guards.
1670–85. The 2nd, or The Queen's Troop of Guards.
1685–1746. The 2nd Troop of Life Guards of Horse : disbanded.
1788 (from). The 2nd Life Guards.

PRINCIPAL CAMPAIGNS, BATTLES, &c.

* " Honours " on the Colours.

1673. Maestricht.
1689–90. Flanders.
1689. Walcourt.
1694–97. Flanders.
1695. Namur.
*1743. Dettingen.

*1812–14. Peninsula.
*1815. Waterloo.
1815. Netherlands.
*1882. Egypt.
*1882. Tel-el-Kebir.
1884–5. Khartoum.

The Second Life Guards—*continued.*

UNIFORM.—Scarlet (from 1690). Facings, Sea-green (1660 to 1690–1742) in honour of Queen Catherine ; blue (since 1742). Plume, White.

REGIMENTAL BADGE.—" The Royal Arms."

NICKNAME.—(See note under " The First Life Guards.")

NOTES.—Similar in origin to " The First Life Guards," and composed of Cavaliers who, having served under Charles I., fled at his death, entering the Spanish service as " His Royal Highness The Duke of York's Troop of Guards."   In 1659 (when peace was declared) they retired to the Netherlands until reorganised by Charles II. in 1660 as " The Third Troop of Life Guards."   In 1670 it became " The Second Troop," and was disbanded in 1746. Cuirasses were worn from 1660 to 1698, and were resumed in 1821.

BIBLIOGRAPHY.—*Historical Record of the Life Guards.* Containing an Account of the Formation of the Corps in the year 1660, and of its Subsequent Services to 1835. [London : Clowes, 1836.]

The Royal Horse Guards (The Blues).

THE ROYAL ARMS.

TITLES.

1661–87. The Royal Regiment of Horse.
1687–1750. The Royal Regiment of Horse Guards.
1750–1819. The Royal Horse Guards Blue.
1819 (from). The Royal Horse Guards (The Blues).

PRINCIPAL CAMPAIGNS, BATTLES, &c.

* "Honours" on the Colours.

1685. Sedgemoor.
1689–90. Flanders.
1689. Walcourt.
1690. Boyne.
1691. Aughrim.
1742–45. Flanders.
*1743. Dettingen.
1745. Fontenoy.
1758–62. Germany.
1759. Minden.
1760. Warbourg.

1761. Kirk Denkern.
1762. Wilhelmstahl.
1794–95. Flanders.
1794. Cateau.
1794. Tournay.
*1812–14. Peninsula.
1813. Vittoria.
*1815. Waterloo.
1815. Netherlands.
*1882. Egypt.
*1882. Tel-el-Kebir.

1884–85. Nile.

The Royal Horse Guards—*continued.*

UNIFORM.—Blue with Scarlet facings (from 1661). Plume, Red.

REGIMENTAL BADGE—" The Royal Arms."

NICKNAMES.—(1) The Oxford Blues, *circa* 1690, from its Colonel's name, the Earl of Oxford, and in distinction to a blue habited Dutch Regiment commanded by the Earl of Portland ; (2) The Blue Guards (1742–45) during the Campaign in Flanders ; and (3) The Blues—a present day sobriquet.

NOTES.—This is the only Cavalry Regiment now extant which formed part of the Parliamentary Army against Charles I., being then known as Colonel Unton Crook's Regiment. King William IV. presented the regiment with a Standard emblazoned with " Dettingen," " Minden," " Warbourg," " Cateau." It wore cuirasses from 1691 to 1698, and resumed them in 1821.

BIBLIOGRAPHY.—*An Historical Record of The Royal Regiment of Horse Guards, or Oxford Blues.* Its Services, and the transactions in which it has been engaged from its first establishment to the present time. By EDMUND PACKE, late Captain Royal Horse Guards. [London : Clowes, 1834.]

The First (The King's) Dragoon Guards.

THE ROYAL CYPHER WITHIN THE GARTER.

TITLES.

1685–1714. The Queen's (or 2nd) Regiment of Horse.
1714–46. The King's Own Regiment of Horse.
1746 (from). The 1st King's Dragoon Guards.

PRINCIPAL CAMPAIGNS, BATTLES, &c.

* " Honours " on the Colours.

1685. Sedgemoor.
1690. Boyne.
1691. Aughrim.
1692–97. Flanders.
1693. Neer Landen.
1695. Namur.
1702–14. Germany.
1702. Liége.
1703. Huy.
1704. Schellenberg.
*1704. Blenheim.
1705. Neer Hespen.
*1706. Ramilies.
*1708. Oudenarde.
1708. Lisle.
1709. Tournay.
*1709. Malplaquet.
1711. Bouchain.
1742–46. Flanders.
*1743. Dettingen.
1745. Fontenoy.
1758–63. Germany.

The First (The King's) Dragoon Guards—*continued.*

PRINCIPAL CAMPAIGNS, BATTLES, &c.—*continued.*

1759. Minden.

1760. Corbach.

1760. Warbourg.

1761. Kirk Denkern.

1762. Wilhelmstahl.

1763. Grœbenstein.

1793–95. Flanders.

1794. Cateau.

1794. Tournay.

*1815. Waterloo.

1815. Netherlands.

*1855. Sevastopol.

1860. China.

*1860. Taku Forts.

*1860. Pekin.

*1879. South Africa.

UNIFORM.—Scarlet (from 1685). Facings, Bright Yellow (the Stuart livery, 1685–1714); Blue Velvet (from 1714). Helmet-plume, Red.

REGIMENTAL BADGE.—"The Royal Cypher within the Garter."

NICKNAMES.—"The Trades' Union" (because employed to quell trade riots in the middle of the present century); "The K. D. G.'s" (its initials).

NOTES.—Raised chiefly near London during the Monmouth Rebellion, and designated "The Queen's Regiment of Horse," the then "King's Regiment" being "The Blues." Cuirasses were worn to 1698, and from 1704 to 1714. The title was changed in 1714 in recognition of brilliant services in Flanders and Germany.

BIBLIOGRAPHY.—*Historical Records of the 1st or King's Regiment of Dragoon Guards.* From 1685 to 1836 Illustrated with plates. [London: Clowes, 1837.]

The Second Dragoon Guards (Queen's Bays).

THE ROYAL CYPHER WITHIN THE GARTER.

TITLES.

1685–88. Colonel the Earl of Peterborough's Regiment of Horse.
1688–1715. The Third Regiment of Horse : also by its Colonel's name.
1715–27. The Princess of Wales's Own Royal Regiment of Horse.
1727–46. The Queen's Own Royal Regiment of Horse.
1746–1872. The 2nd Queen's Dragoon Guards.
1872 (from). The 2nd Dragoon Guards (Queen's Bays).

PRINCIPAL CAMPAIGNS, BATTLES, &c.

* " Honours " on the Colours.

1690. Boyne.
1691. Aughrim.
1695. Namur.
1704–10. Spain.
1707. Almanza.
1710. Almanara.

1710. Saragosa.
1715. Stuart Rebellion.
1745. Stuart Rebellion.
1760–3. Germany.
1760. Corbach.
1760. Cassel.

The Second Dragoon Guards (Queen's Bays)—*continued.*

PRINCIPAL CAMPAIGNS, BATTLES, &c.—*continued.*

1760. Warbourg.
1761. Kirk Denkern.
1762. Wilhelmstahl.
1763. Grœbenstein.
1793. Valenciennes.
1793–5. Flanders.

1793. Dunkirk.
1794. Cateau.
1794. Tournay.
1809. Flushing.
1858. Indian Mutiny.
*1858. Lucknow.

UNIFORM.—Scarlet (from 1685). Facings, Scarlet (1685–1742); Buff (1742–1784); Black Velvet (1784–1855); Buff (from 1855). Helmet-plume, Black.

REGIMENTAL BADGE.—"The Royal Cypher within the Garter."

NICKNAME.—"The Bays." In 1767 an order was made for long-tailed bay mounts, other heavy regiments, except the Scots Greys, having black horses. Also "The Rusty Buckles."

NOTES.—Raised near London, amongst other troops of horse, by Sir Nicholas Wentworth. For three years cuirasses were worn. The facings were changed to buff between 1690 and 1742. The title in 1715 was given in recognition of its services at the battle of Preston; and that of 1727 on the accession of George II.

BIBLIOGRAPHY.—*Historical Record of the 2nd, or Queen's Regiment of Dragoon Guards (Queen's Bays), 1685–1837.* Illustrated with plates. [London: Clowes, 1837.]

The Third (The Prince of Wales's) Dragoon Guards.

THE PRINCE OF WALES'S PLUME.

THE RISING SUN.

TITLES.

1685–87.   Colonel The Earl of Plymouth's Regiment of Horse.
1687–1746.   The 4th Regiment of Horse ; also by its Colonel's name.
1746–65.   The 3rd Regiment of Dragoon Guards.
1765 (from).   The 3rd (Prince of Wales's) Dragoon Guards.

PRINCIPAL CAMPAIGNS, BATTLES, &c.

* " Honours " on the Colours.

1689. Scotland.	*1708. Oudenarde.
1691–97. Flanders.	1708. Wynendale.
1692. Steenkirk.	1708. Landau.
1693. Neer Landen.	1708. Huy.
1695. Namur.	1708. Lisle.
1702–14. Germany.	*1709. Malplaquet.
1704. Schellenberg.	1710. Douai.
*1704. Blenheim.	1710. Bethune.
1705. Neer Hespen.	1710. Aire.
*1706. Ramilies.	1711. Bouchain.

The Third (The Prince of Wales's) Dragoon Guards—*continued.*

PRINCIPAL CAMPAIGNS, BATTLES, &c.—*continued.*

1715 & '45. Jacobite risings.
1758–63. Germany.
1759. Minden.
1760. Corbach.
1760. Warbourg.
1761. Kirk-Denkern.
1762. Wilhelmstahl.
1763. Grœbenstein.
1793–95. Flanders.

1793. Dunkirk.
1794. Cateau.
1794. Tournay.
*1809–14. Peninsula.
*1809. Talavera.
*1811. Albuera.
*1813. Vittoria.
*1868. Abyssinia.

UNIFORM.—Scarlet (from 1685). Facings, Light Green (1685–1765); White (in 1765 and 1785); Blue (in 1818–19); Yellow (from 1819). Helmet-plume, Black and Red.

REGIMENTAL BADGES.—"The Royal Cypher and Crown" (from 1685–1765); "The Prince of Wales's Plume," "The Rising Sun," "The Red Dragon"—ancient badges of the Princes of Wales.

NICKNAME.—"The Old Canaries" (from the facings).

NOTES.—Formed from old Regiments of Horse raised in Worcestershire, Oxfordshire, Bedfordshire, and at St. Albans and Dorking; it wore cuirasses from 1685–88 and from 1704–14.

BIBLIOGRAPHY.—*Historical Record of the 3rd, or Prince of Wales's Regiment of Dragoon Guards.* Illustrated with Plates. [London: Clowes, 1838.]

THE RED DRAGON.

The Fourth (Royal Irish) Dragoon Guards.

" Quis Separabit."

THE HARP AND CROWN.　　　THE STAR OF ST. PATRICK.

TITLES.

1685–90.　Colonel The Earl of Arran's Cuirassiers ; also the 6th Horse.
1690–1746.　The Fifth Horse.
1746–88.　The 1st Irish Horse, or The Blue Horse.
1788 (from).　The 4th Royal Irish Regiment of Dragoon Guards.

PRINCIPAL CAMPAIGNS, BATTLES, &c.

* " Honours " on the Colours.

1691–97. Flanders.
1692. Steenkirk.
1693. Neer Landen.
1695. Namur.
*1811–13. Peninsula.
1812. Ciudad Rodrigo.
1812. Badajos.

1812. Leira.
*1854. Balaclava.
*1855. Sevastopol.
*1882. Egypt.
*1882. Tel-el-Kebir.
1884–5. Nile.

The Fourth (Royal Irish) Dragoon Guards—*continued.*

UNIFORM.—Scarlet (from 1685). Facings, White (1685–1715); Light Blue (1715–1768); Dark Blue (from 1768). Helmet-plume, White.

REGIMENTAL BADGES.—" The Harp and Crown" (on the accession of Her Majesty), "The Star of St. Patrick." "The White Horse of Hanover" also appears on the Standard. Motto : " *Quis separabit.*"

NOTES.—Raised in various English counties—at London, Lichfield, Grantham, Durham, and Morpeth. Cuirasses were worn in 1685. Its title, in 1788, was bestowed for long service in Ireland.

BIBLIOGRAPHY.—*Historical Record of the 4th, or Royal Irish Regiment of Dragoon Guards.* 1685–1838. [London : Longman, 1839.]

THE WHITE HORSE OF HANOVER.

The Fifth (Princess Charlotte of Wales's) Dragoon Guards.

" Vestigia Nulla Retrorsum."

TITLES.

1685–87. Colonel The Duke of Shrewsbury's Regiment of Horse.

1687–1717. The Sixth (or Seventh) Regiment of Horse : also by its Colonel's name (in 1687, Coy's Horse ; in 1794, Cadogan's Horse).

1717–88. The 2nd (or " Green ") Irish Horse.

1788–1804. The Fifth Dragoon Guards.

1804 (from). The Fifth or Princess Charlotte of Wales's Dragoon Guards.

PRINCIPAL CAMPAIGNS, BATTLES, &c.

* " Honours " on the Colours.

1690. Boyne.	1711. Aire.
1692. Enghien.	1711. St. Venant.
1695. Namur.	1711. Quesnoy.
1703–12. Germany.	1759–62. Germany.
1704. Schellenberg.	1794–5. Flanders.
*1704. Blenheim.	1794. Cateau.
1705. Neer Hespen.	*1811–14. Peninsula.
*1706. Ramilies.	1812. Badajos.
*1708. Oudenarde.	1812. Llerena.
1708. Lisle.	*1812. Salamanca.
*1709. Malplaquet.	1812. Burgos.
1709. Tournay.	*1813. Vittoria.
1709. Mons.	*1814. Toulouse.
1710. Douay.	*1854. Balaclava.
1711. Bouchain.	*1855. Sevastopol.
1711. Bethune.	1900. South Africa.

The Fifth (Princess Charlotte of Wales's) Dragoon Guards

—*continued*.

UNIFORM.—Scarlet (from 1685).   Facings, Buff (1685–1717) ; Dark Green (from 1717). Helmet-plume, Red and White.

REGIMENTAL DEVICE.—$\frac{V}{D.G.}$ within the Garter, surrounded by " Princess Charlotte of Wales." Motto, *Vestigia nulla retrorsum* (borne by John Hampden's Regiment in the Civil War).

NICKNAME.—" The Green Horse " (*see* Titles).

NOTES.—Originally raised as a Troop of Cuirassiers at Lichfield, Kingston-on-Thames, Chester, Bridgnorth, Bristol, &c.   It wore cuirasses till 1688, and resumed them from 1707–14.   It captured four Standards at the battle of Blenheim.

BIBLIOGRAPHY.—*Historical Record of the 5th, or Princess Charlotte of Wales's Dragoon Guards*, 1685–1838.   Illustrated with plates.   [London : Longman, 1839.]

The Sixth Dragoon Guards (Carabiniers).

THE REGIMENTAL DEVICE.

TITLES.

1685–90.   The Queen Dowager's Regiment of Horse.
1690–92.   The 8th (or 9th) Regiment of Horse.
1692–1745.   The King's Carabiniers.
1745–88.   The 3rd Irish Horse.
1788 (from).   The 6th Dragoon Guards (Carabiniers).

PRINCIPAL CAMPAIGNS, BATTLES, &c.

* "Honours" on the Colours.

1685. Monmouth's Rebellion.
1690. Boyne.
1691. Aughrim.
1692–97. Flanders.
1692. Steenkirk.
1693. Neer Landen.
1695. Namur.
1702–14. Germany.

1704. Schellenberg.
*1704. Blenheim.
1705. Neer Hespen.
*1705. Ramilies.
*1708. Oudenarde.
*1709. Malplaquet.
1710. Douay.
1760–63. Germany.

The Sixth Dragoon Guards (Carabiniers)—*continued.*

PRINCIPAL CAMPAIGNS, BATTLES, &c.—*continued.*

1760. Warbourg.
1762. Wilhelmstahl.
1793–95. Flanders.
1794. Tournay.
1806. Buenos Ayres.

1807. Monte Video.
*1855. Sevastopol.
1857–58. Indian Mutiny.
*1857. Delhi.
*1879–80. Afghanistan.

1900. South Africa.

UNIFORM.—Scarlet (1685–1853); Blue (from 1853). Facings, Sea-green (1685–1715, the favourite colour of Catherine, the Consort of Charles II.); Yellow (1715–68); White Cloth (from 1768). Helmet-plume, White.

REGIMENTAL DEVICE.—(Unrecognised in *Regulations*) The Crossed Carabines, within the Garter, surrounded by "Sixth Dragoon Guards," with Scroll underneath— "The Carabiniers."

NICKNAMES.—"The Carbs," also "Tichborne's Own" (at the time of the trial of Arthur Orton, Sir Roger Tichborne, Bart., having served in the Regiment).

NOTES.—The Sixth Carabiniers (formerly the First Regiment of Carabiniers in recognition of its gallantry in Ireland, in 1690–91) was formed from Troops of Horse raised in various English counties, and received its title in 1692 from being armed with Carabines. At Ramilies it captured the colours of the Royal Bombardiers, and was conspicuous at Neer Landen for its gallantry.

BIBLIOGRAPHY—*Historical Record of the 6th Regiment of Dragoon Guards, or Carabiniers.* 1685–1839. Illustrated with plates. [London: Longman. 1839.] *A Continuation of the Historical Record of the 6th Dragoon Guards (Carabiniers).* By Captain [now Major] A. SPROT. [Chatham: Gale and Polden. 1888.

The Seventh (The Princess Royal's) Dragoon Guards.

" Quo fata vocant."

TITLES.

1688–90. Colonel The Earl of Devonshire's Regiment of Horse ; also the Tenth Horse.

1690-91. Schomberg's Horse.

1691–1720 (?). Colonel The Duke of Leinster's (or The Eighth) Horse ; also (on succession to the title) Schomberg's Horse.

1720–46. Colonel (afterwards Earl) Ligonier's (The Eighth) Horse.

1746–88. The 4th (or " Black ") Irish Horse.

1788 (from). The 7th (The Princess Royal's) Dragoon Guards.

PRINCIPAL CAMPAIGNS, BATTLES, &c.

* " Honours" on the Colours.

1690. Boyne.
1692–97. Flanders.
1695. Namur.
1702–14. Germany.
1702. Venloo.
1702. Ruremonde.
1702. Liége.
1704. Schellenberg.
*1704. Blenheim.
1705. Neer Hespen.
*1706. Ramilies.
*1708. Oudenarde.
1708. Lisle.
1709. Tournay.
*1709. Malplaquet.
1710. Douay.
1710. Bethune.
1710. St. Venant.

1710. Aire.
1711. Bouchain.
1711. Quesnoy.
1742–45. Flanders.
*1743. Dettingen.
1745. Fontenoy.
1760–63. Germany.
1760. Warbourg.
1761. Kirk Denkern.
1762. Wilhelmstahl.
1763. Grœbenstein.
*1846–47. South Africa (1st Kaffir War).
1857–58. Indian Mutiny.
*1882–84. Egypt.
1882. Kassassin.
*1882. Tel-el-Kebir.
1900. South Africa.

The Seventh (The Princess Royal's) Dragoon Guards—*continued.*

UNIFORM.—Scarlet (from 1688). Facings, Black (from 1688). Note.—In 1751 the waistcoat and breeches were buff. Helmet-plume, Black and White.

REGIMENTAL BADGE.—"The Coronet of Her Majesty the Empress and Queen of Germany and Prussia as Princess Royal of Great Britain and Ireland." Quite recently, however, the War Office has sanctioned the adoption, as the regimental badge, of the arms, crest, and motto of Earl Ligonier. Previously the regimental device consisted of $\frac{7}{DG}$ within the Garter circumscribed " Princess Royal's." On buttons and other appointments the Royal Cypher, Crown, and Wreath are used in one or other combination.

NICKNAMES.—" The Black Horse " or " The Blacks " (from its facings). " Ligoniers " (from its Colonel's name, 1720–49). "Straw-boots" (from wearing wisps of straw to keep the legs dry when engaged in quelling agricultural riots in the south of England, *tempus* George II.). " The Virgin Mary's Body-Guard " (in the reign of George II. the regiment was sent to assist the Archduchess Maria Theresa of Austria).

NOTES.—In 1688 five regiments of horse raised by James II. marched with the Earl of Devonshire to meet the Princess Anne on her flight from London. On accession she commissioned them for permanent service. They wore cuirasses till 1699, and resumed them from 1707–14.

BIBLIOGRAPHY.—*Historical Record of the 7th, or Princess Royal's Regiment of Dragoon Guards.* 1685–1839. Illustrated with plates. [London : Longman. 1839.]

The First (Royal) Dragoons.

"Spectemur Agendo."

THE CREST OF ENGLAND.

THE EAGLE (for capture at Waterloo).

TITLES.

1661–83.   The Tangiers Horse.
1683–90.   The King's Own Royal Regiment of Dragoons.
1690–1751.   The Royal Regiment of Dragoons.
1751 (from).   The 1st (Royal) Dragoons.

PRINCIPAL CAMPAIGNS, BATTLES, &c.

* " Honours " on the Colours.

1661–84. Tangiers.
1690. Boyne.
1694–97. Flanders.
1695. Namur.
1705–10. Spain.
1705. Valencia d'Alcantara.
1706. Albuquerque.
1706. Barcelona.
1707. Almanzar.

1710. Almanara.
1710. Saragossa.
1715. Jacobite rising.
1742–45. Flanders
*1743. Dettingen.
1745. Fontenoy.
1760–63. Germany.
1760. Warbourg.
1760. Campen.

The First (Royal) Dragoons—*continued.*

PRINCIPAL CAMPAIGNS, BATTLES, &c.—*continued.*

1762. Wilhelmstahl.

1793–95. Flanders.

1794. Cateau.

1794. Villers-en-Couché.

1794. Tournay.

*1809–14. Peninsula.

1811. Fuentes d'Onor.

1812. Salamanca.

1813. Vittoria.

1814. Toulouse.

*1815. Waterloo.

1815. Netherlands.

*1854. Balaclava.

*1855. Sevastopol.

1884. Egypt.

1900. South Africa.

UNIFORM.—Scarlet (from 1683). Facings, Dark Blue (from 1683). Helmet-plume, Black.

REGIMENTAL BADGE.—The "Crest of England" within the Garter, circumscribed by "*Spectemur agendo*" and surmounted by a crown (Hanoverian). Also "an Eagle," in commemoration of the capture of the Eagle of the 105th French Regiment at Waterloo.

NICKNAME.—"The Bird-catchers" (also borne by The Second Dragoons and The Royal Irish Fusiliers).

NOTES.—Originating in the Troops of Horse engaged in the defence of Tangiers from 1662 to 1684, the First Royal Dragoons have since figured in nearly every campaign with conspicuous bravery. Among its captured standards are, one from the Moors in 1664, that of the "Mousquetaires Noirs" at the battle of Dettingen, and a French Eagle (see above) at the battle of Waterloo. In 1894 the Emperor of Germany was appointed Colonel-in-Chief.

BIBLIOGRAPHY.—*Historical Record of the 1st or Royal Regiment of Dragoons.* To 1839. Illustrated with plates. [London: Longmans. 1840.]

Historical Record of the 1st, or The Royal Regiment of Dragoons. By General de Ainslie, Colonel of the Regiment. Illustrated with plates. [London: Chapman & Hall. 1887.]

The Second Dragoons (Royal Scots Greys).

"Second to None."

THE THISTLE.

WATERLOO.

TITLES.

1678–1737. The Royal Regiment of Scots Dragoons; also (*c.* 1702)
"The Grey Dragoons," and "The Scots Regiment of White Horses."
1737–51. The Royal Regiment of North British Dragoons.
1751–1866. The 2nd, or Royal North British Dragoons.
1866–77. The 2nd Royal North British Dragoons (Scots Greys).
1877 (from). The 2nd Dragoons (Royal Scots Greys).

PRINCIPAL CAMPAIGNS, BATTLES, &c.

* "Honours" on the Colours.

1694–97. Flanders.
1702–13. Germany.
1704. Schellenberg.
*1704. Blenheim.
1705. Neer Hespen.

*1706. Ramilies.
*1708. Oudenarde.
*1709. Malplaquet.
1711. Bouchain.
1715. Jacobite rising.

The Second Dragoons (Royal Scots Greys)—*continued.*

PRINCIPAL CAMPAIGNS, BATTLES, &c.—*continued.*

1742–48. Flanders.
*1743. Dettingen.
1745. Fontenoy.
1746. Roucoux.
1747. Val.
1758–63. Germany.
1759. Minden.
1760. Warbourg.
1761. Kirk Denkern.
1762. Wilhelmstahl.

1763. Grœbenstein.
1793–95. Flanders.
1794. Tournay.
*1815. Waterloo.
1815. Netherlands.
*1854. Balaclava.
1854. Inkerman.
1855. Tchernaya.
*1855. Sevastopol.
1900. South Africa.

UNIFORM.—Probably Stone-Grey when raised, and afterwards changed to Scarlet. Facings, Blue. Plume, White.

REGIMENTAL BADGES.—"The Thistle" within the Circle, and the motto of St. Andrew, "*Nemo me impune lacessit*," surmounted by a Crown (from the Union of England and Scotland in 1707). Also "an Eagle," with "Waterloo" (from the capture of the Eagle of the 45th French Regiment). Also the motto, "Second to None" (from *circa* 1715).

NICKNAME.—"The Bubbly Jocks," also "The Bird-catchers" (*see* above: likewise applied to The First Dragoons and The Royal Irish Fusiliers).

NOTES.—The oldest regiment of Dragoons in the British Army, and raised in Scotland about 1678 from Troops of Horse, then added to the Establishment. At Ramilies it captured the "Colours" of the French Regiment-du-Roi, whence its distinction of Grenadier caps; also a Standard of the French Guards at Dettingen. At Waterloo, Napoleon spoke of them as "*Ces terribles chevaux gris.*" In 1894 the Emperor of Russia was appointed Colonel-in-Chief of The Greys.

BIBLIOGRAPHY.—*Historical Record of the Royal Regiment of Scots Dragoons, now the 2nd North British Dragoons.* To 1839. Illustrated with plates. [London: Longman. 1840.]

Johnson's *Illustrated Histories of Scottish Regiments.*

The Third (The King's Own) Hussars.

The White Horse (of Hanover) and Motto.

TITLES.

1685–1714. The Queen Consort's Own Regiment of Dragoons.
1714–51. The King's Own Regiment of Dragoons.
1751–1818. The 3rd (King's Own) Dragoons.
1818–61. The 3rd (King's Own) Light Dragoons.
1861 (from). The 3rd (King's Own) Hussars.

PRINCIPAL CAMPAIGNS, BATTLES, &c.

* " Honours " on the Colours.

1690. Boyne.	*1811–14. Peninsula.
1691. Aughrim.	1812. Llereena.
1694–97. Flanders.	*1812. Salamanca.
1695. Namur.	*1813. Vittoria.
1702–8. Spain.	1813. Pampeluna.
1707. Almanza.	*1814. Toulouse.
1715. Jacobite rising.	*1842. Cabool.
1742–45. Flanders.	*1845. Moodkee.
*1743. Dettingen.	*1845. Ferozeshah.
1745. Fontenoy.	*1846. Sobraon.
1745. Jacobite rising.	*1848–49. Punjaub.
1746. Culloden.	*1849. Chillianwallah.
1809. Flushing.	*1849. Goojerat.

The Third (The King's Own) Hussars—*continued.*

UNIFORM.—Scarlet with Blue facings (1685–1818) ; Blue with Scarlet facings (1818–30) ; Scarlet with Scarlet facings (1830–42) ; Blue with Scarlet facings (from 1842). Plume, White.

REGIMENTAL BADGE.—"The White Horse" (of Hanover) within the Garter, with the motto, "*Nec aspera terrent.*"

NICKNAMES.—"Lord Adam Gordon's Life Guards" (from its long detention in Scotland under that officer). "Bland's Dragoons" (in honour of a former Colonel).

NOTES.—The title on formation was bestowed in honour of the Queen Consort.

BIBLIOGRAPHY.—*Historical Record of the 3rd, or King's Own Regiment of Light Dragoons.* 1685–1846. Illustrated with plates. [London : Parker. 1847.]
Historical Record of the 3rd or King's Own Regiment of Light Dragoons. 1685–1857. Illustrated with plates. By George E. F. Kountze, Captain, half-pay, late 3rd Light Dragoons. [London : B. W. Cousins.]
Historical Records of the 3rd, or King's Own Light Dragoons. [Glasgow. 1833.]

The Fourth (The Queen's Own) Hussars.

TITLES.

1685–1702. The Princess Anne of Denmark's Dragoons.
1702–51. [Its Colonel's name] Hussars.
1751–88. The 4th Dragoons.
1788–1818. The 4th, or Queen's Own Dragoons.
1818–61. The 4th, or Queen's Own Light Dragoons.
1861 (from). The 4th, The Queen's Own Hussars.

PRINCIPAL CAMPAIGNS, BATTLES, &c.

* " Honours" on the Colours.

1689. Scotland.	*1809. Talavera.
1690. Boyne.	1810. Busaco.
1692–97. Flanders.	*1811. Albuera.
1692. Steenkirk.	1812. Llerena.
1693. Neer Landen.	*1812. Salamanca.
1695. Namur.	*1813. Vittoria.
1696. Rooselaar.	1814. Tarbes.
1706–8. Spain.	*1814. Toulouse.
1707. Almanza.	*1839. Afghanistan.
1715. Dunblane.	*1839. Ghuznee.
1742–48. Flanders.	*1854. Alma.
*1743. Dettingen.	*1854. Balaclava.
1747. Val.	*1854. Inkerman.
*1809–14. Peninsula.	*1855. Sevastopol.

The Fourth (The Queen's Own) Hussars—*continued.*

UNIFORM.—Scarlet (1685–1815); Blue (1818–30); Scarlet (1830–42); Blue (from 1842). Facings, Light Green (1685–1818); Yellow (1818–36); Light Green (1836–42); Scarlet (1842–61); Blue (from 1861). Helmet-plume, Scarlet.

REGIMENTAL BADGE.—None recognised in *Regulations*, but on pouch are worn the Royal Cypher and Crown; also on Shabraque Q. O. interlaced, surmounted by a Crown, and dominating the regimental number, $\frac{4}{H}$.

NICKNAME.—"Paget's Irregular Horse" (*circa* 1842) from its loose drill after return from India; in the first five years' service it lost, from fever and cholera, no less than 12 officers and 500 non-commissioned officers and men.

NOTES.—Formed from Independent Troops, raised at Warminster, Shaftesbury, Shepton Mallet, Glastonbury, Frome, Wincanton, Ilchester, and Bradford, and named in honour of the youngest daughter of William III. and Mary, afterwards Queen Anne.

BIBLIOGRAPHY.—*Historical Record of the 4th, or Queen's Own Regiment of Light Dragoons.* 1685–1842. Illustrated with a plate. [London: Parker. 1843.]

The Fifth (Royal Irish) Lancers.

"Quis Separabit."

THE HARP AND CROWN.

TITLES.

1689–1704. The Royal Irish Dragoons; also Wynne's Dragoons; also Brigadier Ross's Dragoons (under Marlborough).

1704–[?]. The Royal Dragoons of Ireland.

17[?]–1799. The 5th (Royal Irish) Dragoons; then disbanded, but revived in 1858.

1858 (from). The 5th (Royal Irish) Lancers.

PRINCIPAL CAMPAIGNS, BATTLES, &c.

* "Honours" on the Colours.

1690. Boyne.
1692–97. Flanders.
1702–14. Germany.
*1704. Blenheim.
*1706. Ramilies.
*1708. Oudenarde.

*1709. Malplaquet.
1743–8. Flanders.
1745. Fontenoy.
1798. Irish Rebellion.
*1885. Suakim.
1900. South Africa.

The Fifth (Royal Irish) Lancers—*continued*.

UNIFORM.—Scarlet with Blue facings (1689–1798); Blue with Scarlet facings (from 1858). Lancer-cap plume, Green.

REGIMENTAL BADGE.—"The Harp and Crown." Motto, "*Quis Separabit.*"

NICKNAMES.—"The Daily Advertisers"; also "The Redbreasts."

NOTES.—The old Fifth was the senior of the two regiments of Inniskilling Dragoons, the Second being now represented by the 6th (Inniskilling) Dragoons. Marlborough specially recognised its gallantry at Blenheim; and at Ramilies (with the Scots Greys) it captured two French battalions, for which it, like the Greys, was allowed to wear Grenadier caps. It was disbanded in 1798, after good service, on the discovery of a plot by new recruits to murder the officers and loyal men.

BIBLIOGRAPHY.—Short articles appear in *Grose's Military Antiquities*, and in the *Military Recorder*.

The Sixth (Inniskilling) Dragoons.

INNISKILLING.

TITLES.

1689–1751. Colonel Sir Albert Cunningham's [or its Colonel's name] Regiment of Dragoons; also (*circa* 1715) "The Black Dragoons" (from their black horses).

1751 (from). The 6th, or Inniskilling Dragoons.

PRINCIPAL CAMPAIGNS, BATTLES, &c.

* "Honours" on the Colours.

1690. Boyne.	1759. Minden.
1691. Aughrim.	1760. Warbourg.
1715. Dunblane.	1760. Campen.
1742–48. Flanders.	1761. Kirk Denkern.
*1743. Dettingen.	1762. Wilhelmstahl.
1745. Fontenoy.	1763. Grœbenstein.
1746. Roucoux.	1793–95. Flanders.
1747. Val.	1793. Valenciennes.
1758–63. Germany.	1793. Dunkirk.

The Sixth (Inniskilling) Dragoons—*continued*.

PRINCIPAL CAMPAIGNS, BATTLES, &c.—*continued*.

1793. Landrecies.
1794. Cateau.
1794. Tournay.
*1815. Waterloo.
1815. Netherlands.
*1854. Balaclava.

*1855. Sevastopol.
1881. Transvaal.
1884–90. Bechuanaland, Natal, and Zululand.
1900. South Africa.

UNIFORM.—Scarlet with Yellow facings (from 1689). Plume, White.

REGIMENTAL BADGE.—" The Castle of Inniskilling," with " The St. George's Colours Flying," and the word " Inniskilling " underneath.

NICKNAME.—" The Skillingers "; also " The Old Inniskillings."

NOTES.—Originally the Cavalry arm of the forces raised for the defence of Enniskillen in 1689 (with the Royal Irish Dragoons, and the Inniskilling Fusiliers, or late 27th Foot).

BIBLIOGRAPHY.—*Historical Record of the 6th, or Inniskilling Regiment of Dragoons.* 1689–1843. Illustrated with plates. [London: Parker. 1843.]

The Seventh (The Queen's Own) Hussars.

THE ROYAL CYPHER WITHIN THE GARTER.

TITLES.

1690–1715. The Queen's Own Regiment of Dragoons; also by the Colonels' names, amongst whom at first were Robert Cunningham, the Earl of Eglinton, and Lord Cardross.

1715–27. The Princess of Wales's Own Royal Dragoons.

1727–51. The Queen's Own Dragoons.

1751–83. The 7th, or Queen's Own Dragoons.

1783–1805. The 7th, or Queen's Own Light Dragoons.

1805 (from). The 7th, or Queen's Own Hussars.

PRINCIPAL CAMPAIGNS, BATTLES, &c.

* "Honours" on the Colours.

1694–97. Flanders.
1694. Moorslede.
1695. Namur.
1711–13. Germany.
1715. Jacobite Rising.
1742–49. Flanders.

*1743. Dettingen.
1745. Fontenoy.
1746. Roucoux.
1747. Laffeldt.
1760–63. Germany.
1760. Warbourg.

The Seventh (The Queen's Own) Hussars—*continued.*

PRINCIPAL CAMPAIGNS, BATTLES, &c.—*continued.*

1762. Wilhelmstahl.
1793–95. Flanders.
1793. Valenciennes.
1794. Cateau.
1794. Nimeguen.
1795. Guildermalsen.
1799. Bergen.
1799. Egmont-op-Zee.
1799. Alkmaer.
*1808–09. Peninsula.
1808. Sahagun.
1809. Carrion.

1809. Benevente.
1809. Corunna.
1813–14. Peninsula.
*1814. Orthes.
1814. Touiouse.
*1815. Waterloo.
1815. Netherlands.
1838–39. Canada.
1858. Indian Mutiny.
*1858. Lucknow.
1881. Transvaal.
1896. Rhodesia.

UNIFORM.—Scarlet (1690–1784) ; Blue (1784–1830) ; Scarlet (1830–41) ; Blue (from 1841). Facings, White (1690–1818) ; Blue (from 1818). Helmet-plume, White.

REGIMENTAL BADGE.—" The Royal Cypher within the Garter."

NICKNAMES.—" The Old Saucy Seventh " (in the Peninsula), " The Lily-white Seventh " (from its light blue uniform and white facings, before 1818), " Young Eyes " ; also " Old Straws " or " Strawboots " (for substituting, at Warbourg, 1760, strawbands for worn-out boots).

NOTES.—Formed in Scotland from Independent Troops of Horse that fought at Killiecrankie. Disbanded in 1713, but restored two years later, mainly from two troops of the present 1st, and three troops of the present 2nd Dragoons. It suffered severely at Waterloo, and distinguished itself in the Mutiny.

BIBLIOGRAPHY.—*Historical Record of the 7th, or Queen's Own Regiment of Hussars.* 1690–1842. Illustrated with a plate. [London : Parker. 1842]

The Eighth (The King's Royal Irish) Hussars.

"Pristinæ virtutis memores."

THE HARP AND CROWN.

TITLES.

1693–1751. Colonel Henry Cunningham's [or its Colonel's name] Regiment of Dragoons; "St. George" from 1740–51.

1751–75. The 8th Dragoons.

1775–77. The 8th Light Dragoons.

1777–1822. The 8th, or The King's Royal Irish Light Dragoons.

1822 (from). The 8th, The King's Royal Irish Hussars.

PRINCIPAL CAMPAIGNS, BATTLES, &c.

* "Honours" on the Colours.

1704–13. Spain.	1710. Brehuega.
1706. Barcelona.	1794–95. Flanders.
1707. Almanza.	1795. Cape of Good Hope.
1710. Almanara.	1800. Kaffir War.
1710. Saragossa.	1801. Egypt.

The Eighth (The King's Royal Irish) Hussars—*continued*.

PRINCIPAL CAMPAIGNS, BATTLES, &c.—*continued*.

*1802–22. Hindoostan.
*1803. Leswarree.
1803. Agra.
1804. Aurungabad.
1804. Ferruckabad.
1804. Deeg.
1805. Bhurtpore.
*1854. Alma.

*1854. Balaclava.
*1854. Inkerman.
1855. Eupatoria.
*1855. Sevastopol.
1858. Indian Mutiny.
*1858. Central India.
*1879–80. Afghanistan.
1900. South Africa.

UNIFORM.—Scarlet (1693–1784); Blue (1784–1802); Light Blue or Cavalry Grey (1802–22); Dark Blue (from 1822). Facings, Yellow (1693–1777); Blue (1777–84); Scarlet (1784–1822); Blue (from 1822). Helmet-plume, Red and White.

REGIMENTAL BADGE.—" The Harp and Crown." Motto : *"Pristinæ virtutis memores."*

NICKNAME.—" The Cross Belts " (1768), from its privilege of wearing the sword-belt over the left shoulder, in recognition of services at Saragossa, where it took the belts of the Spanish Cavalry ; of this fact, however, there is no official record ; also " The Georges " (from its Colonel's name, 1740–51) ; also " The Dirty Eighth."

NOTES.—Composed originally of loyal Protestants who had fought at the Boyne. It gained much distinction in Spain and Flanders ; and received its title, crest, and motto in 1777 as special marks of Royal favour. It shared largely in the glory of Leswarree and other Indian actions—in short, few regiments can boast a more honourable record than " The Royal Irish."

BIBLIOGRAPHY.—*Historical Record of the 8th, or King's Royal Irish Regiment of Hussars.* 1693–1843. Illustrated. [London : Parker. 1844.]
Historical Record of the 8th King's Royal Irish Hussars. To 1803. By John Francis Smet, M.D., late Surgeon, 8th Hussars. [London : Mitchell. 1874.]

The Ninth (The Queen's Royal) Lancers.

THE ROYAL CYPHER WITHIN THE GARTER.

TITLES.

1715–51. Major-General Owen Wynne's (or its Colonel's name) Regiment of Dragoons.

1751–83. The 9th Dragoons.

1783–1816. The 9th Light Dragoons.

1816-30. The 9th Lancers.

1830 (from). The 9th, or Queen's Lancers ; and (shortly afterwards) The 9th (Queen's) Royal Lancers.

PRINCIPAL CAMPAIGNS, BATTLES, &c.

* "Honours" on the Colours.

1715. Jacobite rising.
1798. Irish Rebellion.
1806. Buenos Ayres.
1807. Monte Video.
1809. Flushing.

*1811–13. Peninsula.
*1843. Punniar.
*1846. Sobraon.
*1848–49. Punjaub.
*1849. Chillianwallah.

The Ninth (The Queen's Royal) Lancers—*continued.*

PRINCIPAL CAMPAIGNS, BATTLES, &c.—*continued.*

*1849. Goojerat.
1857–58. Indian Mutiny.
*1857. Delhi.
*1858. Lucknow.

*1878–80. Afghanistan.
*1879. Charasiah.
*1879. Kabul.
*1880. Kandahar.

1900. South Africa.

UNIFORM.—Scarlet (1715–84); Blue (1784–1830); Scarlet (1830–41); Blue (from 1841). Facings: Buff (1715–1805); Crimson (1805–30); Blue (1830–41); Scarlet (from 1841). Lancer-cap plume, Black and White.

REGIMENTAL BADGE.—"The Royal Cypher within the Garter."

NICKNAME.—"The Delhi Spearmen" (a native sobriquet).

NOTES.—The senior of several regiments of Dragoons restored in 1715, which had been disbanded after Utrecht. Raised in the southern counties, it served uninterruptedly in Ireland for eighty-six years to 1803, and in its title received special favour at the hands of Queen Adelaide in 1830. It gained distinction for service during the Indian Mutiny, and is the only British cavalry regiment with "Charasiah," "Kabul, 1879," and "Kandahar, 1880" on its Colours.

BIBLIOGRAPHY.—*Historical Record of the 9th, or Queen's Royal Regiment of Light Dragoons (Lancers)*. 1715–1841. Illustrated with a plate. [London: Parker. 1841.]

The Tenth (The Prince of Wales's Own Royal) Hussars.

THE RISING SUN.

THE PLUME OF THE PRINCE
OF WALES.

THE RED DRAGON.

TITLES.

1715–51. Colonel Humphrey Gore's (or its Colonel's name) Regiment of Dragoons.
1751–83. The 10th Dragoons.
1783–1806. The 10th, or Prince of Wales's Own Light Dragoons.
1806–11. The 10th, or Prince of Wales's Own Hussars.
1811 (from). The 10th, The Prince of Wales's Own Royal Hussars.

PRINCIPAL CAMPAIGNS, BATTLES, &c.

* "Honours" on the Colours.

1746. Falkirk.
1746. Culloden.
1758–63. Germany.
1759. Minden.
1760. Warbourg.
1760. Campen.
1761. Kirk Denkern.
1762. Wilhelmstahl.
1763. Grœbenstein.
*1808–14. Peninsula.
1808. Sahagun.
1809. Benevente.
1809. Corunna.

1813. Morales.
1813. Vittoria.
1813. Pyrenees.
1814. Orthes.
1814. Toulouse.
*1815. Waterloo.
1855. Eupatoria.
*1855. Sevastopol.
*1878–79. Afghanistan.
*1878. Ali Masjid.
*1884. Egypt.
1900. South Africa.

The Tenth (The Prince of Wales's Own Royal) Hussars—*continued.*

UNIFORM.—Scarlet (1715–83); Blue (from 1784). Facings, Deep Yellow (1715–1811); Scarlet (1811–1819); Blue (from 1819); Helmet-plume, Black and White.

REGIMENTAL BADGES.—"The Prince's Plume," "The Rising Sun," "The Red Dragon" (from 1783, ancient Badges of the Princes of Wales). Also "The White Horse."

NICKNAMES.—"Baker's Light Bobs" (when under the command of Valentine Baker). "The Don't Dance Tenth" (an officer told his hostess at a ball, "The Tenth Don't Dance"). "The Chainy Tenth" (from the pattern of the pouch belt).

NOTES.—Raised in Hertfordshire and adjoining counties; the regiment received its "baptism of fire" in the Jacobite rising of 1745. Since then its colours show its record.

BIBLIOGRAPHY.—*Historical Record of the 10th, The Prince of Wales's Own Royal Regiment of Hussars.* 1715–1842. Illustrated with plates. [London : Parker. 1843.]

    The Memoirs of the 10th Royal Hussars (Prince of Wales's Own). By Colonel R. S. Liddell, late 10th Hussars. Illustrated. [London : Longmans. 1891.]

THE WHITE HORSE (OF HANOVER).

The Eleventh (Prince Albert's Own) Hussars.

" Treu und Fest."

THE CREST AND MOTTO OF THE LATE
PRINCE CONSORT.

THE SPHINX.

TITLES.

1715–51. Brigadier-General Philip Honeywood's (or its Colonel's name) Regiment of Dragoons.

1751–83. The 11th Dragoons.

1783–1840. The 11th Light Dragoons.

1840 (from). The 11th Prince Albert's Own Hussars.

PRINCIPAL CAMPAIGNS, BATTLES, &c.

* " Honours " on the Colours.

1715. Jacobite rising.	1763. Grœbenstein.
1746. Culloden.	1793–95. Flanders.
1760–63. Germany.	1793. Famars.
1760. Warbourg.	1793. Valenciennes.
1760. Cassel.	1794. Cateau.
1761. Kirk Denkern.	1794. Villers-en-Couché.
1762. Wilhelmstahl.	1794. Tournay.
1762. Capelnhagar.	1794. Martinique.
1762. Foorwohle.	1794. Guadaloupe.

2ND DRAGOONS.

2ND DRAGOON GUARDS.

7TH HUSSARS.

21ST HUSSARS.

ROYAL ARTILLERY.

ROYAL ENGINEERS.

SCOTS GUARDS.

THE ROYAL IRISH REGIMENT
(18TH FOOT)

The Eleventh (Prince Albert's Own) Hussars—*continued.*

PRINCIPAL BATTLES, CAMPAIGNS, &c.—*continued.*

1795. Guildermalsen.	*1812. Salamanca.
1799. Bergen.	1812. Burgos.
1799. Egmont-op-Zec.	1815. Quatre Bras.
1799. Alkmaer.	*1815. Waterloo.
*1801. Egypt.	1815. Netherlands.
1801. Aboukir.	*1826. Bhurtpore.
1801. Mandora.	*1854. Alma.
1801. Alexandria.	*1854. Balaclava.
1805. Hanover.	*1854. Inkerman.
*1811–13. Peninsula.	1855. Eupatoria.
1811. El-Bodon.	*1855. Sevastopol.

UNIFORM.—Scarlet (1715–83); Blue (1783–1830); Scarlet (1830–40); Blue (from 1840). Facings: Buff (1715–1840); Blue (from 1840). Plume, Crimson and White.

REGIMENTAL BADGES.—"The Crest and Motto (*Treu und Fest*) of the late Prince Consort"; also "The Sphinx" for Egypt (1801).

NICKNAMES.—"The Cherry-pickers" (from Peninsula times, a detachment having been taken prisoners in a fruit-garden during the campaign). "The Cherubims" (from the crimson overalls).

NOTES.—Raised in Essex and adjoining counties. It is stated the regiment was first mounted on grey horses, and bore the motto, "*Motus Componere.*" Its present title was bestowed because it escorted the Prince Consort on the occasion of his marriage to Her Majesty.

BIBLIOGRAPHY.—*Historical Record of the 11th, or Prince Albert's Own Regiment of Hussars.* 1715–1842. [London: Parker. 1843.]

The Twelfth (The Prince of Wales's Royal) Lancers.

THE RISING SUN.

THE PLUME OF THE PRINCE
OF WALES.

THE RED DRAGON.

TITLES.

1715–51. Colonel Phineas Bowles's [or its Colonel's name] Regiment of Dragoons.

1751–68. The 12th Dragoons.

1768–1816. The 12th (The Prince of Wales's) Light Dragoons.

1816–17. The 12th (The Prince of Wales's) Lancers.

1817 (from). The 12th (The Prince of Wales's Royal) Lancers.

PRINCIPAL CAMPAIGNS, BATTLES, &c.

* "Honours" on the Colours.

1795. Corsica.

*1801. Egypt.

1801. Aboukir.

1801. Mandora.

1801. Alexandria.

1809. Walcheren.

*1811–14. Peninsula.

1812. Salamanca.

1813. Vittoria.

1814. Bayonne.

*1815. Waterloo.

1815. Netherlands.

*1851–53. South Africa.

1855. Eupatoria.

*1855. Sevastopol.

1858. Indian Mutiny.

*1858. Central India.

1900. South Africa.

The Twelfth (The Prince of Wales's Royal) Lancers--*continued*.

UNIFORM.—Scarlet (1715–84); Blue (1784–1830); Scarlet (1830–42); Blue (from 1842). Facings, White (1715–68); Black (1768–84); Yellow (1784–1817); Scarlet (1817–30); Blue (1830–42); Scarlet (from 1842). Plume, Scarlet.

REGIMENTAL BADGES.—" Plume of the Prince of Wales," " The Rising Sun," " The Red Dragon" (in honour of the Prince of Wales, afterwards George IV., whose crests they were); also " The Sphinx," for Egypt (1801).

NICKNAME.—" The Supple Twelfth."

NOTES.—Originally raised in Berkshire, Buckinghamshire and Hampshire, it served in Ireland, from 1717, for seventy-six years. In Egypt it captured a French Convoy with Colours.

BIBLIOGRAPHY.—*Historical Record of the 12th, Prince of Wales's Royal Regiment of Lancers.* 1715–1842. Illustrated with a plate. [London: Parker. 1842.]

THE SPHINX.

The Thirteenth Hussars.

" Viret in Æternum."

THE ROYAL CYPHER AND CROWN.

TITLES.

1715–51. Colonel Richard Munden's [or its Colonel's name] Regiment of Dragoons.

1751–83. The 13th Dragoons.

1783–1861. The 13th Light Dragoons.

1861 (from). The 13th Hussars.

PRINCIPAL CAMPAIGNS, BATTLES, &c.

* "Honours" on the Colours.

1715. Jacobite rising.
1745. Jacobite rising.
1796. Jamaica.
*1810–14. Peninsula.
1811. Campo Mayor.
*1811. Albuera.
1811. Arroyo dos Molinos.
1812. Badajos.
*1813. Vittoria.

*1814. Orthes.
*1814. Toulouse.
*1815. Waterloo.
1815. Netherlands.
*1854. Alma.
*1854. Balaclava.
*1854. Inkerman.
*1855. Sevastopol.
1900. South Africa.

The Thirteenth Hussars—*continued.*

UNIFORM.—Scarlet (1715–84); Blue (1784–1832); Scarlet (1832–40); Blue (from 1840). Facings, Green (1715–84); Pale Buff (1784–1836); Green (1836–40); Buff (from 1840). Plume, White.

REGIMENTAL BADGE.—None recognised in *Regulations*, but "The Royal Cypher and Crown" appear on appointments. The motto, "*Viret in Æternum*," has been borne since its formation.

NICKNAMES.—Familiar in 18th century as "The Green Dragoons" (from the facings); "The Ragged Brigade" (during the Peninsular War, when its arduous services debarred much attention to appearances); "The Evergreens" (from its facings and punning motto); "The Geraniums" (for smartness of appearance); and "The Great Runaway Prestonpans" (in allusion to the panic which seized some of the men in the fight with the Jacobite rebels).

NOTES.—Raised in the Midlands, the services of this regiment have been of the most distinguished order. It formed part of the Balaclava Light Brigade. In the Peninsula it served in no less than thirty-two affairs, not counting general actions, losing 274 men and 1,009 horses.

BIBLIOGRAPHY.—*Historical Record of the 13th Regiment of Light Dragoons.* 1715–1842. [London: Parker. 1842.]

The Fourteenth (The King's) Hussars.

THE ROYAL CREST WITHIN THE GARTER.

THE PRUSSIAN EAGLE.

TITLES.

1715–20. Brigadier-General James Dormer's Regiment of Dragoons.
1720–76. The 14th Dragoons ; also frequently by its Colonel's name.
1776–98. The 14th Light Dragoons.
1798–1830. The 14th, or Duchess of York's Own Light Dragoons.
1830–61. The 14th King's Light Dragoons.
1861 (from). The 14th, The King's Hussars.

PRINCIPAL CAMPAIGNS, BATTLES, &c.

* "Honours" on the Colours.

1715. Jacobite rising.	*1808–14. Peninsula.
1746. Culloden.	*1809. Douro.
1794–95. Flanders.	*1809. Talavera.
1796. West Indies.	1809. Oporto.

The Fourteenth (The King's) Hussars—*continued.*

PRINCIPAL CAMPAIGNS, BATTLES, &c.—*continued.*

1810. Busaco.
1810. Barca de Avintas.
*1811. Fuentes d'Onor.
1812. Badajos.
1812. Burgos.
1812. Salamanca.
*1813. Vittoria.
*1814. Orthes.
1814. Tarbes.

1814. Toulouse.
1815. New Orleans.
*1848–49. Punjaub.
*1849. Chillianwallah.
*1849. Goojerat.
*1856. Persia.
1858. Indian Mutiny.
*1858. Central India.
1900. South Africa.

UNIFORM.—Scarlet (1715–84); Dark Blue (1784–1830); Scarlet (1830–40): Blue (from 1840).   Facings, Lemon Yellow (1715–1798); Orange (the livery of Brandenburg, 1798–1830); Scarlet (in 1830), and shortly afterwards Blue (1830–40); Scarlet (1840–61); Blue (from 1861).   Plume, White.

REGIMENTAL BADGES.—"The Royal Crest within the Garter," also "The Prussian Eagle" (adopted in 1798 in honour of the Duchess of York, the Princess Royal of Prussia).

NICKNAMES.—"The Ramnuggur Boys" (having encountered enormous odds at the battle in question); "The Emperor's Chambermaids" (bestowed while in India).

NOTES.—Raised in the South of England by Colonel Dormer (*see* Royal Warwickshire Regiment).   Its record of services shows its fame.   Especially in the Peninsula, in the Punjaub, in Persia, and in Central India has it gained distinction.

BIBLIOGRAPHY.—*Historical Record of the* 14th, *or the King's Regiment of Light Dragoons.*   Illustrated with plates.   [London : Parker.   1847.]

The Fifteenth (The King's) Hussars.

" Merebimur."

THE CREST OF ENGLAND WITHIN THE GARTER.

TITLES.

1759-66. The 15th Light Dragoons; also (popularly) Eliott's Light Horse (from its Colonel's name).

1766-69. The 1st, or The King's Royal Light Dragoons.

1769-1806. The 15th, or The King's Royal Light Dragoons.

1806 (from). The 15th, The King's Hussars.

PRINCIPAL CAMPAIGNS, BATTLES, &c.

* "Honours" on the Colours.

1760-63. Germany.
*1760. Emsdorf.
1762. Wilhelmstahl.
1762. Friedburg.

1763. Grœbenstein.
1793-95. Flanders.
1793. Valenciennes.
1794. Cateau.

The Fifteenth (The King's) Hussars—*continued*.

PRINCIPAL CAMPAIGNS, BATTLES, &c.—*continued*.

*1794. Villers-en-Couché.
1794. Tournay.
1794. Nimeguen.
1795. Guildermalsen.
*1799. Egmont-op-Zee.
1799. Alkmaer.
*1808–14. Peninsula.
*1808. Sahagun.
1809. Benevente.
1813. Moraies.

*1813. Vittoria.
1813. Nivelle.
1814. Orthes.
1814. Toulouse.
*1815. Waterloo.
1815. Cambray.
1815. Netherlands.
*1878–80. Afghanistan.
1881. Transvaal.

UNIFORM.—Scarlet (1759–84) ; Blue (from 1784). Facings, Green (1759–66) ; Dark Blue (1766–84) ; Scarlet (1784–1822) ; Blue (from 1822). Plume, Scarlet.

REGIMENTAL BADGE.—"The Crest of England within the Garter." Motto : "*Merebimur*," for valour, in Germany in 1766 ; also a helmet inscription : "Five Battalions of Foot defeated and taken by this Regiment, with their Colours and nine pieces of Ordnance, at Emsdorf, 16 July, 1760." The scarlet plume was also conferred in 1799 as a distinction.

NICKNAMES.—"The Fighting Fifteenth."

NOTES.—This notable regiment was raised near London, and commenced its distinguished career the following year at Emsdorf (*see* above). Subsequently, at Villers-en-Couché, where it captured three guns, in Holland (1799), and in the Peninsula campaigns it gained further renown.

BIBLIOGRAPHY.—*Historical Record of the 15th, or King's Regiment of Light Dragoons* (*Hussars*). 1759–1841. [London : Parker. 1841.]

The Sixteenth (The Queen's) Lancers.

" Aut Cursu, aut Cominus Armis."

THE ROYAL CYPHER WITHIN THE GARTER.

TITLES.

1759–66. The 16th Light Dragoons; also (popularly from its Colonel's name) Burgoyne's Light Horse.

1766–69. The 2nd, Queen's, Light Dragoons.

1769–1815. The 16th, or The Queen's Light Dragoons.

1815 (from). The 16th, The Queen's Lancers.

PRINCIPAL CAMPAIGNS, BATTLES, &c.

* " Honours " on the Colours.

1761. Belle-Isle.	1778. Freehold.
1762. Portugal.	1793–96. Flanders.
1775–78. America.	1793. Valenciennes.
1776. Brooklyn.	1793. Dunkirk.
1776. White Plains.	1794. Cateau.
1777. Brandywine.	1794. Tournay.
1777. Germantown.	1794. West Indies.

The Sixteenth (The Queen's) Lancers—*continued.*

PRINCIPAL CAMPAIGNS, BATTLES, &c.—*continued.*

*1809–14. Peninsula.
*1809. Talavera.
*1811. Fuentes d'Onor.
1812. Llereena.
*1812. Salamanca.
*1813. Vittoria.
*1813. Nive.
*1815. Waterloo.
1815. Netherlands.

*1826. Bhurtpore.
*1839. Afghanistan.
*1839. Ghuznee.
*1843. Maharajpore.
*1846. Aliwal.
*1846. Sobraon.
1897. Dargai.
1900. South Africa.

UNIFORM.—Scarlet (1759–83; possibly for a year or two after formation this may have been red with yellow facings); Blue (1783–1832); Scarlet (from 1832). Facings, Black (1759–66, but see above); Dark Blue (1766–83); Scarlet (1783–1832); Blue (from 1832). Plume, Black.

REGIMENTAL BADGE.—" The Royal Cypher within the Garter." Motto, "*Aut cursu, aut cominus armis*" (bestowed in 1766 for services in Portugal on the regiment becoming " The Queens.")

NICKNAME.—" The Red (or Scarlet) Lancers "; being the only Lancers with the scarlet tunic.

NOTES.—Raised near London during the Seven Years' War. The first Lancer regiment to serve in India.

BIBLIOGRAPHY.—*Historical Record of the 16th, or Queen's Regiment of Light Dragoons* (*Lancers*). 1759–1841. Illustrated with a plate. [London : Parker. 1842.]

The Seventeenth (The Duke of Cambridge's Own) Lancers.

DEATH'S HEAD, WITH MOTTO, "OR GLORY."

TITLES.

1759–63. The 18th Light Dragoons.
1763–66. The 17th Light Dragoons.
1766–69. The 3rd Light Dragoons.
1769–1822. The 17th Light Dragoons.
1822–76. The 17th Lancers.
1876 (from). The 17th (Duke of Cambridge's Own) Lancers.

PRINCIPAL CAMPAIGNS, BATTLES, &c.

* "Honours" on the Colours.

1761. Germany.
1775–83. America.
1775. Bunker's Hill.
1776. Brooklyn.
1778. Freehold.
1795. West Indies.
1806. Buenos Ayres.
1807. Monte Video.
1815–20. Cutch.
1816–18. Pindaree War.

*1854. Alma.
*1854. Balaclava.
*1854. Inkerman.
1855. Eupatoria.
*1855. Sevastopol.
1858. Indian Mutiny.
*1858. Central India.
*1879. South Africa.
1900. South Africa.

The Seventeenth (The Duke of Cambridge's Own) Lancers—*continued.*

UNIFORM.—Scarlet (1759–84); Blue (1784–1830); Scarlet (1830–40); Blue (from 1840). Facings, White (from 1759). Plume, White.

REGIMENTAL BADGE.—"A Death's Head," with the words "Or Glory." This, chosen by Colonel Hale, who raised the corps in Hertfordshire and near London, was intended to commemorate the death of General Wolfe at Quebec (1759). Colonel Hale was with him at the time, and subsequently bore the home despatches.

NICKNAME.—"The Death or Glory Boys," or "The Skulls and Crossbones" (*see* BADGE); "Bingham's Dandies" (*circa* 1826)—one of its Colonels, Lord Bingham, insisting on perfection of fit in uniform, and smartness in accoutrement; "The Gentleman Dragoons;" "The Horse Marines" (when employed as marines on board the *Hermione* frigate on the West India station in 1795).

NOTES.—First raised as the 18th Light Dragoons, and renumbered on the disbandment of the old 17th. This regiment was one of those taking part in the famous charge at Balaclava. Renamed in 1876 in honour of the Duke of Cambridge, who served in its ranks.

BIBLIOGRAPHY.—*Historical Record of the 17th Regiment of Light Dragoons (Lancers).* 1759–1841. Illustrated with plates. [London: Parker. 1841.]
A History of the 17th Lancers (Duke of Cambridge's Own). By the Hon. J. W. Fortescue. [London: Macmillan. 1895.]
The "Death or Glory Boys": The Story of the 17th Lancers. By D. H. Parry. [London: Cassell. 1900.]

The Eighteenth Hussars.

" Pro Rege, pro Lege, pro Patria Conamur."

TITLES.

1759–63. The 19th Light Dragoons ; popularly, " The Drogheda Light Horse."

1763–1807. The 18th Light Dragoons.

1807–22. The 18th King's Irish Hussars (then disbanded and revived).

1858 (from). The 18th Hussars.

PRINCIPAL CAMPAIGNS, BATTLES, &c.

* " Honours " on the Colours.

1795. Jamaica.

1796. St. Domingo.

1799. Holland.

*1808–14. Peninsula.

1808. Sahagun.

1809. Benevente.

1809. Corunna.

1813. Vittoria.

1813. Nive.

1814. Orthes.

1814. Toulouse.

*1815. Waterloo.

1900. South Africa.

UNIFORM.—Scarlet (1759——?) ; subsequently, and at disbandment, Dark Blue ; ?
  (from 1858). Facings, White (1759–1821) ; Blue (from 1858). Plume, Scarlet
  and White.

The Eighteenth Hussars—*continued.*

REGIMENTAL BADGE.—None recognised in *Regulations*; but in the case of both the late and the present 18th " The Royal Cypher and Crown" appeared and appears on the appointments. Motto, "*Pro Rege, pro Lege, pro Patria Conamur*"—" We Strive for Sovereign, Laws, and Country."

NOTES.—The first 18th is now the 17th Lancers; the present 18th, raised at Leeds in 1858, was allowed to revive the " honours" of the old corps, disbanded in 1821 ; the motto and the scarlet and white plume were restored in 1878.

BIBLIOGRAPHY.—*Historical Record of the 18th Hussars.* By Captain Harold Esdaile Malet. [London : Clowes. 1869.]

THE ROYAL CYPHER AND CROWN.

The Nineteenth (Princess of Wales's Own) Hussars.

THE ELEPHANT.

TITLES.

1759–63. The 19th Light Dragoons (popularly the Drogheda Light Horse); re-numbered 18th in 1763, disbanded as 18th Hussars in 1821.

1779–83. The 19th Light Dragoons: disbanded.

1781–86. The 23rd Light Dragoons: then re-numbered.

1786–1817. The 19th Light Dragoons.

1817–21. The 19th Lancers: then disbanded.

1858–61. The Hon. East India Company's 1st Bengal European Cavalry.

1861 (from). The 19th (Princess of Wales's Own) Hussars.

PRINCIPAL CAMPAIGNS, BATTLES, &c.

* "Honours" on the Colours :—(1) Honours of the old 19th Lancers, disbanded in 1821; (2) Honours of the present 19th Hussars, raised in 1858, (3) Not on present Colours, but worn by the old 19th Lancers.

1799. Mallavelly.

*1799. Seringapatam (3).

1800–1. Deccan.

*1800–1. Mysore (1).

*1803. Assaye (1).

1805. Vellore.

*1813. Niagara. (1).

*1882–4. Egypt (2).

*1882. Tel-el-Kebir (2).

1883. El Teb.

*1884–5. Nile (2).

*1885. Abu-Klea (2).

1900. South Africa.

The Nineteenth (Princess of Wales's Own) Hussars—*continued.*

UNIFORM.—Scarlet, and Green facings (1779–83) ; Dark Blue, and Light Yellow facings (in 1821) ; Blue, with Blue facings (from 1858). Plume, White.

REGIMENTAL BADGE. —"The Elephant" (for the distinguished services of the old 19th Light Dragoons in India).

NICKNAMES.—"The Dumpies" (when raised in 1858, from the small stature of its men) ; "The Droghedas" (of the first 19th).

NOTES.—The old 19th received a honorary Standard from the late Hon. East India Company for distinction at Assaye ; its badge, "The Elephant," was also then bestowed.

BIBLIOGRAPHY.—*Colburn's United Service Magazine.* 1873. [Art.]
   The Nineteenth and their Times. By Colonel John Biddulph. [London : Murray. 1900.]

The Twentieth Hussars.

TITLES.

1759–63. The 20th Inniskilling Light Dragoons : disbanded.

1779–83. The 20th Light Dragoons : disbanded.

1791–1802. The 20th Jamaica Light Dragoons : renamed.

1802–1818. The 20th Light Dragoons : disbanded.

1858–60. The 2nd Bengal European Light Cavalry.

1860 (from). The 20th Hussars.

PRINCIPAL CAMPAIGNS, BATTLES, &c.

* "Honours" on the Colours.

1795–6. Maroon War.	1807. Monte Video.	1812–13. Spain.
1806. Cape of Good Hope.	1807. Egypt.	1814. Genoa.
	*1808. Peninsula.	1884–5. Nile.
1806. Maida.	*1808. Vimiera.	*1885. Suakim.
1806. Buenos Ayres.	1808–12. Sicily.	

UNIFORM.—Scarlet and Yellow (afterwards Black) facings (1759–63); Scarlet and Yellow facings (1779–83); Blue and Yellow (afterwards Orange) facings (1791–1814); Blue and Blue facings (from 1858). Plume, Yellow.

REGIMENTAL BADGE.—None recognised in *Regulations:* on appointments "The Royal Cypher and Crown with $\frac{XX}{H}$."

BIBLIOGRAPHY.—*Colburn's United Service Magazine.* 1876. [Art.]

The Twenty=First (Empress of India's) Lancers.

TITLES.

1759–63. The 21st Light Dragoons, or Royal Windsor Foresters : disbanded.

1779–83. The 21st Light Dragoons : disbanded.

1794–1819. The 21st Light Dragoons : disbanded.

1858. The East India Company's 3rd Bengal European Cavalry.

1858–62. The 3rd Bengal European Cavalry.

1862–1897. The 21st Hussars.

1897–9. The 21st Lancers.

1899 (from). The 21st (Empress of India's) Lancers.

PRINCIPAL CAMPAIGNS, BATTLES, &c.

1795–8. San Domingo (the Toussaint l'Ouverture Revolution).

1807. Monte Video.

1812. Cape of Good Hope.

1814–15. Kaffraria.

*1899. Khartoum.

UNIFORM.—Scarlet and Dark Blue facings (1759–63); Scarlet and White facings (1779–83); Blue and Yellow facings (when raised in 1794); Blue and Pink facings (in 1814); Blue and Black Velvet facings (in 1815); Blue and Blue facings (from 1858–97); Blue and French Grey facings (from 1897).   Plume, White.

REGIMENTAL BADGE.—None recognised in *Regulations:* on appointments "The Royal Cypher and Crown with **XXI.**" **H**

NOTES.—A detachment of this regiment served at St. Helena as guard to the Emperor Napoleon when in exile. The recent title was conferred in recognition of its brilliant services at Omdurman.

THE ROYAL ARTILLERY.

The Royal Regiment of Artillery.

THE ROYAL ARMS.

THE GUN AND MOTTOES.

TITLES.

16th century to 1716. The Train of Artillery.

1716 (from). The Royal Regiment of Artillery : comprising (Mar. 1900).

(1) Horse Artillery (27 Batteries).

(2) Field Artillery (121 Batteries).

(3) Mountain Artillery (10 Batteries).

(4) Garrison Artillery (83 Batteries) ; with

(5) Artillery Militia : also incorporated.

(6) The Royal Malta Artillery.

(7) The (late) Bengal Artillery.

(8) The (late) Madras Artillery.

(9) The (late) Bombay Artillery.

PRINCIPAL CAMPAIGNS, BATTLES, &c.

One arm or other of this branch of the Service has, obviously, taken part in every campaign : a particularised list is therefore unnecessary. The guns are the " Colours " of the Artillery, and as such are entitled to all " parade honours." Formerly, regimental honours appear to have been worn by certain companies. Amongst such were " Niagara," " Leipsic," " Waterloo," and " The Dragon of China."

The Royal Regiment of Artillery—*continued.*

UNIFORM.—Blue with Scarlet facings. Plume, White.

REGIMENTAL BADGES.—The Royal Arms and Supporters, with a Cannon. The mottoes, "*Ubique*" (Everywhere) over, and "*Quo fas et gloria ducunt*" ("Whither Right and Glory lead us") under the gun.

NICKNAMES.—"The Gunners;" "The Four-wheeled Hussars" (of the Royal Horse Artillery).

NOTES.—Trains of artillery seem first to have been raised in the time of Henry VIII.; and up to 1716 appear to have been disbanded after each campaign. In 1716 several companies received permanent corporate existence, since which the exigencies of modern warfare have led to an enormous increase in the number of batteries. But, from first to last the record of the Royal Artillery has been one of distinction, and it may fitly be said to share the honours of all other regiments. The Royal Irish Artillery were absorbed in 1801, and the East India Company's Artillery in 1858.

BIBLIOGRAPHY.—*History of the Royal Regiment of Artillery.* Compiled from the original Records. By Captain Francis Duncan, M.A., D.C.L. 2 vols. [London : Murray. 1872.]

History of the Horse Brigade. [London : Mitchell.]

History of the Regiment of Bengal Artillery. By F. W. Stubbe. 2 vols. [1877.]

Proceedings of the Royal Artillery Institution. Passim.

THE ROYAL ENGINEERS.

The Corps of Royal Engineers

THE ROYAL ARMS.

TITLES.

1717–88. The Soldier Artificer Company.
1788–1813. The Corps of Royal Military Artificers.
1813–56. The Corps of Royal Sappers and Miners.
1856 (from). The Corps of Royal Engineers.

CAMPAIGNS, BATTLES, &c.

Like the Artillery, this Corps has necessarily taken part in every campaign. Its services have been pre-eminent from the first, and few regiments, if any, can show a longer or more distinguished list of honoured names. Amongst many others may be mentioned Jones, Burgoyne, Pasley, Colby, Denison, Napier of Magdala, Simmons, Gordon of Khartoum, Gerald Graham, Kitchener of Khartoum, Warren, and others.

UNIFORM.—Scarlet and Black velvet facings (in 1717); Scarlet and Orange facings (1772–88); Dark Blue and Black facings (1788–1813); Scarlet and Dark Blue facings (from 1813).

The Corps of Royal Engineers—*continued.*

REGIMENTAL BADGE.—"The Royal Arms and Supporters," with the mottoes, " *Ubique*" over, and " *Quo fas et gloria ducunt*" below.

NICKNAME.—"The Mudlarks"; "The Measurers"; "The Flying Bricklayers" (of the mounted contingent).

NOTES.—A company of Engineer Militia is attached to the corps: also incorporated (from 1858) the Bengal, Bombay, and Madras Engineers.

BIBLIOGRAPHY.—*History of the Royal Sappers and Miners.* By T. W. J. Connolly. 2 vols. [London: 1855.]

The Royal Engineers. By the Right Hon. Sir Francis B. Head, Bart. [London: Murray. 1869.]

History of the Corps of Royal Engineers. By Whitworth Porter, Major-General, Royal Engineers. 2 vols. [London: Longmans 1889.]

THE FOOT GUARDS.

The Grenadier Guards.

3 Batts.

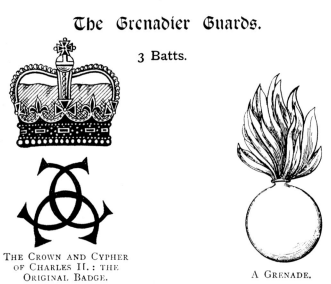

THE CROWN AND CYPHER
OF CHARLES II.: THE
ORIGINAL BADGE.

A GRENADE.

TITLES.

1660-85. The King's Royal Regiment of Guards.
1685–1815. The First Regiment of Foot Guards.
1815 (from). The First, or Grenadier Regiment of Foot Guards.

PRINCIPAL CAMPAIGNS, BATTLES, &c.

* "Honours" on the Colours.

1680–83. Tangier.
1685. Sedgemoor.
1691–97. Flanders.
1692. Steenkirk.
1693. Neer Landen.
1695. Namur.
1702–13. Germany.
1704. Schellenberg.
*1704. Blenheim.
1704–8. Spain.
1705. Gibraltar.
1705–6. Barcelona.
*1706. Ramilies.
1707. Almanza.
1708. Lisle.
*1708. Oudenarde.
1708. Ghent.

1709. Tournay.
*1709. Malplaquet.
1710. Menin.
1710. Douai.
1729. Gibraltar.
1742–47. Flanders.
*1743. Dettingen.
1745. Fontenoy.
1745. Jacobite rising.
1747. Val.
1758. Cherbourg.
1759–62. Germany.
1762. Denkern.
1762. Wilhelmstahl.
1776–81. America.
1776. Brooklyn.
1777. Brandywine.

1777. Germantown.
1778. Freehold.
1781. Guildford.
1793. Famars.
1793. Valenciennes.
*1793. Lincelles.
1793–95. Flanders.
1794. Cateau.
1799. Helder.
1799. Crabbendam.
1799. Bergen.
1799. Egmont-op-Zee.
1799. Alkmaer.
1806–7. Sicily.
*1808–14. Peninsula.
1809. Flushing.
*1809. Corunna.

The Grenadier Guards—*continued.*

PRINCIPAL CAMPAIGNS, BATTLES, &c.—*continued.*

*1811. Barossa.	1814–15. Netherlands.	*1854. Inkerman.
1813. St. Sebastian.	1814. Bergen-op-Zoom.	*1855. Sevastopol.
1813. St. Marcial.	1815. Quatre Bras.	*1882. Egypt.
1813. Bidassoa.	*1815. Waterloo.	*1882. Tel-el-Kebir.
1813. Nive.	1826–27. Portugal.	*1885. Suakim.
1813. Nivelle.	1838–42. Canada.	*1898. Khartoum.
1814. Bayonne.	*1854. Alma.	1900. South Africa.

UNIFORM.—Scarlet with Blue facings (from formation).

REGIMENTAL AND OTHER BADGES.—On formation "The Red Cross of St. George" on a white ground ; also (till 1815) "The Royal Cypher and Crown." From 1815 "A Grenade," with three of the ancient company badges in rotation (as Colours are renewed). Also, 1st Batt.—The Imperial Crown. 2nd. Batt.—The Royal Cypher, interlaced and reversed, surmounted by the Imperial Crown. 3rd Batt.—The same as 2nd Batt. The company badges are :—

(1) The Royal Crest of England.
(2) The Red and White Rose.
(3) The Fleur de Lys.
(4) The Golden Portcullis.
(5) The Rose en Soleil.
(6) The Scottish Thistle.
(7) The Harp of Erin.
(8) The Red Dragon of Wales.
(9) The White Greyhound with Golden Collar and Chain.
(10) The Sun in Splendour.
(11) The Unicorn of the Royal Crown of Scotland.
(12) The Antelope.
(13) A Royal Hart.
(14) A Silver Falcon within a Golden Fetterlock.
(15) The Red Rose of Lancaster.
(16) A White Swan.
(17) The Falcon and Sceptre.
(18) A Stock of a Tree putting forth a Green Shoot.
(19) A Sword and Sceptre crossed.
(20) The Boscobel Oak.
(21) The Sun in the Clouds.
(22) A Blazing Beacon.
(23) Crossed Plumes.
(24) The Royal Crest of Ireland.
(25) The Cross of St. George.
(26) The Lion of Nassau.
(27) The Badge of the Order of the Bath.
(28) The Crest of Old Saxony.
(29) The Irish Shamrock.
(30) The Crest of H.R.H. the late Prince Consort.

NICKNAMES.—"The Sand Bags," "The Coal-heavers," "Old Eyes," "The House-maids' Pets," "The Bermuda Exiles."

NOTES.—First raised in London by Colonel John Russell, and incorporated with the Royal Guards of Charles II., raised by Lord Wentworth in the Low Countries in 1656. The title received in 1815 was in recognition of having defeated the French Imperial Guards at Waterloo.

BIBLIOGRAPHY.—*The Origin and History of the 1st or Grenadier Guards.* By Lieut.-Gen. Sir T. W. Hamilton, K.C.B. 3 vols. With Illustrations. [London : Murray. 1874.]

The Coldstream Guards.

3 Batts.

THE STAR OF THE GARTER.

THE SPHINX.

TITLES.

1650–60. Colonel Monck's Regiment of Foot: also (popularly) Monck's Coldstreamers.
1660–61. The Lord General's Regiment of Foot.
1661–70. The Lord General's Regiment of Foot Guards.
1670–1817. The Coldstream Regiment of Foot Guards.
1817 (from). The Coldstream Guards.

PRINCIPAL CAMPAIGNS, BATTLES, &c.

* " Honours" on the Colours.

1680–83. Tangier.	1745. Jacobite rising.	1799. Crabbendam.
1689–97. Flanders.	1758. Cherbourg.	1799. Bergen.
1689. Walcourt.	1760–62. Germany.	1799. Egmont-op-Zee.
1692. Steenkirk.	1761. Denkern.	1799. Alkmaer.
1693. Neer Landen.	1762. Wilhelmstahl.	*1801. Egypt.
1695. Namur.	1776–81. America.	1801. Aboukir.
1704–8. Spain.	1776. Brooklyn.	1801. Alexandria.
1704. Gibraltar.	1777. Brandywine.	1801. Marabout.
1705–6. Barcelona.	1777. Germantown.	1805. Hanover.
1707. Almanza.	1778. Freehold.	1807. Copenhagen.
1707–13. Germany.	1781. Guildford.	*1809–14. Peninsula.
*1708. Oudenarde.	1793–95. Flanders.	1809. Flushing.
1708. Ghent.	1793. St. Amand.	1809. Douro.
*1709. Malplaquet.	1793. Valenciennes.	*1809. Talavera.
1711. Bouchain.	*1793. Lincelles.	1811. Fuentes d'Onor.
1742–45. Flanders.	1794. Tournay.	*1811. Barossa.
*1743. Dettingen.	1794. Cateau.	1812. Ciudad Rodrigo.
1745. Fontenoy.	1799. Helder.	1812. Badajos.

The Coldstream Guards—*continued.*

PRINCIPAL CAMPAIGNS, BATTLES, &c.—*continued.*

1812. Burgos.	1814. Bayonne.	*1854. Inkerman.
1812. Salamanca.	1814–15. Netherlands.	*1855. Sevastopol.
1813. St. Sebastian.	1814. Bergen-op-Zoom.	*1882. Egypt.
1813. Vittoria.	1815. Quatre Bras.	*1882. Tel-el-Kebir.
1813. Pyrenees.	*1815. Waterloo.	*1885. Suakim.
1813. Bidassoa.	1827–28. Portugal.	1900. South Africa.
1813. Nive.	1838–42. Canada.	
1813. Nivelle.	*1854. Alma.	

UNIFORM.—Scarlet faced with Green (1650–70) ; Scarlet faced with Blue (from 1670).

REGIMENTAL AND OTHER BADGES.—In 1660 a red cross on a green ground with six white balls ; in 1684 a St. George's Cross, bordered white on a blue ground. The *Regulation* device is for 1st and 3rd Batts., the Star of the Order of the Garter, surmounted by the Imperial Crown ; 2nd Batt., a Star of eight points within the Garter, surmounted by the Imperial Crown, the Union within the dexter canton. Also in twos, in succession, as the Colours are renewed, the following company badges conferred by Royal Authority in 1751 :—

(1) A White Lion.
(2) The Prince of Wales's Feathers.
(3) A Spotted Panther.
(4) Two Crossed Swords.
(5) The George and Dragon.
(6) A Red Rose within the Garter.
(7) A Centaur.
(8) Two Golden Sceptres crossed.
(9) The Golden Knot of the Collar of the Garter.
(10) An Escarbuncle.
(11) A White Boar with golden bristles.
(12) A Dun Cow.
(13) A Red and White Rose empaled with a Pomegranate.
(14) The White Horse of Hanover.
(15) The Electoral Bonnet of Hanover.
(16) The Hanover Horse.

Also " The Sphinx " for Egypt.

NICKNAMES, &c.—" The Coldstreamers." " The Nulli Secundus Club."

NOTES.—The Regiment of Coldstream Guards is the direct and only descendant of the Parliamentary Infantry, all other corps having been disbanded at the Restoration. It derives its name from Monck's march from Coldstream to restore Charles II.

BIBLIOGRAPHY.—*The Origin and Services of the Coldstream Guards.* By Colonel Sir Daniel MacKinnon. 2 vols. [London : Bentley. 1833.]
A History of the Coldstream Guards from 1815 to 1895. By Lieut.-Col. Ross of Bladensburg, C.B. [London : 1896.]

The Scots Guards.

3 Batts.

ROYAL ARMS OF SCOTLAND.   THE THISTLE.   THE SPHINX.

TITLES.

1660–1713. The Scots Regiment of Guards.
1713–1831. The 3rd Foot Guards.
1831–77. The Scots Fusilier Guards.
1877 (from). The Scots Guards.

PRINCIPAL CAMPAIGNS, BATTLES, &c.

* "Honours" on the Colours.

1689–95. Flanders.	1758. Cherbourg.	1793–95. Flanders.
1689. Walcourt.	1759–62. Germany.	*1793. Lincelles.
1690. Boyne.	1761. Denkern.	1799. Helder.
1693. Neer Landen.	1762. Wilhelmstahl.	1799. Crabbendam.
1695. Namur.	1776–83. America.	1799. Bergen.
1709–13. Spain.	1776. Brooklyn.	1799. Egmont-op-Zee.
1710. Saragossa.	1777. Brandywine.	1799. Alkmaer.
1742–48. Flanders.	1777. Germantown.	1801. Aboukir.
*1743. Dettingen.	1778. Freehold.	*1801. Egypt.
1745. Fontenoy.	1781. Guildford.	1801. Alexandria.
1747. Val.	1793. Valenciennes.	1801. Marabout.

The Scots Guards—*continued.*

PRINCIPAL CAMPAIGNS, BATTLES, &c.—*cont'nued.*

1807. Copenhagen.	1812. Ciudad Rodrigo.	*1854. Alma.
*1809–14. Peninsula.	1813. St. Sebastian.	*1854. Inkerman.
1809. Flushing.	1814–15. Netherlands.	*1854. Sevastopol.
1809. Douro.	1814. Bayonne.	*1882. Egypt.
*1809. Talavera.	1814. Bergen-op-Zoom.	*1882. Tel-el-Kebir
*1811. Barossa.	1815. Quatre Bras.	*1885. Suakim.
1812. Badajos.	*1815. Waterloo.	1900. South Africa.
1812. Burgos.	1826–28. Portugal.	

UNIFORM.—Scarlet and White facings (from 1660 to *circa* 1713); Scarlet and Blue facings (from *circa* 1713).

REGIMENTAL AND OTHER BADGES.—The 1st Batt. : The Royal Arms of Scotland, with motto, "*En! Ferus Hostis*," surmounted by the Imperial Crown ; 2nd Batt. : The Union Badge, viz., the Rose, Thistle, and Shamrock, with the motto, "*Unita Fortior*," surmounted by the Imperial Crown. Also two of sixteen company badges, with mottoes borne in rotation, as follows :—

(1) The Royal Crest of Scotland, with "*Nemo me impune lacessit.*"

(2) A Bombshell, with "*Terrorem affero.*"

(3) A Lion erect, with "*Intrepidus.*"

(4) The Badge and Motto of the Order of the Thistle.

(5) The Red Lion rampant of Scotland, with collar and chain of gold, and "*Timiere nescius.*"

(6) A Blue Griffin, with "*Belloque ferox.*"

(7) A Phœnix in flames, with "*Per funera vitam.*"

(8) A Thunderbolt, with "*Horror ubique.*"

(9) A Cannon firing, with "*Concussæ cadent urbes.*"

(10) A Salamander, with "*Pascua nota mihi.*"

(11) St. Andrew's Cross, with "*In hoc signo vinces.*"

(12) A Trophy, with "*Honores præfero.*"

(13) A Dog, with "*Intaminata fide.*"

(14) The Label of the Duke of Connaught, with "*Te duce vincimus.*"

(15) The Galley of Lorne, with "*Ne obliviscaris.*"

(16) The Rose and Thistle, with "*Facit eos en gentem unam.*"

Also "The Sphinx," for Egypt (1801).

NICKNAME.—"The Jocks."

NOTES.—Raised in Scotland by the Earl of Linlithgow.

The Irish Guards.

THE HARP AND CROWN.

THE STAR OF THE ORDER OF ST. PATRICK.

By an Army Order (No. 77, April, 1900), "Her Majesty the Queen, having deemed it desirable to commemorate the bravery shown by the Irish regiments in the recent operations in South Africa, has been graciously pleased to command that an Irish regiment of Foot Guards be formed. This regiment will be designated 'The Irish Guards.'"

The details of the Uniform have not yet been fully settled; the Harp and Crown appear on the buttons, and the Shamrock on the collar, while the regimental badge is the Star of the Order of St. Patrick.

The Irish Guards commenced their public service as the guard of honour at the reception by H.R.H. the Prince of Wales, at Paddington, of Lord Roberts, the Commander-in-Chief, on the occasion of his return from the field of operations in South Africa, 1899–190[?].

TERRITORIAL REGIMENTS.

The Royal Scots (Lothian Regiment),

COMPRISING

1st & 2nd Batts. (formerly) The 1st (The Royal Scots) Regiment; with
3rd Batt. The Edinburgh Light Infantry Militia.

"Nemo me impune lacessit."

THE THISTLE AND CROWN.   THE ST. ANDREW'S CROSS.   THE SPHINX.

TITLES.

1633–78. Le Régiment de Douglas.

1678–84. Colonel the Earl of Dumbarton's Regiment of Foot.

1684–1751. The Royal Regiment of Foot.

1751–1812. The 1st, or The Royal Regiment of Foot.

1812–21. The 1st, or The Royal Scots Regiment of Foot.

1821–71. The 1st, or The Royal Regiment of Foot.

1871–81. The 1st, the Royal Scots.

1881 (from). The Royal Scots (Lothian Regiment).

PRINCIPAL CAMPAIGNS, BATTLES, &c.

* "Honours" on the Colours.

1673. Maestricht.
1680–83. Tangier.
1689–97. Flanders.
1689. Walcourt.
1692. Steenkirk.
1693. Neer Landen.

1695. Namur.
1701–14. Germany.
1702. Venloo.
1704. Schellenberg.
*1704. Blenheim.
*1706. Ramilies.

*1708. Oudenarde.
1708. Wynendale.
1708. Lisle.
1708. Ghent.
1709. Tournay.
*1709. Malplaquet.

The Royal Scots (Lothian Regiment)—*continued.*

PRINCIPAL CAMPAIGNS, BATTLES, &c.—*continued.*

1710. Douay.	*1799. Egmont-op-Zee.	1814. Bayonne.
1743–49. Flanders.	1801. Aboukir.	*1814. Niagara.
1745. Fontenoy.	*1801. Egypt.	1814. Bergen-op-Zoom.
1746. Culloden.	1801. Mandora.	1815. Quatre Bras.
1747. Hulst.	1801. Alexandria.	*1815. Waterloo.
1757–60. Canada.	*1803. St. Lucia.	*1817. Nagpore.
*1758. Louisbourg.	*1809–14. Peninsula.	*1817. Maheidpore.
1758. Ticonderoga.	*1809. Corunna.	1819. Asseerghur.
1759. Guadaloupe.	1809. Flushing.	*1824–26. Ava.
1761. Dominica.	1810. Guadaloupe.	1838–39. Canada.
1762. Martinique.	*1810. Busaco.	*1854. Alma.
1762. Havannah.	*1812. Salamanca.	*1854. Inkerman.
1793. Toulon.	*1813. Vittoria.	*1855. Sevastopol.
1794. Corsica.	*1813. St. Sebastian.	*1860. Taku Forts.
1799. Helder.	*1813. Nive.	*1860. Pekin.
1799. Crabbendam.	1814–15. Netherlands.	1900. South Africa.

UNIFORM.—Scarlet with White facings (from 1678 probably to 1684); Scarlet and Blue facings (since 1684).

REGIMENTAL BADGES.—"The Royal Cypher" within the Collar of St. Andrew and the Crown over it. Also "The Thistle and Crown," with the Motto of the Order, "*Nemo me impune lacessit.*" Also, The Sphinx, for Egypt (1801). In 1633 it bore the St. Andrew's Cross, with the Thistle and Crown; and, in 1751, the distinction of the Colours of the 2nd Batt. was a flaming ray of gold from the upper corner of each Colour to the centre.

NICKNAME.—"Pontius Pilate's Body-guard" (from its antiquity).

NOTES.—Traditionally regarded as the ancient body-guard of the Scottish kings, this famous corps was in the service of Sweden, as "Hepburn's Regiment," from 1625 to 1633; and in that of France from 1633 to 1678, when (under Dumbarton) it came to England. It received its title in 1684 in recognition of the capture of a Colour from the Moors at Tangier. At Sedgemoor (1685) it also captured the Duke of Monmouth's Standard.

BIBLIOGRAPHY.—*Historical Record of the 1st, or Royal Regiment of Foot.* To 1838. Illustrated. [London : Longman. 1838.]

The Queen's (Royal West Surrey Regiment).

COMPRISING

1st & 2nd Batts. (formerly)   The 2nd (Queen's Royal) ; with
3rd Batt.   The 2nd Royal Surrey Militia.

" *Pristinæ virtutis memor.*"   " *Vel exuviæ triumphant.*"

THE PASCHAL LAMB.   THE ROYAL CYPHER   THE SPHINX.
WITHIN THE GARTER.

TITLES.

1661–84. The Tangierenes, or Queen's Own Regiment of Foot.

1684–1703. The Queen Dowager's Regiment of Foot.

1703–15. The Queen's Royal Regiment of Foot.

1715–27. The Princess of Wales's Own Regiment of Foot.

1727–51. The Queen's Own Regiment of Foot.

1751–1881. The 2nd (Queen's Royal) Regiment of Foot.

1881 (from). The Queen's (Royal West Surrey Regiment).

PRINCIPAL CAMPAIGNS, BATTLES, &c.

* "Honours" on the Colours.

1662–83. Tangier.
1690. Boyne.
1691. Aughrim.
1692–5. Flanders.
1693. Neer Landen.
1695. Namur.
1702. Cadiz.

1703–4. Germany.
1703. Tongres.
1704–8. Spain.
1707. Almanza.
1711. Quebec.
1799. Helder.
1799. Bergen.

1799. Egmont-op-Zee.
1801. Mandora.
*1801. Egypt.
1801. Alexandria.
1807. Rosetta.
*1808–14. Peninsula.
*1808. Vimiera.

The Queen's (Royal West Surrey Regiment)—*continued.*

PRINCIPAL CAMPAIGNS, BATTLES, &c.—*continued*

1809. Flushing.	*1814. Toulouse.	*1860. Taku Forts.
*1809. Corunna.	*1839. Afghanistan.	*1860. Pekin.
1809. Talavera.	*1839. Ghuznee.	*1886-8. Burma.
*1812. Salamanca.	*1839. Khelat.	*1897-8. Tirah.
*1813. Vittoria.	1842. Cabool.	1900. South Africa.
*1813. Pyrenees.	*1851-2-3 & 6-7. South	
*1813. Nivelle.	Africa.	

UNIFORM.—Scarlet and Sea-Green facings (1661–1768; sea-green was the favourite colour of Queen Catherine; see also " Badges "); Scarlet with Blue facings (from 1768).

TERRITORIAL BADGES.—"The Paschal Lamb" (the crest of the house of Braganza) with the mottoes, "*Pristinæ virtutis memor*" and "*Vel exuviæ triumphant.*" Also "The Royal Cypher within the Garter." Also "The Sphinx," for Egypt (1801).

NICKNAMES.—" Kirke's Lambs " (during the Monmouth Rebellion, 1685, under the Colonelcy of Piercy Kirke the reputation of the regiment was none of the best). "The Sleepy Queen's" (at Almeida, 1810, they carelessly allowed General Brennier to escape). " The Governor's Regiment " (on its formation for service in Tangier).

NOTES.—Tangier was part of the dowry of Catherine of Braganza, the Queen of Charles II. " The Paschal Lamb " is the crest of the royal house of Braganza, and the facings (sea-green) on formation were also in honour of the Queen. For gallantry at Tongres it received its title in 1703; also possibly its *second* motto (" Even the Remnant Triumph "), a most desperate resistance of twenty-eight hours' duration having there been offered to the French attack. The other motto (" Mindful of Ancient Valour ") is thought to refer to Marlborough's Spanish campaigns, in which it saw much service, besides having been specially selected for reinforcements.

BIBLIOGRAPHY.—*Historical Record of the 2nd, or Queen's Royal Regiment of Foot* 1661-1837. [London : Clowes. 1837.]

History of the 2nd Queen's Royal Regiment, now the Queen's (Royal West Surrey) Regiment. By Colonel John Davis, F.S.A. Maps and Illustrations. Vol. 1, 1661-84. Vols. 2 and 3, 1684-1799. [London: Bentley. 1887-95.]

G

The Buffs (East Kent Regiment),

1st & 2nd Batts. (formerly) The 3rd (East Kent—The Buffs) Regiment of Foot ; with a

3rd Batt. The East Kent Militia.

" Veteri frondescit honore."

| THE DRAGON | THE UNITED ROSE AND CROWN. | THE WHITE HORSE OF KENT. |

TITLES.

1665–89. The Holland Regiment (from 1572—*temp.* Queen Elizabeth — in service of Holland).

1689–1708. Prince George of Denmark's Regiment.

1708–51. The Buffs.

1751–82. The 3rd (or The Buffs) Regiment of Foot.

1782–1881. The 3rd (East Kent—The Buffs) Regiment of Foot.

1881 (from). The Buffs (East Kent) Regiment of Foot.

The Buffs (East Kent Regiment)—*continued.*

PRINCIPAL CAMPAIGNS, BATTLES, &c.

1689–97. Flanders.	1745. Fontenoy.	*1813. Pyrenees.
1689. Walcourt.	1747. Val.	*1813. Nivelle.
1693. Neer Landen.	1759. Guadaloupe.	*1813. Nive.
1703–13. Germany.	1761. Belle Isle.	*1814. Orthes.
1704. Schellenberg.	1781. America.	*1814. Toulouse.
*1704. Blenheim.	1782. Jamaica.	1814. Plattsburg.
*1706. Ramilies.	1794–95. Flanders.	*1843. Punniar.
*1708. Oudenarde.	1794. Nimeguen.	*1855. Sevastopol.
1708. Lisle.	1796. Grenada.	*1860. Taku Forts.
1709. Tournay.	*1808–14. Peninsula.	*1879. South Africa.
*1709. Malplaquet.	*1809. Douro.	*1895. Chitral.
1715. Jacobite rising.	*1809. Talavera.	1900. South Africa.
1742–49. Flanders.	*1811. Albuera.	
*1743. Dettingen.	*1813. Vittoria.	

UNIFORM.—Scarlet with Buff facings (from 1665).

REGIMENTAL BADGES.—" The Dragon " (a badge of Queen Elizabeth). Also " The United Red and White Rose with the Imperial Crown " (also probably dating back to the Virgin Queen). Also " The White Horse of Kent," with " *Invicta* " (in 1751 " The White Horse " was that of Hanover, but with the territorial classification the change was made). Motto, " *Veteri frondescit honore.*" In 1686 the regiment bore " The Red Cross of St. George," bordered with white on a green ground.

NICKNAMES, &C.—" The Buff Howards " (1737–49—from its Colonel's name). " The Nutcrackers," and " The Resurrectionists " (at Albuera it is said to have shown despatch in cracking the heads, and to have rallied after dispersal at the hands of the Polish Lancers). " The Old Buffs " (to distinguish it from the 31st, the " Young Buffs ").

NOTES.—The Regiment of Buffs possesses the privilege of marching unhindered through the City of London with drums beating—a relic of Elizabethan days. At Punniar it captured eleven guns and a standard.

BIBLIOGRAPHY.—*Historical Record of the 3rd Regiment of Foot, or The Buffs.* To 1838. Illustrated with plates. [London : Longman. 1839.]

The King's Own (Royal Lancaster Regiment),

COMPRISING

1st & 2nd Batts. (formerly) The 4th (The King's Own Royal); with

3rd & 4th Batts. The 1st Royal Lancashire Militia.

THE LION OF ENGLAND.   THE ROYAL CYPHER WITHIN   THE RED ROSE OF LANCASTER.
THE GARTER.

TITLES.

1680–84. The 2nd Tangier Regiment; also The Tangierenes.

1684–85. The Duchess of York and Albany's Regiment.

1685–88. The Queen's Regiment.

1688–1702. The Queen Consort's Regiment.

1702–15. The Queen's Marines.

1715–51. The King's Own Regiment.

1751–1867. The 4th, or The King's Own Regiment.

1867–1881. The 4th (The King's Own Royal) Regiment.

1881 (from). The King's Own (Royal Lancaster Regiment).

The King's Own (Royal Lancaster Regiment)—*continued.*

PRINCIPAL CAMPAIGNS, BATTLES, &c.

* "Honours" on the Colours.

1685. Sedgemoor.	1762. Martinique.	1812. Burgos.
1690. Boyne.	1762. Havannah.	1813. Bidassoa.
1692–95. Flanders.	1775–78. America.	*1813. Vittoria.
1692. Steenkirk.	1775. Lexington.	*1813. St. Sebastian.
1693. Neer-Landen.	1775. Bunker's Hill.	*1813. Nive.
1695. Namur.	1776. Brooklyn.	*1814. Bladensburg.
1704–9. Spain.	1777. Germantown.	1814. Washington.
1704. Malaga.	1778. St. Lucia.	1815. New Orleans.
1705. Gibraltar.	1799. Egmont-op-Zee.	*1815. Waterloo.
1705. Barcelona.	1799. Alkmaer.	1815. Netherlands.
1707. Almanza.	1807. Copenhagen.	*1854. Alma.
1708. Minorca.	*1808–14. Peninsula.	*1854. Inkerman.
1711. Quebec.	*1809. Corunna.	*1855. Sevastopol.
1746. Culloden.	1809. Flushing.	1858. Indian Mutiny.
1756. Minorca.	1812. Cadiz.	*1868. Abyssinia.
1759. Guadaloupe.	*1812. Badajos.	*1879. South Africa.
1761. Dominica.	*1812. Salamanca.	1900. South Africa.

UNIFORM.—Scarlet, with bright Yellow facings (the Stuart livery, 1680–88), Scarlet, with Blue facings (from 1688).

REGIMENTAL AND OTHER BADGES.—"The Lion of England" (conferred by William III.). Also "The Royal Cypher within the Garter. Also "The Red Rose of Lancaster," since its territorial assignment to the County of Lancaster.

NICKNAMES.—"Barrell's Blues" (from its Colonel's name, *circa* 1734–9, and long afterwards). "The Lions" (from its badge).

NOTES.—This regiment was, like The Queen's, originally raised near London, and in the West of England, for the defence of Tangier. It became a "Royal" regiment in recognition of its devotion to William III. From 1704 to 1710 it served as a Marine corps. The present 2nd Battalion was formed in 1858.

BIBLIOGRAPHY.—*Historical Record of the 4th, or The King's Own Regiment of Foot.* 1680–1839. Illustrated with plates. [London : Longman. 1839.]

The Northumberland Fusiliers,

COMPRISING

1st to 4th Batts. (formerly) The 5th (Northumberland Fusiliers); with **5th Batt.** The Northumberland Militia.

" Quo fata vocant."

St. George and the Dragon. · The United Rose (slipped) and Crown.

TITLES.

1674–88. A "Holland Regiment" (in service of Prince of Orange: previous to 1684 "The Irish Regiment).

1688–94. Colonel Edmond Lloyd's Regiment of Foot.

1694–1751. (Its Colonel's name) Regiment of Foot.

1751–82. The 5th Regiment of Foot.

1782–1836. The 5th (Northumberland) Regiment of Foot.

1836–81. The 5th (Northumberland Fusiliers) Regiment of Foot.

1881 (from). The Northumberland Fusiliers.

PRINCIPAL CAMPAIGNS, BATTLES, &c.

* "Honours" on the Colours.

1690. Boyne.	1727. Gibraltar.	1775–78. America.
1691. Athlone.	1758. Cherbourg.	1775. Lexington.
1691. Limerick.	1760–63. Germany.	1775. Bunker's Hill.
1692–97. Flanders.	1760. Corbach.	1776. Brooklyn.
1695. Namur.	1760. Warbourg.	1776. Long Island.
1707–13. Spain.	1761. Denkern.	1776. White Plains.
1709. Caya.	*1762. Wilhelmsthal.	1776. Brunx.

The Northumberland Fusiliers—*continued.*

PRINCIPAL CAMPAIGNS, BATTLES, &c.—*continued.*

1777. Brandywine.	*1808. Roleia.	*1813. Vittoria.
1777. Germantown.	*1808. Vimiera.	*1813. Nivelle.
1778. St. Lucia (La Vigie).	*1809. Corunna.	*1814. Orthes.
1787–97. Canada.	1809. Flushing.	*1814. Toulouse.
1799. Bergen.	1809. Talavera.	1814. Plattsburg.
1799. Egmont-op-Zee.	*1810. Busaco.	1857–58. Indian Mutiny.
1799. Crabbendam.	1811. El Bodon.	*1857. Lucknow.
1799. Alkmaer.	*1812. Ciudad Rodrigo.	*1878–80. Afghanistan.
1806. Buenos Ayres.	*1812. Badajos.	*1898. Khartoum.
*1808–14. Peninsula.	*1812. Salamanca.	1900. South Africa.

UNIFORM.—Scarlet (since 1688). Facings.—At first Yellow, subsequently changed to Green; in 1832 a "faded-leaf" Green; afterwards White, and now (1900) Gosling-green.

REGIMENTAL AND OTHER BADGES.—"St. George and the Dragon" (adopted when "The Irish Regiment" became English). Also "The United Red and White Rose, with the Royal Crest," and the Motto "*Quo fata vocant*" (from 1751).

NICKNAMES.—(1) "The Shiners" (at the time of "The Seven Years' War," from its smart appearance). Also (from Peninsula times) "The Old Bold Fifth" and "The Fighting Fifth." Also known, through being at headquarters in 1811, "Lord Wellington's Body-guard."

NOTES.—For defeating a French division of Grenadiers at Wilhelmstahl (1762) it was granted the privilege of wearing Fusilier caps; also a white plume for gallantry at St. Lucia, and when it took the feathers from the caps of their French opponents. The 5th is now the only regiment retaining the distinction by a red and white hackle. At Wilhelmstahl Phoebe Hassell, the notorious "female soldier," served in the ranks. Its investment of Ciudad Rodrigo was specially commended by Lord Wellington. The territorial title was bestowed in 1782 in compliment to its Colonel, Earl Percy.

BIBLIOGRAPHY.—*Historical Record of the Fifth Regiment of Foot, or Northumberland Fusiliers.* 1674 to 1837. [London: Clowes. 1838.]
   A Short Narrative of the 5th Regiment of Foot, or Northumberland Fusiliers. Printed for Private Circulation. [London: Howard, Jones, and Parkes. 1873.]

The Royal Warwickshire Regiment,

COMPRISING

1st & 2nd Batts. (formerly) The 6th (Royal First Warwickshire) Regiment of Foot; the 3rd and 4th Batts. have been recently sanctioned, with two Militia Battalions.

5th Batt. The 1st Warwick Militia.

6th Batt. The 2nd Warwick Militia.

THE ANTELOPE.   THE UNITED ROSE AND CROWN.   THE BEAR AND RAGGED STAFF.

TITLES.

1673–88. A "Holland Regiment." Also (when raised) Colonel Sir Walter Vane's Regiment of Foot.

1688–1702. [Its Colonel's name] Regiment of Foot.

1702–[?]. The "Sea Service" Regiment of Foot.

17[?]–1832. The 6th (1st Warwickshire) Regiment of Foot.

1832–81. The 6th (Royal 1st Warwickshire) Regiment of Foot.

1881 (from). The Royal Warwickshire Regiment.

THE CAMERONIANS,
SCOTTISH RIFLES (26TH & 90TH FOOT)

THE ROYAL SUSSEX REGIMENT
(35TH & 107TH FOOT)

THE DORSETSHIRE REGIMENT

(39TH & 54TH FOOT)

THE OXFORDSHIRE LIGHT INFANTRY
(43RD & 52ND FOOT)

THE PRINCE OF WALES' (NORTH STAFFORDSHIRE REGIMENT)
(64TH & 98TH FOOT)

THE HIGHLAND LIGHT INFANTRY

(71ST & 74TH FOOT)

SEAFORTH HIGHLANDERS
(ROSS-SHIRE BUFFS, THE DUKE OF ALBANY'S)
(72ND & 78TH FOOT)

THE LEICESTERSHIRE REGIMENT
(17TH FOOT)

The Royal Warwickshire Regiment—*continued.*

PRINCIPAL CAMPAIGNS, BATTLES, &c.

* " Honours " on the Colours.

1690. Boyne.	*1808–14. Peninsula.	1832. Baloochistan.
1690–96. Flanders.	*1808. Roleia.	1840–41. Aden.
1702. Cadiz.	*1808. Vimiera.	*1846–47. South Africa.
1704–10. Spain.	*1809. Corunna.	*1851–2–3. South Africa.
1707. Almanza.	1809. Flushing.	1856–57. South Africa.
1710. Saragossa.	*1813. Vittoria.	1857–58. Indian Mutiny.
1741. Carthagena.	*1813. Pyrenees	1860. Thibet.
1745. Jacobite rising.	(Eschalar).	1865. Jamaica.
1772. St. Vincent.	*1813. Nivelle.	1868. Hazara.
1776–77. America.	*1813. Niagara.	1869. Punjaub.
1794. Martinique.	*1814. Orthes.	*1898. Atbara.
1794. Guadaloupe.	1814. Bordeaux.	*1898. Khartoum.
1796–98. Ireland.	1821–7. Kaffraria.	1900. South Africa.
1799–1806. Canada.	1832. Scinde.	

UNIFORM.—Red and Deep Yellow facings (1673–1832); Scarlet with Blue facings (since 1832).

REGIMENTAL AND OTHER BADGES.—" The Antelope " (an ancient Royal Badge—in Henry VI.'s reign one of the supporters of the Royal Arms). Also " The United Red and White Rose with the Imperial Crown " (the rose is with stalk and leaves —the Tudor rose had none of these appendages—and is thought to have been the badge of all the " Holland regiments.") Also " The Rampant Bear Chained to a Ragged Staff"—" Old Neville's Crest "—borne only since the territorial reorganisation.

NICKNAMES.—" Guise's Geese," " The Warwickshire Lads," " The Saucy Sixth."

NOTES.—As in the case of the Northumberland Fusiliers, this is one of the regiments that returned, after service in Holland, with William of Orange in 1688. Its service has always been distinguished—it was cut up at Almanza in 1707—and the Iron Duke characterised its performance at Eschalar (Pyrenees, 1813) as " the most gallant and finest thing I have ever witnessed." Also at Niagara it won special distinction, since when its general Colonial service has been unique.

BIBLIOGRAPHY.—*Historical Record of the 6th, or 1st Royal Warwickshire Regiment of Foot.* 1674–1838. Illustrated. [London : Longman. 1839.]

The Royal Fusiliers (City of London Regiment),

1st & 2nd Batts. (formerly) The 7th (Royal Fusiliers) Regiment; Batts. 3 and 4 recently sanctioned; with Militia (three Battalions).

5th Batt. The Royal Westminster Militia.

6th Batt. The Royal London Militia ; and

7th Batt. The Royal South Middlesex Militia.

THE UNITED ROSE AND GARTER.

THE WHITE HORSE.

TITLES.

1685–89. " Our Royal Regiment of Fusiliers "; also " Our Ordnance Regiment"; formerly " The Tower Guards."

1689–1881. The 7th (Royal Fusiliers).

1881 (from). The Royal Fusiliers (City of London Regiment).

The Royal Fusiliers (City of London Regiment)—*continued.*

PRINCIPAL CAMPAIGNS, BATTLES, &c.

* " Honours " on the Colours.

1689–90. Flanders.
1690. Cork.
1690. Kinsale.
1692–96. Flanders.
1693. Neer Landen.
1695. Namur.
1702. Cadiz.
1704–9. Spain.
1705–6. Barcelona.
1707. Lerida.
1773–82. America.
1775. Quebec.

1807. Copenhagen.
*1809. Peninsula.
*1809. Talavera.
*1809. Martinique.
1810. Busaco.
*1811. Albuera.
*1812. Badajos.
*1812. Salamanca.
*1813. Vittoria.
*1813. Pyrenees.
1813. Bidassoa.
*1814. Orthes.

*1814. Toulouse.
1814. Bordeaux.
1814. America.
1815. New Orleans.
*1854. Alma.
*1854. Inkerman.
*1855. Sevastopol.
1857–58. Indian Mutiny.
*1879–80. Afghanistan.
*1880. Kandahar.
1900. South Africa.

UNIFORM.—Red, with Yellow facings (1685) ; Red and Dark Blue facings (in 1742) ; now Scarlet and Blue facings.

REGIMENTAL AND OTHER BADGES.—" The United Red and White Rose within the Garter, with the Crown over it."   Also " The White Horse."

NICKNAMES, &c.—" The Hanoverian White Horse."   " The Elegant Extracts."

NOTES.—Raised at the time of the Monmouth Rebellion.

BIBLIOGRAPHY.—*Historical Record of the 7th Regiment, or Royal Fusiliers.* 1685–1846. Illustrated. [London : Parker. 1847.]
    Historical Record of the 7th, or Royal Regiment of Fusiliers.   Printed for private circulation.   By Colonel G. H. Waller, Royal Fusiliers. [Dublin. 1877.]

The King's (Liverpool Regiment),

1st & 2nd Batts. (formerly) The 8th (The King's) Regiment of Foot; the 3rd and 4th Batts. recently sanctioned ; with Militia Battalions.

5th & 6th Batts. The 2nd Lancashire Militia.

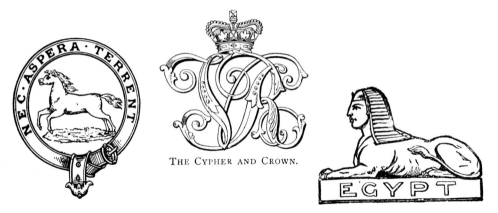

THE CYPHER AND CROWN.

THE WHITE HORSE AND GARTER.

THE SPHINX.

TITLES.

1685–1702. The Princess Anne of Denmark's Regiment.

1702–16. The Queen's Regiment.

1716–51. The King's Regiment ; also the King's Hanoverian White Horse.

1751–1881. The 8th (The King's) Regiment.

1881 (from). The King's (Liverpool Regiment).

The King's (Liverpool Regiment)—*continued.*

PRINCIPAL CAMPAIGNS, BATTLES, &c.

* " Honours " on the Colours.

1690. Boyne.	1746. Falkirk.	1801. Mandora.
1691. Limerick.	1746. Culloden.	1801. Alexandria.
1696–97. Flanders.	1746. Roucoux.	1807. Copenhagen.
1701–14. Germany.	1747. Val.	*1809. Martinique.
1702. Venloo.	1760–63. Germany.	1809. Flushing.
1702. Liége.	1760. Corbach.	1812–14. America.
1704. Schellenberg.	1760. Warbourg.	1813–14. Quebec.
*1704. Blenheim.	1760. Zierenberg.	1814. Plattsburg.
*1706. Ramilies.	1760. Campen.	*1814. Niagara.
*1708. Oudenarde.	1761. Kirch Denkern.	1857–58. Indian Mutiny.
1708. Lisle.	1761. Grafenstein.	1857. Cawnpore.
1709. Tournay.	1762. Wilhelmstahl.	*1857. Delhi.
*1709. Malplaquet.	1768. America.	1857. Pillour.
1710. Douay.	1794–95. Flanders.	*1857. Lucknow.
1715. Jacobite rising.	1794. Martinique.	1857. Agra.
1715. Dunblane.	1794. Guadaloupe.	*1876–80. Afghanistan.
1742–48. Flanders.	1794. Nimeguen.	*1878. Peiwar Kotal.
*1743. Dettingen.	1794. St. Lucia.	*1885–87. Burma.
1745. Fontenoy.	1796. Grenada.	1900. South Africa.
1745. Jacobite rising.	*1801. Egypt.	

UNIFORM.—Scarlet and bright Yellow facings (1685 to 1716); Scarlet and Blue facings (from 1716).

REGIMENTAL AND OTHER BADGES.—" The White Horse within the Garter" (for services during the Jacobite rising of 1715, the corps suffering heavily at Dunblane. At the same time and for a similar reason it received its title of " King's"). Also ".The Royal Cypher and the Imperial Crown." Also " The Sphinx," for Egypt (1801). Motto, " *Nec aspera terrent*" (" Nor do difficulties terrify us").

NOTES.—Raised chiefly in Derbyshire at the time of the Monmouth Rebellion.

BIBLIOGRAPHY.—*Historical Record of the 8th, or King's Regiment of Foot.* 1685–1844. Illustrated. [London : Parker. 1844.]

Historical Record of The King's (Liverpool) Regiment of Foot. 1685–1881. By General Cunningham Robertson. Illustrated. [London : Harrison. 1883.]

The Norfolk Regiment,

COMPRISING

1st & 2nd Batts. (formerly) The 9th (East Norfolk) Regiment of Foot ; with Militia Battalions.

3rd Batt. The 1st Norfolk Militia.

4th Batt. The 2nd Norfolk Militia.

THE FIGURE OF BRITANNIA.

TITLES.

1685–88. Colonel Henry Cornwell's Regiment of Foot.

1688–1751. (Its Colonel's name) Regiment of Foot.

1751–82. The 9th Regiment of Foot.

1782–1881. The 9th (East Norfolk) Regiment of Foot.

1881 (from). The Norfolk Regiment.

PRINCIPAL CAMPAIGNS, BATTLES, &c.

* " Honours " on the Colours.

1689. Londonderry.
1690. Boyne.
1691. Aughrim.
1701–4. Germany.
1702. Liége.

1702. Kaiserswerth.
1702. Venloo.
1702. Huy.
1704–10. Spain.
1707. Almanza.

1707. Valencia d'Alcantara.
1707. Albuquerque.
1710. Almanara.
1710. Badajos.

The Norfolk Regiment—*continued.*

PRINCIPAL CAMPAIGNS, BATTLES, &c.—*continued.*

1710. Vellina.	*1808. Vimiera.	*1813. Nive.
1761. Belle Isle.	*1809. Corunna.	1813. Nivelle.
1762. Havannah.	1809. Flushing.	1814. Bayonne.
1775–81. America.	1809. Douro.	*1842. Cabool.
1777. Stillwater.	*1810. Busaco.	*1845. Moodkee.
1794. Martinique.	1811. Barossa.	*1845. Ferozeshah.
1794. St. Lucia.	1811. Tarifa.	*1846. Sobraon.
1796. Guadaloupe.	1811. Tarragona.	*1855. Sevastopol.
1796. Grenada.	1811. Fuentes d'Onor.	*1879–80. Afghanistan.
1799. Bergen.	1812. Badajos.	*1879. Cabool.
1799. Egmont-op-Zee.	*1812. Salamanca.	1889. Burma.
1799. Alkmaer.	*1813. Vittoria.	1900. South Africa.
*1808–14. Peninsula.	*1813. St. Sebastian.	
*1808. Roleia.	1813. Bidassoa.	

UNIFORM.—Scarlet with Blue facings (from 1685 to well on in the 18th Century); Scarlet and Yellow facings (in 1751). In Irish Army Lists, *circa* 1718–46, it is set down as with Orange facings. At present Scarlet and White facings.

REGIMENTAL BADGE.—"The Figure of Britannia"—"This distinguished badge was given to you for your gallantry at the battle of Almanza, during the War of Succession in Spain, by Queen Anne. On the occasion of that battle it is recorded that you lost 24 officers and had 300 killed and wounded out of 467. In retiring from the field the regiment covered the retreat of General Lord Galway, a most arduous, hazardous, and difficult service. The regiment thus upheld the honour of Great Britain, and was rewarded for it by Queen Anne by allowing them to wear the figure of Britannia on their breastplates."—General BAINBRIDGE, *in* 1848, *when presenting new Colours.*

NICKNAMES, &c.—"The Holy Boys" (tradition says, for selling Bibles for drink in the Peninsula; but tradition likewise says because the Spaniards mistook the figure of Britannia on their belts for the Virgin Mary. "The Fighting Ninth." "The Norfolk Howards."

NOTES.—It captured the Colours of the 2nd Hampshire Regiment at Fort Anne in 1777.

BIBLIOGRAPHY.—*Historical Record of the 9th, or East Norfolk Regiment of Foot.* 1685–1847. Illustrated with plates. [London : Parker. 1848.]

The Lincolnshire Regiment,

COMPRISING

st & 2nd Batts. The 10th (North Lincolnshire) Regiment of Foot; with Militia Battalions.

3rd Batt. The Royal North Lincoln Militia.

4th Batt. The Royal South Lincoln Militia.

THE SPHINX.

TITLES.

1685–95. Colonel Sir John Greville's (The Earl of Bath) Regiment of Foot.

1695–1751. [Its Colonel's name] Regiment of Foot.

1751–82. The 10th Regiment of Foot.

1782–1881. The 10th (North Lincolnshire) Regiment of Foot.

1881 (from). The Lincolnshire Regiment.

PRINCIPAL CAMPAIGNS, BATTLES, &c.

* "Honours" on the Colours.

1690–96. Flanders.
1692. Steenkirk.
1701–13. Germany.
1702. Kaiserswerth.

1702. Liége.
1704. Schellenberg.
*1704. Blenheim.
1705. Neer Hespen.

*1706. Ramilies.
*1708. Oudenarde.
1708. Lisle.
1708. Ghent.

The Lincolnshire Regiment—*continued.*

PRINCIPAL CAMPAIGNS, BATTLES, &c.—*continued.*

1709. Tournay.	1777. Brandywine.	*1849. Mooltan.
*1709. Malplaquet.	1777. Germantown.	*1849. Goojerat.
1711. Bouchain.	1778. Freehold.	1857–58. Indian Mutiny.
1712. Quesnoy.	1798. Grenada.	*1857. Lucknow.
1767–78. America.	*1801. Egypt.	1875–76. Perak.
1775. Lexington.	1809. Flushing.	1888. Burma.
1775. Bunker's Hill.	1809. Ionian Islands.	*1898. Atbara.
1776. Long Island.	*1812–14. Peninsula.	*1898. Khartoum.
1776. White Plains.	*1846. Sobraon.	1900. South Africa.
1776. Brunx.	*1848–49. Punjaub.	

UNIFORM.—Blue faced with Red (when raised); Scarlet and Yellow facings (subsequently, but when is unknown); Scarlet with White facings (present time).

REGIMENTAL BADGE.—"The Sphinx," for Egypt (1801).

NICKNAME.—"The Springers" (during American War: also applied to the 62nd).

NOTES.—The 10th were the only regiment of Foot dressed in Blue when raised. Amongst other distinctions this regiment has been wrecked, has lost its way in the Arabian desert, has been attacked by plague, and took part in a gallant dash without the loss of a man. In the Mutiny it did much hard work.

BIBLIOGRAPHY.—*Historical Record of the 10th (or North Lincolnshire) Regiment of Foot.* 1685–1847. Illustrated. [London: Parker. 1847.]

The Devonshire Regiment,

COMPRISING

1st & 2nd Batts. (formerly) The 11th (North Devonshire) Regiment of Foot; with Militia Batts.

3rd Batt. The 2nd Devon Militia.

4th Batt. The 1st Devon Militia.

THE CASTLE OF EXETER AND MOTTO.

TITLES.

1685–87. Colonel the Duke of Beaufort's Regiment of Foot.

1687–1751. [Its Colonel's name] Regiment of Foot.

1751–82. The 11th Regiment of Foot.

1782–1881. The 11th (North Devonshire) Regiment of Foot.

1881 (from). The Devonshire Regiment.

PRINCIPAL CAMPAIGNS, BATTLES, &c.

* "Honours" on the Colours.

1690. Boyne.	1703–4. Germany.	1709. Mons.
1690. Athlone.	1706–8. Spain.	1709. Pont-à-Vendin.
1690. Limerick.	1707. Almanza.	1710. Douay.
1690–96. Flanders.	1708–11. Germany.	1710 Bethune.
1692. Steenkirk.	1709. Malplaquet.	1710. Aire.

The Devonshire Regiment—*continued.*

PRINCIPAL CAMPAIGNS, BATTLES, &c.—*continued.*

1710. St. Venant.
1711. Quebec.
1715. Jacobite rising.
1715. Dunblane.
1742–8. Flanders.
*1743. Dettingen.
1745. Fontenoy.
1745. Jacobite rising.
1746. Roucoux.
1760–3. Germany.
1760. Corbach.
1760. Warbourg.

1760. Campen.
1762. Wilhelmstahl.
1793. Toulon.
1794. Corsica.
1809. Flushing.
*1809–14. Peninsula.
1810. Busaco.
1811. Sabugal.
*1812. Salamanca.
1812. Burgos.
1813. Vittoria.
*1813. Pyrenees.

*1813. Nivelle.
*1813. Nive.
*1814. Orthes.
*1814. Toulouse.
1837–38. Ionian Islands.
1838–39. Canada.
*1879–80. Afghanistan.
1895. Chitral.
*1897–98. Tirah.
1900. South Africa.

UNIFORM.—Scarlet and "Tawny" facings (in 1685); Scarlet and Green facings (in 1742); Scarlet and White facings (present time).

REGIMENTAL AND OTHER BADGES.—"The Castle of Exeter." Motto, "*Semper fidelis*" (an allusion to the Civil Wars).

NICKNAME.—"The Bloody Eleventh" (from its having been cut to pieces at Salamanca by the French, when capturing a standard).

NOTES.—The regiment captured the drums of the 11th French Infantry at Flushing. Its service is fitly and truly described by its motto (" Always faithful ").

BIBLIOGRAPHY.—*Historical Record of the 11th, or North Devon Regiment.* 1685–1845. Illustrated. [London: Parker. 1845.]

The Suffolk Regiment,

COMPRISING

1st & 2nd Batts. (formerly) The 12th (East Suffolk) Regiment of Foot; with Militia Batts.

3rd Batt. The West Suffolk Militia ; and

4th Batt. The Cambridge Militia.

THE CASTLE, THE KEY, AND MOTTO.

TITLES.

1685 (*ante*). Colonel The Duke of Norfolk's Regiment of Foot.

1685–86. Colonel The Earl of Lichfield's Regiment of Foot.

1685–1751. [Its Colonel's name] Regiment of Foot.

1751–82. The 12th Regiment of Foot.

1782–1881. The 12th (East Suffolk) Regiment of Foot.

1881 (from). The Suffolk Regiment.

The Suffolk Regiment—*continued.*

PRINCIPAL CAMPAIGNS, BATTLES, &c.

* "Honours" on the Colours.

1690. oyne.	1761. Denkern.	1799. Mallavelly.
1691. Aughrim.	1762. Wilhelmstahl.	*1799. Seringapatam.
1694–97. Flanders.	1779–83. Gibraltar.	1810. Bourbon.
1719. Messina.	1794. Martinique.	1810. Mauritius.
1742–45. Flanders.	1794. Guadaloupe.	*1851–53. South Africa.
*1743. Dettingen.	1794–95. Flanders.	*1863–66. New Zealand.
1745. Fontenoy.	1794. Nimeguen.	*1878–80. Afghanistan.
1758–63. Germany.	1795. Guildermalsen.	1888. Hazara.
*1759. Minden.	*1798–1807. India.	1900. South Africa.

UNIFORM.—Scarlet and White facings (in 1685); Scarlet and Yellow facings (in 1751); Scarlet and White facings (present time). †

REGIMENTAL AND OTHER BADGES.—"The Castle and Key" (the arms of Gibraltar, where it served on defensive for many years), and the Motto, "*Montis insignia calpe.*"

NICKNAME.—"The Old Dozen" (from the late regimental number).

NOTES.—This regiment was first raised in Norfolk and Suffolk. At the storming of Seringapatam it captured eight stand of colours.

BIBLIOGRAPHY.—*Historical Record of The 12th, or East Suffolk Regiment.* 1685–1847. Illustrated. [London: Parker. 1847.]

† Whilst this book was passing through the press the Yellow facings have been restored.

The Prince Albert's (Somersetshire Light Infantry),

COMPRISING

1st & 2nd Batts. (formerly) The 13th (1st Somersetshire) (Prince Albert's Light Infantry) Regiment; with Militia.

3rd Batt. The 1st Somerset Militia; and

4th Batt. The 2nd Somerset Militia.

THE SPHINX.

THE MURAL CROWN.

TITLES.

1685–88. Colonel The Earl of Huntingdon's Regiment of Foot.

1688–1751. [Its Colonel's name] Regiment of Foot.

1751–82. The 13th Regiment of Foot.

1782–1822. The 13th (First Somersetshire) Regiment of Foot.

1822–42. The 13th (First Somersetshire Light Infantry) Regiment.

1842–1881. The 13th (1st Somersetshire) (Prince Albert's Light Infantry) Regiment.

1881 (from). The Prince Albert's (Somersetshire Light Infantry).

PRINCIPAL CAMPAIGNS, BATTLES, &c.

* "Honours" on the Colours.

1689. Killicrankie.
1690. Boyne.
1690. Cork.
1690. Kinsale.
1701–3. Flanders.
1702. Kaiserwerth.

1702. Venloo.
1702. Ruremonde.
1702. Huy.
1702. Limberg.
1702. Liége.
1704–11. Spain.

1704–5. Gibraltar.
1705. Barcelona.
1707. Almanza.
1709. Caya.
1711. Tortosa.
1711. St. Matheo.

The Prince Albert's (Somersetshire Light Infantry)—*continued.*

PRINCIPAL CAMPAIGNS, BATTLES, &c.—*continued.*

1727. Gibraltar.
1742–48. Flanders.
*1743. Dettingen.
1745. Fontenoy.
1745. Jacobite rising.
1746. Roucoux.
1747. Val.
1793–95. San Domingo.
*1801. Egypt.

1801. Mandora.
1801. Alexandria.
*1809. Martinique.
1810. Guadaloupe.
1813–15. America.
1814. Plattsburg.
*1824–26. Ava.
1825–27. Burma.
*1839. Afghanistan.

*1839. Ghuznee.
*1842. Jellalabad.
*1842. Cabool.
*1855. Sevastopol.
1858. Indian Mutiny.
*1878–79. South Africa.
*1885–87. Burma.
1900. South Africa.

UNIFORM.—Scarlet and Yellow facings (1685–1842); Scarlet and Blue facings (from 1842).

REGIMENTAL AND OTHER BADGES.—"A Mural Crown" superscribed "Jellalabad" (where it captured three standards from the Afghans). Also "The Sphinx" for "Egypt" (1801).

NICKNAMES.—"The Bleeders," "The Illustrious Garrison," "The Jellalabad Heroes."

NOTES.—Chiefly raised in Buckinghamshire. For its services at Culloden (1746) it wears the sash knots on the right side.

BIBLIOGRAPHY.—*Historical Record of The 13th, 1st Somerset, or Prince Albert's Light Infantry.* 1685–1848. Illustrated. [London: Parker. 1848.]
 Historical Record of The 13th, 1st Somersetshire, or Prince Albert's Light Infantry. By Thomas Carter. Illustrated. [London: Mitchell. 1867.]

The Prince of Wales's Own (West Yorkshire Regiment),

COMPRISING

1st & 2nd Batts. (formerly) The 14th (Buckinghamshire—The Prince of Wales's Own) Regiment of Foot ; with Militia Batts.

3rd Batt. The 2nd West York Militia ; and

4th Batt. The 4th West York Militia.

THE WHITE HORSE AND MOTTO.

THE PLUME OF THE PRINCE OF WALES.

THE ROYAL TIGER.

TITLES.

1685–88. Colonel Sir Edward Hales's Regiment of Foot.

1688–1751. [Its Colonel's name] Regiment of Foot.

1751–82. The 14th Regiment of Foot.

1782–1809. The 14th (Bedfordshire) Regiment of Foot.

1809–76. The 14th (Buckinghamshire) Regiment of Foot.

1876–81. The 14th (Buckinghamshire—The Prince of Wales's Own) Regiment of Foot.

1881 (from). The Prince of Wales's Own (West Yorkshire Regiment).

PRINCIPAL CAMPAIGNS, BATTLES, &c.

* "Honours" on the Colours.

1692–96. Flanders.
1693. Neer-Landen.
1695. Namur.
1727. Gibraltar.

1745. Flanders.
1746. Falkirk.
1746. Culloden.
1766–71. America.

1793–95. Flanders.
1793. Famars.
1793. Valenciennes.
1793. Dunkirk.

The Prince of Wales's Own (West Yorkshire Regiment)—*continued.*

PRINCIPAL CAMPAIGNS, BATTLES, &c.—*continued.*

*1794. Tournay.
1795. Guildermalsen.
1796. St. Lucia.
*1807–31. India.
1808–9. Peninsula.
*1809. Corunna.
1809. Flushing.

1810. Mauritius.
1811. Tarifa.
*1811. Java.
1814. Genoa.
1815. Netherlands.
*1815. Waterloo.
1815. Cambray.

*1826. Bhurtpore.
*1855. Sevastopol.
*1860–66. New Zealand.
*1879–80. Afghanistan.
1900. South Africa.

UNIFORM.—Red and Yellow facings (in 1685); Scarlet with Buff facings (in 1742); Scarlet with White facings (present time).

REGIMENTAL AND OTHER BADGES.—"The Prince of Wales's Plume" (from 1876). Also "The White Horse," and Motto, "*Nec aspera terrent*" (from 1765). Also "The Royal Tiger" (for service in India 1807–31).

NICKNAMES, &c.—"The Old and Bold." "Calvert's Entire" (from 1806 to 1826 its Colonel was Sir Harry Calvert, at whose request the county title was changed in 1809. He had large estates in mid-Buckinghamshire, now represented by the Verneys). "The Powos."

NOTES.—This regiment was one of the trio known in the 1793–95 Flanders campaign as "The Fighting Brigade." Characterised by the Earl of Albemarle as "composed of boys, but fine boys," they suffered heavily at Waterloo. The regiment was first raised in Kent.

BIBLIOGRAPHY.—*Historical Record of The* 14*th, or the Buckinghamshire Regiment.* 1685–1845. Illustrated. [London: Parker. 1845.]
Historical Records of the 14*th Regiment* (*now Prince of Wales's Own West Yorkshire*). *From its formation in* 1685 *to* 1892. By Captain H. O'Donnell. With full-page coloured and other illustrations, and illustrations in the text. [Devonport: Swiss. 1893.]

The East Yorkshire Regiment,

COMPRISING

1st & 2nd Batts. (formerly)   The 15th (Yorkshire East Riding) Regiment of Foot ; with Militia Batt.

3rd Batt.   The East York Militia.

THE WHITE ROSE AND STAR.

TITLES.

1685–86. Colonel Sir William Clifton's Regiment.

1686–1751. [Its Colonel's name] Regiment of Foot.

1751–82. The 15th Regiment of Foot.

1782–1881. The 15th (York, East Riding) Regiment of Foot.

1881 (from). The East Yorkshire Regiment.

PRINCIPAL CAMPAIGNS, BATTLES, &c

* " Honours " on the Colours.

1694–97. Flanders.
1695. Namur.
1702–12. Germany.
1702. Liége.
1704. Schellenberg.

*1704. Blenheim.
*1706. Ramilies.
*1708. Oudenarde.
1708. Lisle.
1709. Tournay.

*1709. Malplaquet.
1709. Mons.
1710. Douai.
1711. Bouchain.
1741. Carthagena.

The East Yorkshire Regiment—*continued.*

PRINCIPAL CAMPAIGNS, BATTLES, &c.—*continued.*

1745. Jacobite rising.
1758–60. Canada.
*1758. Louisburg.
*1759. Quebec.
1760. Sillery.
1762. Martinique.

1762. Havannah.
1776–78. America.
1776. Brooklyn.
1777. Brandywine.
1777. Germantown.
1778. St. Lucia.

1794. Martinique.
1794. Guadaloupe.
*1809. Martinique.
*1810. Guadaloupe.
1815. Martinique.
*1879–80. Afghanistan.

UNIFORM.—Scarlet faced with Yellow (in 1685); Scarlet with White facings (present time).

REGIMENTAL BADGE.—" The White Rose " (of York).

NICKNAMES.—" The Snappers," " The Poona Guards."

NOTES.—This regiment is specially distinguished for West India service—note its repeated capture of Martinique and Guadaloupe during the campaigns against France.

BIBLIOGRAPHY.—*Historical Record of the 15th (East Yorkshire) Regiment.* 1685–1848. Illustrated. [London : Parker. 1848.]

The Bedfordshire Regiment,

COMPRISING

1st & 2nd Batts. (formerly)   The 16th (the Bedfordshire) Regiment of Foot ; with
Militia Batts.

3rd Batt.   The Bedford Militia.

4th Batt.   The Hertford Militia.

THE UNITED RED AND WHITE ROSE.

TITLES.

1688–1751. Colonel James Douglas's Regiment of Foot (when raised); subsequently by the name of successive Colonels (in 1689 Colonel James Stanley).

1751–82. The 16th Regiment of Foot.

1782–1809. The 16th (Buckinghamshire) Regiment of Foot.

1809–81. The 16th (Bedfordshire) Regiment of Foot (the county title was exchanged with the 14th at the request of the Colonel of that regiment).

1881 (from). The Bedfordshire Regiment.

The Bedfordshire Regiment—*continued*.

PRINCIPAL CAMPAIGNS, BATTLES, &c.

* " Honours " on the Colours.

1689–97. Flanders.
1689. Walcourt.
1692. Steenkirk.
1693. Neer Landen.
1695. Namur.
1702–12. Germany.
1702. Liége.
1704. Schellenberg.

*1704. Blenheim.
*1706. Ramilies.
*1708. Oudenarde.
1708. Lisle.
1709. Tournay.
*1709. Malplaquet.
1741. Carthagena.
1742. Cuba.

1778. Baton Rouge.
1779–81. America.
1781. Pensacola.
1793–94. San Domingo.
1795. Jamaica.
*1804. Surinaam.
*1895. Chitral.
1900. South Africa.

UNIFORM.—Scarlet with White facings (in 1688); Scarlet and deep Yellow facings (in 1742); Scarlet and White facings (present time).

REGIMENTAL BADGE.—"The United Red and White Rose."

NICKNAMES.—"The Old Bucks" (before 1809, when the county title was exchanged with the 14th). "The Peacemakers." "The Featherbeds."

NOTES.—One of twelve regiments raised in 1688. It and the 17th Foot alone remain (1900).

BIBLIOGRAPHY.—*Historical Record of the 16th, or Bedfordshire Regiment.* 1688–1848. Illustrated. [London : Parker. 1848.]

The Leicestershire Regiment,

COMPRISING

1st & 2nd Batts. (formerly) The 17th (Leicestershire) Regiment of Foot; with Militia Batt.

3rd Batt. The Leicestershire Militia.

HINDOOSTAN.

THE ROYAL TIGER.

TITLES.

1688–89. Colonel Solomon Richards' Regiment of Foot.

1689–1751. [Its Colonel's name] Regiment of Foot (in 1702 Colonel Holcroft Blood).

1751–82. The 17th Regiment of Foot.

1782–1881. The 17th (Leicestershire) Regiment of Foot.

1881 (from). The Leicestershire Regiment.

PRINCIPAL CAMPAIGNS, BATTLES, &c.

"Honours" on the Colours.

1693–97. Flanders.
1693. Neer Landen.
1695. Namur.
1702–4. Germany.
1702. Venloo.

1702. Huy.
1702. Liége.
1704–9. Spain.
1707. Almanza.
1715. Jacobite rising.

1757–60. Canada.
*1758. Louisbourg.
1762. Martinique.
1762. Havannah.
1775–81. America.

The Leicestershire Regiment—*continued.*

PRINCIPAL CAMPAIGNS, BATTLES, &c.—*continued.*

1776. Brooklyn.
1777. Brandywine.
1777. Germantown.
1778. Freehold.
1796. San Domingo.
1799. Helder.

1799. Crabbendam.
1799. Bergen.
1799. Egmont-op-Zee.
*1804–23. Hindoostan.
*1839. Afghanistan.
*1839. Ghuznee.

*1839. Khelat.
*1855. Sevastopol.
*1878–79. Afghanistan.
*1878. Ali Masjid.
1900. South Africa.

UNIFORM.—Scarlet with Greyish-white facings (1688–1790); Scarlet and White facings (from 1790).

REGIMENTAL BADGE.—"The Royal Tiger within a Wreath," superscribed "Hindoostan" (for services in India from 1804–23).

NICKNAMES.—(1) "The Bengal Tigers" (from its badge); (2) "The Lily-whites" (from its facings).

NOTES.—Mainly raised near London: twelve regiments in all were formed in 1688, but this and The 16th (The Bedfordshire) are alone in commission now.

BIBLIOGRAPHY.—*Historical Record of The 17th, or Leicestershire Regiment.* 1688–1848. [London: Parker. 1848.]

The Royal Irish Regiment,

COMPRISING

1st & 2nd Batts. (formerly) The 18th (The Royal Irish) Regiment of Foot ;
with Militia Batts.

3rd Batt. The Wexford Militia.
4th Batt. The North Tipperary Militia.
5th Batt. The Kilkenny Militia.

THE HARP AND CROWN.

THE DRAGON OF CHINA.

THE LION OF NASSAU.

THE SPHINX.

TITLES.

1684–86. Colonel the Earl of Granard's Regiment of Foot.

1686–1695. [Its Colonel's name] Regiment of Foot.

1695–1751. The Royal Regiment of Ireland.

1751–1881. The 18th (The Royal Irish) Regiment of Foot.

1881 (from). The Royal Irish Regiment.

The Royal Irish Regiment—*continued.*

PRINCIPAL CAMPAIGNS, BATTLES, &c.

* "Honours" on the Colours.

1690. Boyne.
1691. Limerick.
1691. Aughrim.
1693–97. Flanders.
1695. Namur.
1702–15. Germany.
1702. Venloo.
1702. Liége.
1704. Schellenberg.
*1704. Blenheim.
1705. Neer-Hespen.
*1706. Ramilies.
*1708. Oudenarde.
1708. Lisle.

1709. Tournay.
*1709. Malplaquet.
1711. Bouchain.
1715. Aire.
1727. Gibraltar.
1745. Flanders.
1775–76. America.
1775. Lexington.
1775. Bunker's Hill.
1793. Toulon.
1794. Corsica.
*1801. Egypt.
1801. Mandora.
1801. Alexandria.

1809. San Domingo.
*1840–42. China.
1852. Rangoon.
*1852–53. Pegu.
*1855. Sevastopol.
*1863–66. New Zealand.
*1879–80. Afghanistan.
*1882. Egypt.
1882. Kassassin.
*1882. Tel-el-Kebir.
*1884–85. Nile.
1900. South Africa.

UNIFORM.—Scarlet with Blue facings (from 1684).

REGIMENTAL AND OTHER BADGES.—"The Harp and Crown." Also "The Lion of Nassau," with Motto, "*Virtutis Namurcensis Præmium*"—"the reward of valour at Namur"—(both bestowed by William III. for prowess in assault at the siege of Namur). Also "The Sphinx," for Egypt (1801). Also "The Dragon," for China (1840–42). Also (till 1695) "The Cross of St. Patrick."

NOTES.—The only regiment now in existence out of nineteen raised in Ireland from the Independent Garrison Companies of the Commonwealth.

NICKNAMES.—"Paddy's Blackguards," "The Namurs."

BIBLIOGRAPHY.—*Historical Record of the 18th, or Royal Irish Regiment.* 1684–1848. [London: Parker. 1848.]

The Princess of Wales's Own (Yorkshire Regiment),

COMPRISING

1st & 2nd Batts. (formerly) The 19th (1st Yorkshire, North Riding—Princess of Wales's Own) Regiment of Foot; with Militia Batts.

3rd Batt. The 5th West York Militia.

4th Batt. The North York Militia.

THE WHITE ROSE.

THE PRINCESS OF WALES'S
CYPHER WITH CROWN AND CORONET.

TITLES.

1688–91. Colonel Francis Luttrell's Regiment of Foot.

1691–1751. [Its Colonel's name] Regiment of Foot (in 1693 Colonel Earl's).

1751–82. The 19th Regiment of Foot.

1782–1875. The 19th (1st Yorkshire, North Riding) Regiment of Foot.

1875–81. The 19th (1st Yorkshire, North Riding—Princess of Wales's Own) Regiment of Foot.

1881 (from). The Princess of Wales's Own (Yorkshire Regiment).

The Princess of Wales's Own (Yorkshire Regiment)--*continued.*

PRINCIPAL CAMPAIGNS, BATTLES, &c.

* "Honours" on the Colours.

1692–96. Flanders.	1745. Fontenoy.	1817–19. Ceylon.
1692. Steenkirk.	1746. Roucoux.	*1854. Alma.
1693. Neer Landen.	1747. Val.	*1854. Inkerman.
1695. Namur.	1761. Belle Isle.	*1855. Sevastopol.
1709–13. Germany.	1781–82. America.	1858. Indian Mutiny.
*1709. Malplaquet.	1793. Nieuport.	1868. Hazara.
1709. Pont-à-Vendin.	1794–95. Flanders.	1884–85. Nile.
1710. Douay.	1795. Guildermalsen.	*1897–98. Tirah.
1711. Bouchain.	1799. Seringapatam.	1900. South Africa.
1744–48. Flanders.	1810. Mauritius.	

UNIFORM.—Scarlet with Grass-Green facings (to 1881); Scarlet and White facings (since 1881). Recently (1900) the grass-green facings have been restored.

REGIMENTAL AND OTHER BADGES.—"The White Rose" (of York) in the *Regulations.* Also a special device on various appointments—" H.R.H. the Princess of Wales's Cypher and Coronet, combined with a Cross "; on the cross, 1875.

NICKNAMES.—"The Green Howards," "Howard's Garbage," or "Howard's Greens," from its facings and Colonel's name (1738–48); also " The Bounders."

NOTES.—Raised from independent companies of pikemen and musketeers in Devonshire.

BIBLIOGRAPHY.—*Historical Record of The 19th, or 1st Yorkshire, North Riding Regiment.* 1688–1848. Illustrated. [London : Parker. 1848.]
   The Nineteenth and their Times. By Colonel John Biddulph. [London : Murray. 1900.]

The Lancashire Fusiliers,

COMPRISING

1st and 2nd Batts. (formerly) The 20th (The East Devonshire) Regiment of Foot; two other batts. have been sanctioned; also Militia Batts.

5th and 6th Batts. The 7th Royal Lancashire Militia.

" Omnia audax."

THE SPHINX WITH WREATH AND CROWN.

TITLES.

1688–89. Colonel Sir Robert Peyton's Regiment of Foot.

1689–1751. [Its Colonel's name] Regiment of Foot (in 1689 Colonel Gustavus Hamilton, afterwards Viscount Boyne).

1751–82. The 20th Regiment of Foot.

1782–1881. The 20th (East Devonshire) Regiment of Foot.

1881 (from). The Lancashire Fusiliers.

PRINCIPAL CAMPAIGNS, BATTLES, &c.

* " Honours" on the Colours.

1690. Boyne.	1709. Caya.	1745. Fontenoy.
1691. Athlone.	1727. Gibraltar.	1745. Culloden.
1691. Aughrim.	1742–45. Flanders.	1758. Cherbourg.
1707–12. Spain.	*1743. Dettingen.	1758–63. Germany.

The Lancashire Fusiliers—*continued.*

PRINCIPAL CAMPAIGNS, BATTLES, &c.—*continued.*

*1759. Minden.
1760. Warbourg.
1760. Campen.
1761. Denkern.
1762. Wilhelmstahl.
1776–81. America.
1777. Stillwater.
1799. Crabbendam.
1799. Bergen.
*1799. Egmont-op-Zee.

1799. Alkmaer.
1800. Quiberon.
*1801. Egypt.
*1806. Maida.
*1808–14. Peninsula.
*1808. Vimiera.
*1809. Corunna.
1809. Flushing.
*1813. Vittoria.
*1813. Pyrenees.

1813. St. Sebastien.
*1814. Orthes.
*1814. Toulouse.
*1854. Alma.
*1854. Inkerman.
*1855. Sevastopol.
1857–58. Indian Mutiny.
*1858. Lucknow.
*1898. Khartoum
1900. South Africa.

UNIFORM.—Scarlet and Pale Yellow (at formation) ; Scarlet and White (present time).

REGIMENTAL BADGE.—" The Sphinx " with a laurel wreath surmounted by a Crown for " Egypt " (1801). Also (time uncertain) the Motto, "*Omnia audax.*"

NICKNAMES.—" The Two Tens " (XXth). " The Minden Boys " (at Minden, in 1759, the regiment sported roses, obtained from a garden close by, in their hats ; in memory of distinction then won, a custom still obtains of wearing " Minden Roses " every 1st of August). " Kingsley's Stand " (also from its conduct at Minden and its Colonel's name).

NOTES.—Raised in Devonshire on the landing of William of Orange, afterwards William III.

BIBLIOGRAPHY.—*Historical Record of The 20th, or East Devonshire Regiment.* 1688–1848. Illustrated. [London : Parker. 1848.]

Orders, Memoirs, &c., connected with The 20th Regiment. By Lieut. F. W. BARLOW, 2nd Batt. 20th Regiment. [Minden Press. 1868.]

History of The 20th Regiment. 1688–1888. By Lieutenant and Quartermaster B. SMYTH, 1st Lancashire Fusiliers. [London : Simpkin Marshall & Co. 1889.]

The Royal Scots Fusiliers,

COMPRISING

1st & 2nd Batts. (formerly)   The 21st (Royal Scots Fusiliers) Regiment of Foot; with Militia Batt.

3rd Batt.   The Royal Ayr and Wigtown Militia.

THE THISTLE WITHIN CIRCLE OF
ST. ANDREW.

ROYAL CYPHER AND CROWN.

TITLES.

1678–86. Colonel The Earl of Mar's Regiment of Foot (afterwards Fusiliers).

1686–1707. [Its Colonel's name] Regiment of Fusiliers; also (popularly) The Scots Fusiliers Regiment of Foot.

1707–12. The Scots Fusiliers Regiment of Foot.

1712–51. The Royal North British Fusiliers Regiment of Foot.

1751–1877. The 21st (Royal North British) Fusiliers Regiment of Foot.

1877–81. The 21st (Royal Scots Fusiliers) Regiment of Foot.

1881 (from). The Royal Scots Fusiliers.

The Royal Scots Fusiliers—*continued.*

PRINCIPAL CAMPAIGNS, BATTLES, &c.

* " Honours " on the Colours.

1689–1697. Flanders.
1689. Walcourt.
1692. Steenkirk.
1693. Neer-Landen.
1702–12. Germany.
1704. Schellenberg.
*1704. Blenheim.
1705. Neer Hespen.
*1706. Ramilies.
*1708. Oudenarde.
1708. Lisle.
*1709. Malplaquet.
1710. Douay.

1711. Bouchain.
1742–48. Flanders.
*1743. Dettingen.
1745. Fontenoy.
1747. Val.
1761. Belle-Isle.
1776–81. America.
1777. Stillwater.
1794. Martinique.
1794. St. Lucia.
1794. Guadaloupe.
1809. Ionian Islands.
1809. Scylla.

1814. Bergen-op-Zoom.
1814. Netherlands.
*1814. Bladensburg.
1814. Baltimore.
1815. New Orleans.
*1854. Alma.
*1854. Inkerman.
*1855. Sevastopol.
*1879. South Africa.
*1885–87. Burma.
*1897–8. Tirah.
1900. South Africa.

UNIFORM.—Scarlet with Scarlet facings (1678–1712); Scarlet and Blue facings (from 1712).

REGIMENTAL AND OTHER BADGES.—" The Thistle within the Circle of St. Andrew," with the Motto, "*Nemo me impune lacessit.*" Also " The Royal Cypher and Crown."

NICKNAME.—" The Earl of Mar's Grey-breeks " (from the colour of the breeches and its Colonel's name when raised).

NOTES.—Armed, when raised, with fusils instead of muskets—hence its title. Formerly (1751) " The White Horse of Hanover " and Motto appeared on some appointments.

BIBLIOGRAPHY.—*Historical Record of The 21st, or Royal North British Fusiliers.* 1678–1849. Illustrated. [London : Parker. 1849.]
    Historical Record of The Royal Scots Fusiliers. 1678–1885. By James Clarke, late Sergeant Royal Scots Fusiliers. Illustrated. [Edinburgh : Banks & Co. 1885.]

The Cheshire Regiment,

COMPRISING

1st & 2nd Batts. (formerly) The 22nd (The Cheshire) Regiment of Foot; with Militia Batts.

3rd Batt. The 1st Royal Cheshire Militia.

4th Batt. The 2nd Royal Cheshire Militia.

THE UNITED ROSE.

THE ACORN AND LEAVES.

TITLES.

1689. Colonel the Duke of Norfolk's Regiment of Foot.

1689–1751. [Its Colonel's name] Regiment of Foot.

1751–82. The 22nd Regiment of Foot.

1782–1881. The 22nd (The Cheshire) Regiment of Foot.

1881 (from). The Cheshire Regiment.

PRINCIPAL CAMPAIGNS, BATTLES, &c.

* " Honours " on the Colours.

1690. Boyne.
1691. Athlone.
1691. Limerick.
1691. Aughrim.
1727. Gibraltar.
1757–60. Canada.
*1758. Louisberg.
1759. Quebec.
1761. Dominica.

1762. Martinique.
1762. Havannah.
1775–79. America.
1775. Bunker's Hill.
1776. Brooklyn.
1794. Guadaloupe.
1794. St. Lucia.
1794. San Domingo.
1800. Cape of Good Hope.

1804. Deig.
1805. Bhurtpore.
1810. Mauritius.
*1843. Meanee.
*1843. Hyderabad.
*1843. Scinde.
1887. Burma.
1900. South Africa.

The Cheshire Regiment—*continued.*

UNIFORM.—Scarlet with Buff facings (in 1689); Scarlet and White facings (present time).

REGIMENTAL AND OTHER BADGES.—" The United Red and White Rose" (this, though given in *Army List,* is not worn). Also " An Acorn and Oak Leaves."

NICKNAMES.—" The Two Twos" (22nd). "The Red Knights" (in 1795 it was served with red jackets, waistcoats, and breeches, instead of the proper uniform).

NOTES.—First raised at Chester. At Hyderabad (1743) it captured seventeen standards.

BIBLIOGRAPHY.—*Historical Record of The 22nd, or Cheshire Regiment of Foot.* 1689–1849. Illustrated. [London : Parker. 1849.]

The Royal Welsh Fusiliers,

COMPRISING

1st & 2nd Batts. (formerly) The 23rd (Royal Welsh Fusiliers) Regiment of Foot; with Militia Batts.

3rd Batt. The Royal Denbigh and Flint Militia.

4th Batt. The Royal Carnarvon and Merioneth Militia.

THE PLUME OF THE PRINCE OF WALES.

THE RISING SUN.

THE RED DRAGON.

THE WHITE HORSE.

THE SPHINX.

TITLES.

1688–89. Colonel Lord Herbert's Regiment of Foot.

1689–1714. [Its Colonel's name] Regiment of Foot.

1714–27. The Prince of Wales's Own Royal Welsh Fusiliers.

1727–51. The Royal Welsh Fusiliers.

1751–1881. The 23rd (Royal Welsh Fusiliers) Regiment of Foot.

1881 (from). The Royal Welsh Fusiliers.

The Royal Welsh Fusiliers—*continued.*

PRINCIPAL CAMPAIGNS, BATTLES, &c.

* "Honours" on the Colours.

1690. Boyne.	*1759. Minden.	1809. Flushing.
1691. Aughrim.	1760. Warbourg.	*1809. Martinique.
1692–97. Flanders.	1760. Campen.	*1811. Albuera.
1695. Namur.	1775–81. America.	*1812. Badajos.
1702–12. Germany.	1775. Lexington.	*1812. Salamanca.
1702. Liége.	1775. Bunker's Hill.	1812. Burgos.
1704. Schellenberg.	1776. Brooklyn.	*1813. Vittoria.
*1704. Blenheim.	1777. Brandywine.	1813. San Sebastian.
1705. Neer-Hespen.	1778. Freehold.	*1813. Pyrenees.
*1706. Ramilies.	1780. Camden.	*1813. Nivelle.
1708. Wynendale.	1781. Guildford.	*1814. Orthes.
*1708. Oudenarde.	1792. San Domingo.	*1814. Toulouse.
1708. Lisle.	1799. Helder.	1815. Quatre-Bras.
*1709. Malplaquet.	1799. Crabberdam.	*1815. Waterloo.
1710. Douay.	1799. Bergen.	1815. Netherlands.
1711. Bouchain.	1799. Egmont-op-Zee.	*1854. Alma.
1742–48. Flanders.	1799. Alkmaer.	*1854. Inkerman.
*1743. Dettingen.	1801. Aboukir.	*1855. Sevastopol.
1745. Fontenoy.	*1801. Egypt.	1857–58. Indian Mutiny.
1747. Val.	1801. Alexandria.	*1858. Lucknow.
1756. Minorca.	1807. Copenhagen.	*1874. Ashantee.
1758. Cherbourg.	*1808–14. Peninsula.	*1885–87. Burma.
1758–62. Germany.	*1809. Corunna.	1900. South Africa.

UNIFORM.—Scarlet (from 1688, the colour of facings being unknown, but probably Blue); Scarlet and Blue (from 1742).

REGIMENTAL AND OTHER BADGES.—"The Prince of Wales's Plume," with "*Ich Dien.*" "The Rising Sun." "The Red Dragon." (The two last are ancient badges of the Princes of Wales.) Also "The White Horse" (of Hanover), with the Motto, "*Nec aspera terrent.*" Also "The Sphinx" for "Egypt" (1801).

NICKNAMES.—"The Nanny Goats" and "The Royal Goats" (it has a goat as a regimental pet, which is led with garlanded horns and a shield at the head of the drums—how the custom arose is unknown).

NOTES.—Raised in Wales. Its officers wear the "flash," a relic of the old queue. A leek is also worn in the cap on St. David's Day. Its title in 1714 was bestowed in honour of the Prince of Wales.

BIBLIOGRAPHY.—*Historical Record of The 23rd, or Royal Welsh Fusiliers.* 1689–1850. Illustrated. [London: Parker. 1850.]
Historical Record of The Royal Welsh Fusiliers. By Major Rowland Broughton Mainwaring, Royal Welsh Fusiliers. Illustrated. [London: Hatchards. 1889.]

The South Wales Borderers,

COMPRISING

1st & 2nd Batts. (formerly)   The 24th (The 2nd Warwickshire) Regiment; with Militia Batts.

3rd Batt.   The Royal South Wales Borderers Militia.

4th Batt.   The Royal Montgomery Militia.

THE WELSH DRAGON AND LAUREL WREATH.

THE SPHINX.

TITLES.

1689–1751. Col. Sir Edward Dering's [or its Colonel's name] Regiment of Foot (amongst these were Marlborough in 1702 until transferred to the Guards).

1751–82. The 24th Regiment of Foot.

1782–18—. The 24th (2nd Warwickshire) Regiment of Foot.

1881 (from). The South Wales Borderers.

The South Wales Borderers—*continued.*

PRINCIPAL CAMPAIGNS, BATTLES, &c.

* "Honours" on the Colours.

1690-1. Ireland.
1694. La Hague.
1694. Brest.
1695. Namur.
1697. Brabant.
1702-10. Germany.
1704. Schellenberg.
*1704. Blenheim.
1705. Neer-Hespen.
*1706. Ramilies.
*1708. Oudenarde.
1708. Menin.
1708. Lisle.
*1709. Malplaquet.
1710. Douay.
1741. Carthagena.
1756. Minorca.

1758. Cherbourg.
1759. Guadaloupe.
1760-62. Germany.
1760. Corbach.
1760. Warburg.
1761. Denkern.
1762. Wilhelmstahl.
1776-81. America.
1777. Stillwater.
*1801. Egypt.
1801. Alexandria.
*1806. Cape of Good
      Hope.
*1809-14. Peninsula.
*1809. Talavera.
*1811. Fuentes d'Onor.
*1812. Salamanca.

1812. Burgos.
*1813. Vittoria.
1813. St. Sebastian.
*1813. Pyrenees.
*1813. Nivelle.
*1814. Orthes.
1814. Toulouse.
1814-15. Nepaul.
*1848-49. Punjaub.
*1849. Chillianwallah.
*1849. Goojerat.
1857-58. Indian Mutiny.
*1877-79. South Africa.
*1885-87. Burma.
1900. South Africa.

UNIFORM.—Scarlet and Green facings (till 1881); Scarlet and White facings (from 1881).

REGIMENTAL AND OTHER BADGES.—"The Sphinx," for "Egypt" (1801). Also "The Welsh Dragon" within a Laurel Wreath.

NICKNAME.—"Howard's Greens" (from 1717 till 1737, during which period its Colonel's name was Howard and its facings Green). Also (as with the Leicestershires—the 17th) "The Bengal Tigers" (having seen much service in India).

BIBLIOGRAPHY.—*Rambling Reminiscences of the Punjab Campaign,* 1848–49; *with a brief History of the 24th Regiment from* 1689–1889. By Lieutenant-Colonel Andrew John Macpherson. [Chatham : Mackay. 1889.]

Historical Records of The 24th Regiment. 1689–1892. With numerous coloured and other illustrations. Edited by Colonel George Paton, late 24th Regimental District; Colonel Farquhar Glennie, late 24th Foot ; and Colonel William Penn Symons, late 24th Foot. [Devonport: Swiss. 1892.]

The King's Own Scottish Borderers,

COMPRISING

1st & 2nd Batts. (formerly) The 25th (The King's Own Borderers) Regiment of Foot ; with Militia Batt.

3rd Batt. The Scottish Borderers Militia.

" In veritate Religionis confido."

" Nisi Dominus frustra."

THE ROYAL CREST.

THE CASTLE OF EDINBURGH.

THE WHITE HORSE.

THE SPHINX.

TITLES.

1689–1751. The Edinburgh Regiment of Foot ; also Leven's Foot.

1751–82. The 25th (Edinburgh) Regiment of Foot.

1782–1805. The 25th (Sussex) Regiment of Foot.

1805–87. The 25th (The King's Own Borderers) Regiment of Foot.

1887 (from). The King's Own Scottish Borderers.

The King's Own Scottish Borderers—*continued.*

PRINCIPAL CAMPAIGNS, BATTLES, &c.

* "Honours" on the Colours.

1689. Killiecrankie.
1691. Athlone.
1691. Galway.
1691. Limerick.
1692–97. Flanders.
1692. Steenkirk.
1693. Neer Landen.
1695. Namur.
1715. Jacobite rising.
1727. Gibraltar.
1743–47. Flanders.
1745. Fontenoy.
1745. Jacobite rising.

1746. Roucoux.
1747. Val.
1758. Cherbourg.
1758–63. Germany.
*1759. Minden.
1760. Warbourg.
1760. Campen.
1761. Kirk Denkern.
1762. Wilhelmstahl.
1782–83. Gibraltar.
1794. Toulon.
1794. Corsica.
1799. Helder.

*1799. Egmont-op-Zee.
*1801. Egypt.
1801. Alexandria.
*1809. Martinique.
1815. Martinique.
1815. Guadaloupe.
*1878–80. Afghanistan.
1889. Soudan (Gemazieh).
*1895. Chitral.
*1897–8. Tirah.
1900. South Africa.

UNIFORM.—Scarlet, with deep Yellow facings (1689–1805); Scarlet and Blue facings (from 1805).

REGIMENTAL AND OTHER BADGES.—"The Royal Crest," with Motto, "*In veritate Religionis confido*" (conferred in 1805 by George III. on change of Title). Also "The Castle of Edinburgh," with Motto, "*Nisi Dominus frustra*" (the Regiment was raised to defend the City of Edinburgh). Also "The White Horse" (of Hanover), with Motto, "*Nec aspera terrent.*" Also "The Sphinx," for "Egypt" (1801).

NICKNAME.—"The K.O.B.s" (its initials); also "The Botherers," and "The Kokky-Olly Birds."

NOTES.—Said to have been raised to the number of 800 men in two hours. It captured two standards at Val (1747).

BIBLIOGRAPHY.—*Records of The King's Own Borderers, or Old Edinburgh Regiment.* By Captain R. T. Higgins. [London : Chapman and Hall. 1873.]

The Cameronians (Scottish Rifles),

1st Batt. (formerly)   The 26th (The Cameronians) Regiment of Foot.

2nd Batt. (formerly)   The 90th (Perthshire Volunteers—Light Infantry) Regiment ;
with Militia Batts.

3rd & 4th Batts.   The 2nd Royal Lanark Militia.

THE SPHINX.

THE DRAGON OF CHINA.

TITLES.

1st Batt.	2nd Batt.
1688. The Cameronian Guard.	1759–63. The 90th (Irish Light Infantry) Regiment : disbanded.
1689–1751. The Earl of Angus's (or successive Colonels') Regiment of Foot ; also for a considerable part of this period, " The Cameronians."	1775–83. The 90th Regiment of Foot : disbanded.
1751–86. The 26th Regiment of Foot.	1794–18—. The 90th (Perthshire Volunteers—Light Infantry) Regiment.
1786-1881. The 26th (The Cameronians) Regiment of Foot.	

1881 (from). The Cameronians (Scottish Rifles).

The Cameronians (Scottish Rifles)—*continued.*

PRINCIPAL CAMPAIGNS, BATTLES, &c.

* " Honours," the figures showing the Battalion concerned.

1689. Dunkeld.	*1709. Malplaquet (1).	1808–9. Peninsula.
1691–95. Flanders.	1709. Pont-à-Vendin.	*1809. Corunna (1).
1692. Steenkirk.	1710. Douay.	1809. Flushing.
1693. Neer Landen.	1711. Bouchain.	*1809. Martinique (2).
1695. Namur.	1715. Jacobite rising.	*1810. Guadaloupe (2).
1702–13. Germany.	1727. Gibraltar.	1811–12. Peninsula.
1704. Schellenberg.	1761. Belleisle.	*1840–42. China (1).
*1704. Blenheim (1).	1762. Havannah.	*1846–47. South Africa(2).
*1706. Ramilies (1).	1775–81. America.	*1855. Sevastopol (2).
1707. Dendermonde.	1775. St. John's.	1857–58. Indian Mutiny.
1707. Ath.	1795. Quiberon.	*1857. Lucknow (2).
1708. Wynendale.	1798. Minorca.	*1868. Abyssinia (1).
*1708. Oudenarde (1).	*1801. Egypt (1 & 2).	*1877–79. South Africa(2).
1708. Lisle.	*1801. Mandora (2).	1900. South Africa.
1708. Ghent.	1801. Alexandria.	

UNIFORM.—1st Batt., Scarlet and White facings (in 1689); Scarlet and Pale Yellow facings (in 1713); 2nd Batt., Scarlet and Buff (in 1794). Now Dark Green and Rifle Green for both Batts.

REGIMENTAL AND OTHER BADGES.—" The Sphinx " with " Egypt " (for 1801). Also " The Dragon " (for China, 1840–42). *See* " Notes."

NICKNAMES, &c.—The old 26th (1st Batt.) was familiarly known as " The Scots," *circa* 1762 ; while the late 90th, when raised, was dubbed " The Perthshire Greybreeks " (from the colour of their breeches).

NOTES.—The 1st Batt. of The Cameronians trace a direct descent from the old " Cameronian Guard " of the " Lords of Convention," the name itself being derived from Richard Cameron, a famous preacher. The Cameronians, as a rifle corps, carry no colours—its honours are displayed on various appointments.

BIBLIOGRAPHY.—*Historical Record of The 26th, or Cameronian Regiment.* By T. Carter. [London : Byfield, Stanford & Co. 1867.]
Records of the 90th Regiment (Perthshire Light Infantry). With Roll of Officers from 1795 to 1800. By Captain A. L. Delavoye, 56th Foot (late 90th Light Infantry). [London: Richardson & Co. 1880.]

The Royal Inniskilling Fusiliers,

COMPRISING

1st Batt. (formerly) The 27th (Inniskilling) Regiment of Foot.

2nd Batt. („) The 108th (Madras Infantry) Regiment of Foot; with Militia Batts.

3rd Batt. The Fermanagh Militia.

4th Batt. The Tyrone Militia.

5th Batt. The Donegal Militia.

THE WHITE HORSE.   THE CASTLE OF INNISKILLING.   THE SPHINX.

TITLES.

1st Batt.

1689–1751. Colonel Zachariah Tiffin's (or successive Colonels' names) Regiment of Foot.

1751–1881. The 27th (Inniskilling) Regiment of Foot.

1881 (from). The Royal Inniskilling Fusiliers.

2nd Batt.

1760–63. The 108th Regiment of Foot: disbanded.

1794–96. The 108th Regiment of Foot: dispersed between 64th and 85th Foot.

1854–58. The Hon. East India Company's 3rd (Madras Infantry) Regiment.

1858–61. The 3rd (Madras) Regiment.

1861–81. The 108th (Madras Infantry) Regiment.

1881 (from). The Royal Inniskilling Fusiliers.

The Royal Inniskilling Fusiliers—*continued.*

PRINCIPAL CAMPAIGNS, BATTLES, &c.

* "Honours" on the Colours, the figures showing the Battalion concerned.

1690. Boyne.	1779. Grenada.	*1812. Badajos (1).
1691. Aughrim.	1793. Nieuport.	*1812. Salamanca (1).
1715. Jacobite rising.	1794–95. Flanders.	*1813. Vittoria (1).
1739. Porto Bello.	1794. Nimeguen.	1813. St. Sebastian.
1741. Carthagena.	1795. Guildermalsen.	1813. Bidassoa.
1745. Jacobite rising.	1796. Grenada.	*1813. Pyrenees (1).
1756–60. Canada.	*1796. St. Lucia (1).	*1813. Nivelle (1).
1758. Ticonderoga.	1799. Helder.	*1814. Orthes (1).
1762. Martinique.	1799. Bergen.	*1814. Toulouse (1).
1762. Grenada.	1799. Egmont-op-Zee.	1814. Plattsburg.
1762. Havannah.	1799. Alkmaer.	*1815. Waterloo (1).
1775–78. America.	*1801. Egypt (1).	1815. Netherlands.
1776. Brooklyn.	1801. Alexandria.	*1834–35. South Africa (1).
1776. Long Island.	*1806. Maida (1).	*1846–47. South Africa (1).
1776. White Plains.	*1808–14. Peninsula (1).	*1857–58. Central India (2).
1777. Germantown.	1809. Scylla.	1857–58. Indian Mutiny.
1778. St. Lucia.	1811. Albuera.	1900. South Africa.

UNIFORM.—1st Batt., Scarlet and Buff facings (in 1689). 2nd Batt., Scarlet and Yellow facings (in 1854). Both wear Scarlet and Blue facings at the present time.

REGIMENTAL AND OTHER BADGES.—"The Castle of Inniskilling with St. George's Colours" (in recognition of the defence of the Castle of Inniskilling in 1691). Also "The White Horse" (of Hanover), with the Motto, "*Nec aspera terrent*" (for services during the Jacobite rising of 1715). Also "The Sphinx" for "Egypt" (1801).

NOTES.—Formed from three Companies of the Inniskilling forces. It is unique in using the old Irish war-pipes. While employed on the Isthmus of Darien all but nine of six hundred men succumbed. For distinguished gallantry at St. Lucia, in 1696, it was directed that the French garrison in marching out should lay down their arms to the 27th, other marks of favour being likewise accorded to the officers and men of the regiment.

NICKNAME.—"The Lumps."

BIBLIOGRAPHY.—*Historical Record of The 27th Inniskillings.*

A History of The 27th Regiment, now The 1st Battalion of the Royal Inniskilling Fusiliers. From its formation in 1689 to 1893. Compiled by Lieut.-Col. C. J. Lloyd Davidson. Illustrated with coloured plates of costumes and other illustrations.

The Gloucestershire Regiment,

COMPRISING

1st Batt. (formerly) The 28th (North Gloucestershire) Regiment of Foot.

2nd Batt. („) The 61st (South Gloucestershire) Regiment of Foot; with Militia Batts.

3rd Batt. The Royal South Gloucester Militia; and

4th Batt. The Royal North Gloucester Militia.

THE SPHINX.

TITLES.

1st Batt.

1694–1751. Colonel Sir John Gibson's (or successive Colonels' names) Regiment of Foot.

1751–82. The 28th Regiment of Foot.

1782–1881. The 28th (North Gloucestershire) Regiment of Foot.

1881 (from). The Gloucestershire Regiment.

2nd Batt.

1742–48. The 61st Regiment of Foot: disbanded.

1755–59. The 61st Regiment of Foot: re-numbered as The 59th Foot (the present 2nd East Lancashire Regiment).

1758–82. The 61st Regiment of Foot.

1782–1881. The 61st (South Gloucestershire) Regiment of Foot.

1881 (from). The Gloucestershire Regiment.

PRINCIPAL CAMPAIGNS, BATTLES, &c.

* "Honours" on the Colours, the figures showing the Battalion concerned.

1702–6. Flanders.
1702. Huy.
1705. Neer Hespen.
*1706. Ramilies (1).
1706–12. Spain.
1707. Almanza.

1742–47. Flanders.
1745. Fontenoy.
1747. Hulst.
1757–60. Canada.
*1758. Louisberg (1).
1758. Cape Breton.

*1759. Quebec (1).
1759. Martinique.
1760. Salery.
1761. Belle Isle.
1762. Martinique.
1762. Havannah.

The Gloucestershire Regiment—*continued.*

PRINCIPAL CAMPAIGNS, BATTLES, &C.—*continued.*

1776–78. America.
1776. Brooklyn.
1776. White Plains.
1776. Brunx.
1777. Brandywine.
1777. Germantown.
1778. St. Lucia.
1782. Minorca.
1794–95. Flanders.
1794. Nimeguen.
1795. Guildermalsen.
1796. St. Lucia.
1796. Grenada.
1798. Minorca.
1800. Kaffraria.
*1801. Egypt (1 & 2).
1801. Aboukir.
1801. Mandora.
1801. Alexandria.

*1806. Maida (2).
1807. Copenhagen.
1809. Flushing.
*1809–14. Peninsula (1 & 2).
*1809. Corunna (1).
1809. Douro.
*1809. Talavera (2).
1810. Busaco.
1810. Torres Vedras.
1810. Almeida.
*1811. Barossa (1).
*1811. Albuera (1).
1811. Arroyo-des-Molinos.
1812. Ciudad Rodrigo.
*1812. Salamanca (2).
1812. Almaraj.
1812. Burgos.

1812. Badajos.
*1813. Vittoria (1).
*1813. Pyrenees (1 & 2).
*1813. Nivelle (1 & 2).
*1813. Nive (1 & 2).
*1814. Orthes (1 & 2).
*1814. Toulouse (1 & 2).
1815. Quatre Bras.
*1815. Waterloo (1).
1815. Netherlands.
*1848–49. Punjab (2).
*1849. Chillianwallah (2).
*1849. Goojerat (2).
*1854. Alma (1).
*1854. Inkerman (1).
*1855. Sevastopol (1).
1857–58. Indian Mutiny.
*1857. Delhi (2).
1900. South Africa.

UNIFORM.—Scarlet and Yellow facings (1st Batt. in 1742), and Scarlet and Buff facings (2nd Batt. in 1758). Now Scarlet with White facings.

REGIMENTAL BADGE.—"The Sphinx" for "Egypt," 1801. [The unique distinction of wearing the Regimental number both in front and at the back of the cap was bestowed on the old 28th for distinguished conduct at Alexandria (1801), having been then engaged with the enemy front and rear. "The Sphinx" is now so worn.]

NICKNAMES.—"The Old Braggs" (from its Colonel's name, 1734–51). Also "The Slashers" (the current stories to account for this sobriquet are mythical). "The Whitewashers" (of the 61st). "The Right-abouts."

NOTES.—At Almanza the old 28th was all but cut to pieces: at Waterloo it captured a flag of the 25th French Infantry. The old 61st was formerly the 2nd Batt. of The 3rd Buffs, and so retained its Buff facings.

BIBLIOGRAPHY.—*Narrative of The Campaigns of The 28th Regiment.* From 1862. By Lieutenant-Colonel Charles Cadell. [London: Whittaker. 1835.]
    Historical Records of The 28th, North Gloucestershire Regiment. 1692–1882. By Lieutenant-Colonel F. Brodigan. [London: Blackfriars Publishing Co. 1884.]
    Historical Record of The 61st or South Gloucestershire Regiment. 1758–1844. [London: Parker. 1844.]

The Worcestershire Regiment,

COMPRISING

1st Batt. (formerly)   The 29th (Worcestershire) Regiment of Foot.
2nd Batt. („   )   The 36th (Herefordshire) Regiment of Foot; the 3rd and 4th Batts. are authorised; with Militia Batts.
5th Batt.   The 1st Worcestershire Militia.
6th Batt.   The 2nd Worcestershire Militia.

THE UNITED RED AND WHITE ROSE.

FIRM.

TITLES.

1st Batt.

1694–1751. Colonel Thomas Farington's (or successive Colonels' names) Regiment of Foot.

1751–82. The 29th Regiment of Foot.

1782–1881. The 29th (Worcestershire) Regiment of Foot.

2nd Batt.

1701–51. Colonel Viscount Charlemont's (or successive Colonels' names) Regiment of Foot.

1751–82. The 36th Regiment of Foot.

1782–1881. The 36th (Herefordshire) Regiment of Foot.

1881 (from). The Worcestershire Regiment.

PRINCIPAL CAMPAIGNS, BATTLES, &c.

* "Honours" on the Colours, the figures showing the Battalion concerned.

1704–8. Spain.	1715. Jacobite rising.	1761. Belle Isle.
1704–6. Germany.	1727. Gibraltar.	1776–81. America.
1705. Neer Hespen.	1744–48. Flanders.	1776. Quebec.
*1706. Ramilies (1)	1745. Jacobite rising.	*1783–98. Hindoostan (2).
1706. Barcelona.	1746. Culloden.	1791. Bangalore.
1707. Almanza.	1747. Val.	1791. Nundy-Droog.
1711. Quebec.	1758. Cherbourg.	1792. Seringapatam.

The Worcestershire Regiment—*continued.*

PRINCIPAL CAMPAIGNS, BATTLES, &c.—*continued.*

1793. Pondicherry.
1796. Grenada.
1799. Helder.
1799. Oud-Karspel.
1799. Bergen.
1799. Egmont-op-Zee.
*1800-1. Mysore (2).
1800. Quiberon.
1806. Buenos Ayres.
1807. Monte Video.
*1808-14. Peninsula (1 & 2).

*1808. Roleia (1 & 2).
*1808. Vimiera (1 & 2).
1809. Douro.
*1809. Corunna (2).
1809. Flushing.
*1809. Talavera (1).
1811. Badajos.
*1811. Albuera (1).
*1812. Salamanca (2).
*1813. Pyrenees (2).
*1813. Nivelle (2).

*1813. Nive (2).
*1814. Orthes (2).
*1814. Toulouse (2).
*1845. Ferozeshah (1).
*1846. Sobraon (1).
*1848-49. Punjab (1).
1848. Chenab.
1848. Ionian Islands.
*1849. Chillianwallah (1).
*1849. Goojerat (1).
1900. South Africa.

UNIFORM.—1st Batt., Scarlet with Yellow facings (in 1702); Scarlet with White facings (present time) for both Battalions. The old 36th Foot wore Scarlet with Green facings from 1742 to the time of the territorial re-arrangement, when all non-"Royal" regiments assumed "White" for their facings.

REGIMENTAL AND OTHER BADGES.—"The United Red and White Rose" (since 1881). Also "Firm" (worn by the old 36th since, if not before, 1773, but why is not known).

NICKNAMES.—"The Ever-Sworded 29th" (supposed to date back to 1746, from a regimental usage that all officers wore their swords at mess; now confined to the Captain and Subaltern of the day). "The Old Bold" (of the 29th). "The Saucy Greens" (of the 36th Foot from their facings). "The Star (or Guard) of the Line." The "Vein-openers."

NOTES.—The 29th captured a standard from the French at Talavera (1809). Its quick-step—the Royal Windsor March—was presented by the Princess Augusta.

BIBLIOGRAPHY.—*History of Thomas Farrington's Regiment; afterwards 29th (Worcestershire) Foot.* 1694-1891. By Major H. Everard. [Worcester: Littlebury & Co. 1891.]

Historical Records of The 3rd and 4th Battalions Worcestershire Regiment. By Captain R. Holden.

Historical Records of The 36th, or Herefordshire Regiment. 1701-1852. Illustrated. [London: Parker. 1853.]

Historical Records of The 36th Regiment. 1852-81. [London: Mitchell. 1883.]

The East Lancashire Regiment,

COMPRISING

1st Batt. (formerly)   The 30th (Cambridgeshire) Regiment of Foot.

2nd Batt. („   )   The 59th (2nd Nottinghamshire) Regiment of Foot; with Militia Batt.

3rd Batt.   The 5th Lancashire Militia.

THE SPHINX.

THE RED ROSE OF LANCASTER.

TITLES.

1st Batt.

1702-14. Colonel Thomas Sanderson's (or its Colonel's name) Regiment of Marines.

1714-51. Colonel Charles Willis's (or its Colonel's name) Regiment of Foot.

1751-82. The 30th Regiment of Foot.

1782-1881. The 30th (Cambridgeshire) Regiment of Foot.

1881 (from). The East Lancashire Regiment.

2nd Batt.

1741-48. The 59th Regiment of Foot: renumbered The 48th Foot.

1755. The 59th Regiment of Foot: renumbered The 56th Foot.

1755-57. The 61st Regiment of Foot: renumbered The 59th Foot.

1757-82. The 59th Regiment of Foot.

1782-1881. The 59th (2nd Nottingham- (shire Regiment of Foot.

1881 (from).   The East Lancashire Regiment.

The East Lancashire Regiment—*continued.*

PRINCIPAL CAMPAIGNS, BATTLES, &c.

* " Honours " on the Colours, the figures showing the Battalion concerned.

1704–5. Gibraltar.
1704. Malaga.
1704–6. Spain.
1705. Barcelona.
1706. Alicante.
1706. Tortosa.
1707. Lerida.
1708. Cagliari.
1758. Cherbourg.
1761. Belle Isle.
1775–76. America.
1775. Bunker's Hill.
1781. Carolina.
1782–83. Gibraltar.
1794. Toulon.
1794. Corsica.
1794–95. Flanders.
1794. Nimeguen.
1796. St. Vincent.
1798. Minorca.

1800. Malta.
1801. Mandora.
*1801. Egypt (1).
1801. Alexandria.
1801. Marabout.
*1806. Cape of Good Hope (2).
1806–7. Madras.
1808–9. Peninsula.
*1809. Corunna (2).
1810. Mauritius.
*1811. Java (2).
*1810–13. Peninsula (1 & 2).
*1812. Badajos (1).
*1812. Salamanca.
*1813. Vittoria (2).
*1813. St. Sebastien (2).
*1813. Nive (2).
1814. Bayonne.
1814–15. Netherlands.

1815. Quatre Bras.
*1815. Waterloo (1).
1815–19. Hindoostan.
1817–19. Mahratta War.
1819. Asseerghur.
*1826. Bhurtpore (2).
*1854. Alma (1).
*1854. Inkerman (1).
*1855. Sevastopol (1).
1857–58. China.
*1857. Canton (2).
1858. Nantow.
*1878–80. Afghanistan (2).
*1879. Ahmed Khel (2).
1879. Ghuznee.
1879. Cabool.
1880. Candahar.
*1895. Chitral.
1900. South Africa.

UNIFORM.—1st Batt., Red with Yellow facings (the latter probably from formation, but certainly since 1742 till 1881 (?)). 2nd Batt., Red and Purple facings (in 1755); Scarlet and " lily "-White (in 1815). Now Scarlet and White facings for both Batts.

REGIMENTAL BADGES.—"The Sphinx," for " Egypt " (1801): the honour was won by the 1st Batt. Also (since territorial re-organisation) "The Red Rose of Lancaster."

NICKNAMES.—1st Batt., " The Triple X's," or " The Three Tens " (the regimental number). 2nd Batt., " The Lily-Whites " (from the facings).

BIBLIOGRAPHY.—*Historical Records of The XXX Regiment.* [London : Clowes. 1887.]

The East Surrey Regiment,

COMPRISING

1st Batt. (formerly). The 31st (The Huntingdonshire) Regiment of Foot.
2nd Batt.   ,,   The 70th (Surrey) Regiment of Foot; with Militia Batts.
3rd Batt. The 1st Royal Surrey Militia.
4th Batt. The 3rd Royal Surrey Militia.

THE UNITED ROSE.

THE STAR AND ARMS OF GUILDFORD.

TITLES.

1st Batt.

1702–14. Col. George Villiers' (or successive Colonels') Regiment of Marines.

1714–51. Colonel Sir Harry Goring's (or successive Colonels') Regiment of Foot.

1751–82. The 31st Regiment of Foot.

1782–1881. The 31st (Huntingdonshire) Regiment of Foot.

2nd Batt.

1756–58. The 31st Regiment of Foot (2nd Batt.).

1758–82. The 70th Regiment of Foot.

1782–1813. The 70th (Surrey) Regiment of Foot.

1813–25. The 70th (Glasgow Lowland) Regiment of Foot.

1825–81. The 70th (Surrey) Regiment of Foot.

1881 (from). The East Surrey Regiment.

PRINCIPAL CAMPAIGNS, BATTLES, &c.

* "Honours" on the Colours, the figures showing the Battalion concerned.

1702. Cadiz.
1702. Vigo Bay.
1704–6. Spain.
1704–5. Gibraltar.
1705. Barcelona.

1706. Carthagena.
1706. Ivica.
1706. Majorca.
1706. Sardinia.
1707. Toulon.

1708. Cagliari.
1708. Minorca.
1742–45. Flanders.
*1743. Dettingen (1).
1745. Fontenoy.

The East Surrey Regiment—*continued.*

PRINCIPAL CAMPAIGNS, BATTLES, &c.—*continued.*

1772. St. Vincent.
1776–81. America.
1794. Martinique.
1794. St. Lucia.
*1794. Guadaloupe (2).
1796. St. Lucia.
1799. Egmont-op-Zee.
1799. Alkmaer.
1800. Isle de Huet.
1807. Egypt.
1807. Rosetta.
*1809–14. Peninsula (1).
*1809. Talavera (1).

1810. Guadaloupe.
*1811. Albuera (1).
1813–14. Canada.
*1813. Vittoria (1).
*1813. Pyrenees (1).
*1813. Nivelle (1).
*1813. Nive (1).
1813. Bayonne.
*1814. Orthes (1).
1814. Plattsburg.
1824–46. Hindoostan.
*1842. Cabool (1).
*1845. Moodkee (1).

*1845. Ferozeshah (1).
*1846. Aliwal (1).
*1846. Sobraon (1).
*1855. Sevastopol (1).
1857–58. Indian Mutiny.
1860. China.
*1860. Taku Forts (1).
*1863–65. New Zealand (2).
*1878–79. Afghanistan (2).
*1885. Suakim (2).
1885. Tamai.
1900. South Africa.

UNIFORM.—1st Batt., Scarlet with Buff facings (when raised). 2nd Batt., Scarlet with Grey facings (1758–68); Scarlet and Black facings (1768). Both Batts. (from 1881), Scarlet with White facings.

REGIMENTAL AND OTHER BADGES.—"The United Red and White Rose" was suggested for this as for other regiments when territorialised, and, though not used, still retains a place in official papers. Also "A Star and Arms of Guildford"—these are the old badges of the Militia battalions.

NICKNAMES, &c.—"The Young Buffs" (of the late 31st, King George II. having, through the similarity of the facings, mistaken it at Dettingen for the 3rd (or "Old") Buffs). "The Glasgow Greys" (of the late 70th), from its facings and many Glasgow men serving in its ranks.

NOTES.—On its way to Bengal in 1824, part of the old 31st was on board the East Indiaman *Kent* when burnt in the Bay of Biscay. It specially distinguished itself in the Sikh War by capturing a colour at Ferozeshah, another at Aliwal, and two more at Sobraon.

BIBLIOGRAPHY.—*Historical Record of The* 31st (*or Huntingdonshire*) *Regiment of Foot.* 1702–1850. With Services of the Marine Corps, 1664–1748. Illustrated. [London: Parker. 1850.]

Historical Record of The 70th *Surrey Regiment of Foot.* 1758–1848. Illustrated. [London: Parker. 1849.]

Duke of Cornwall's Light Infantry,

COMPRISING

1st Batt. (formerly) The 32nd (Cornwall—Light Infantry) Regiment.

2nd Batt. („) The 46th (South Devonshire) Regiment of Foot; with Militia Batt.

3rd Batt. The Royal Cornwall Rangers Militia.

THE COLLAR BADGE.

THE UNITED RED AND WHITE ROSE.

ORNAMENT ON HELMET PLATE.

TITLES.

1st Batt.

1702–14. Colonel Edward Fox's (or Jacob Borr's) Regiment of Marines.

1714–51. Colonel Jacob Borr's (or successive Colonels') Regiment of Foot.

1751–82. The 32nd Regiment of Foot.

1782–1858. The 32nd (Cornwall) Regiment of Foot.

1858–81. The 32nd (Cornwall—Light Infantry).

2nd Batt.

1741–51. Colonel James Price (or successive Colonels') Regiment of Foot.

1751–82. The 46th Regiment of Foot.

1782–1881. The 46th (South Devonshire) Regiment of Foot.

1881 (from). Duke of Cornwall's Light Infantry.

PRINCIPAL CAMPAIGNS, BATTLES, &c.

* "Honours" on the Colours, the figures showing the Battalion concerned.

1702. Cadiz.	1742–47. Flanders.	1758. Ticonderoga.
1702. Vigo.	*1743. Dettingen (1).	1759. Niagara.
1704–5. Gibraltar.	1745. Fontenoy.	1761. Martinique.
1704–6. Spain.	1747. Val.	1762. Havannah.
1705. Barcelona.	1757–60. Canada.	1776–78. America.

Duke of Cornwall's Light Infantry—*continued.*

PRINCIPAL CAMPAIGNS, BATTLES, &c.—*continued.*

1776. Brooklyn.	1810. Guadaloupe.	*1849. Mooltan (1).
1777. Brandywine.	1812. Badajos.	*1849. Goojerat (1).
1778. St. Lucia.	*1812. Salamanca (1).	1854. Alma.
1792. Gibraltar.	1812. Burgos.	1854. Inkerman.
1794. Martinique.	*1813. Pyrenees (1).	1854. Balaclava.
1795–96. St. Vincent.	*1813. Nivelle (1).	*1855. Sevastopol (2).
*1805. Dominica (2).	*1813. Nive (1).	1857–58. Indian Mutiny.
*1808–14. Peninsula (1).	*1814. Orthes (1).	*1857. Lucknow (1).
*1808. Roleia (1).	1815. Quatre-Bras.	1857. Cawnpore.
*1808. Vimiera (1).	*1815. Waterloo (1).	*1882. Egypt (2).
*1809. Corunna (1).	1815. Netherlands.	*1882. Tel-el-Kebir (2).
1809. Martinique.	*1848–49. Punjaub (1).	*1884–85. Nile (2).
1809. Flushing.	1848. Soorajkhoond.	1900. South Africa.

UNIFORM.—1st Batt., Scarlet with White facings (at formation as now). 2nd Batt., Scarlet with Yellow facings (in 1741 : the latter now White as with all non-"Royal" regiments).

REGIMENTAL AND OTHER BADGES.—Officially, "The United Red and White Rose," but not worn. On appointments various special devices—combining "A Bugle with Strings," "The Coronet of the Duke of Cornwall," "The County Badge," with Motto, "One and All," "A Turreted Archway," and "Two Feathers" (red). [The "Turreted Archway" commemorates the defence of "Lucknow;" and the "Two Red Feathers" is a distinction of the 46th, a Light company of which, in 1777, with others were brigaded as "The Light Battalion." The Americans were so harassed by the Brigade that they vowed "No Quarter." In derision, to prevent mistakes, The Light Battalion dyed their feathers red : the 46th Foot alone has retained the distinction.]

NICKNAMES, &c.—These pertain to the late 46th : "Murray's Bucks" (from Colonel's name [1743–64] and its smart appearance on home duty in Scottish Royal livery). "The Surprisers" (from an incident [1777] in the American War). "The Lacedemonians" (its Colonel once, when under heavy fire, made a disciplinarian speech concerning the Lacedemonians). Also, in early days, "The Edinburgh Regiment." "The Red Feathers." "The Docs" (the initials).

BIBLIOGRAPHY.—*Historical Records of The 32nd (Cornwall) Light Infantry, now 1st Battalion Duke of Cornwall's Light Infantry.* 1702–1892. By Colonel G. C. Swiney. [Devonport: Swiss. 1893.]

The Duke of Wellington's (West Riding Regiment),

COMPRISING

1st Batt. (formerly) The 33rd (Duke of Wellington's) Regiment of Foot.

2nd Batt. („) The 76th Regiment of Foot; with Militia Batt.

3rd Batt. The 6th West York Militia.

THE CREST AND MOTTO OF THE
DUKE OF WELLINGTON.

THE ELEPHANT WITH HOWDAH.

TITLES.

1st Batt.

1702–51. Colonel The Earl of Huntingdon's (or successive Colonels') Regiment of Foot.

1751–82. The 33rd Regiment of Foot.

1782–1853. The 33rd (1st York, West Riding) Regiment of Foot.

1853–81. The 33rd (Duke of Wellington's) Regiment.

2nd Batt.

1756–63. The 76th Regiment of Foot: disbanded.

1777–84. The 76th (Macdonald's Highlanders) Regiment of Foot: disbanded.

1787–1812. The 76th (Hindoostan) Regiment of Foot.

1812–81. The 76th Regiment of Foot.

1881 (from). The Duke of Wellington's (West Riding Regiment).

The Duke of Wellington's (West Riding Regiment)—*continued.*

PRINCIPAL CAMPAIGNS, BATTLES, &c.

* " Honours " on the Colours, the figures showing the Battalion concerned.

1702–4. Germany.	1778. Freehold.	1810. Mauritius.
1704–10. Spain.	1780. Camden.	*1813. Nive (2).
1705. Valentia d'Alcantara.	1781. Guildford.	1813–14. Peninsula.
1707. Almanza.	*1780–1806. Hindoostan(2).	1813. Pyrenees.
1742–47. Flanders.	1791. Bangalore.	1813. Bidassoa.
*1743. Dettingen (1).	1791. Savendroog.	1813. Nive.
1745. Fontenoy.	1792. Seringapatam.	1814. Bayonne.
1745. Jacobite rising.	1794–95. Flanders.	1814–15. Netherlands.
1746. Roucoux.	1795. Guildermalsen.	1814. Antwerp.
1746. Tongres.	1799. Malvelly.	1814. Bergen-op-Zoom.
1747. Val.	*1799. Seringapatam (1).	1814. Canada.
1758. Cherbourg.	*1800–1. Mysore (2).	1814. Plattsburg.
1760–63. Germany.	*1803. Allyghur (2).	1815. Quatre Bras.
1760. Corbach.	*1803. Delhi (2).	*1815. Waterloo (1).
1761. Kerk Denkern.	1803. Agra.	*1854. Alma (1).
1761. Belle-Isle.	*1803. Leswarree (2).	*1854. Inkerman (1).
1762. Martinique.	*1804. Deig (2).	*1855. Sevastopol (1).
1776–81. America.	1805. Bhurtpore.	1857–58. Indian Mutiny.
1776. Brooklyn.	*1808–9. Peninsula (2).	*1868. Abyssinia (1).
1777. Brandywine.	1809. Corunna.	1868. Magdala.
1777. Germantown.	1809. Flushing.	1900. South Africa.

UNIFORM.—Scarlet (or Red) with Scarlet facings for both regiments till the introduction of the territorial system. Now Scarlet, faced with White.

REGIMENTAL AND OTHER BADGES.—(1) "The Crest and Motto of the Duke of Wellington" (the 33rd was the first regiment commanded by "The Hero of Waterloo," and is the only corps in the British Army named after a subject); also (2) "The Elephant" to the 76th for valour in India. In 1808 The East India Company presented it with honorary colours: in conjunction with the 8th Hussars it captured 44 standards and 72 guns at Leswarree (1803).

NICKNAMES, &c.—1st Batt., "Havercake Lads" (the recruiting sergeants, *circa* 1782, carried oaten cakes on their sword-points when beating up). 2nd Batt., "The Immortals" (from most of its men having been wounded in Lake's Campaigns). "The Pigs" (from its "Elephant" badge). "The Old Seven and Sixpennies" (from its number, and the amount of a lieutenant's pay).

The Border Regiment,

COMPRISING

1st Batt. (formerly) The 34th (Cumberland) Regiment of Foot.
2nd Batt. („) The 55th (Westmoreland) Regiment of Foot ; with Militia Batts.
3rd Batt. The Royal Cumberland Militia.
4th Batt. The Royal Westmoreland Militia.

THE LAUREL WREATH.　　　　THE DRAGON OF CHINA.

TITLES.

1st Batt.

1702–51. Colonel Lord Lucas's (or successive Colonels') Regiment of Foot.

1751–82. The 34th Regiment of Foot.

1782–1881. The 34th (Cumberland) Regiment of Foot.

2nd Batt.

1742–48. The 55th Regiment of Foot: now the 1st Essex.

1756–58. The 55th Regiment of Foot: now The 1st Shropshire Light Infantry.

1755–57. The 57th Regiment of Foot: renumbered in

1757–82. The 55th Regiment of Foot.

1782–1881. The 55th „ (Westmoreland) Regiment of Foot.

1881 (from). The Border Regiment.

PRINCIPAL CAMPAIGNS, BATTLES, &c.

* "Honours" on the Colours, the figures showing the Battalion concerned.

1705–7. Spain.	1727. Gibraltar.	1757–60. Canada.
1705. Barcelona.	1744. Flanders.	1758. Ticonderoga.
1706. Montjuich.	1745. Fontenoy.	1759. Niagara.
1709–12. Germany.	1745. Jacobite rising.	1758. Louisberg.
1710. Douay.	174–. Falkirk.	1758. Cherbourg.
1711. Bouchain.	174–. Culloden.	1762. Havannah.
1718. Vigo.	1757. Minorca.	1775–78. America.

The Border Regiment—*continued.*

PRINCIPAL CAMPAIGNS, BATTLES, &c.—*continued.*

1776. Brooklyn.	1799. Egmont-op-Zee.	1814–15. Netherlands.
1776. Long Island.	1799. Alkmaer.	1814. Bergen-op-Zoom.
1777. Brandywine.	1800. Kaffraria.	1820. Kaffraria.
1777. Germantown.	1800–23. Hindoostan.	*1840–2. China (2).
1777. Stillwater.	1809. San Domingo.	1842. Chusan.
1778. St. Lucia.	*1809–14. Peninsula (1).	1842. Chinghai.
1794–95. Flanders.	*1811. Albuera.	1842. Ningpoo.
1794. Nimeguen.	*1811. Arroyo - dos -	1842. Ching-Kiang-Foo.
1794. Martinique.	Molinos (1).	*1854. Alma (2).
1794. Guadaloupe.	*1813. Vittoria (1).	*1854. Inkerman (2).
1796. St. Lucia.	1813. Maya.	*1855. Sevastopol (1 & 2).
1796. St. Vincent.	*1813. Pyrenees (1).	1857–58. Indian Mutiny.
1796. Grenada.	*1813. Nivelle (1).	1857. Cawnpore.
1799. Helder.	*1813. Nive (1).	*1858. Lucknow (1).
1799. Crabbendam.	*1814. Orthes (1).	1900. South Africa.
1799. Bergen.	1814. Toulouse.	

UNIFORM.—1st Batt., Red (or Scarlet) with bright Yellow facings (when raised); the latter changed to White when territorialised in 1881; 2nd Batt., Red and Dark Green facings (1755); Scarlet with White facings (present time).

REGIMENTAL AND OTHER BADGES.—" A Laurel Wreath " (an old 34th Badge for services at Fontenoy: *see* NOTES). Also " The Dragon of China " (to the 55th); the two are variously combined for different appointments.

NICKNAME.—" The Two Fives " (to the 55th, for its number; *cf.* " The Two XX's " = the late 20th).

NOTES.—A red and white pompon, or tuft, was formerly worn by the 34th in recognition of the capture of the 34th French Infantry at Arroyo-dos-Molinos. The Royal Arms appear in the lace of the drummers' coats in memory of Fontenoy: *see* BADGES.

BIBLIOGRAPHY.—*Historical Record of The 34th (The Cumberland) Regiment of Foot.* 1702–1844. Illustrated. [London : Parker. 1844.]
Historical Account of The 34th and 55th Regiments. By George Noakes, Quartermaster-Sergeant, 2nd Brigade Depôt. [Carlisle : Thurnam & Sons. 1875.]

The Royal Sussex Regiment,

COMPRISING

1st Batt. (formerly) The 35th Royal Sussex Regiment of Foot.

2nd Batt. („) The 107th (Bengal Infantry) Regiment; with Militia Batt.

3rd Batt. The Royal Sussex Militia.

THE UNITED RED AND WHITE ROSE.

THE COLLAR BADGE.

TITLES.

1st Batt.

1701–51. Colonel The Earl of Donegal's (or successive Colonels') Regiment of Foot: also popularly "The Belfast Regiment."

1751–82. The 35th Regiment of Foot.

1782–1805. The 35th (Dorsetshire) Regiment of Foot.

1805–32. The 35th (Sussex) Regiment of Foot.

1832–1881. The 35th (Royal Sussex) Regiment of Foot.

2nd Batt.

1854–58. The Hon. East India Company's 3rd (Bengal European Light Infantry) Regiment.

1858–61. The 3rd (Bengal Light Infantry) Regiment.

1861–1881. The 107th Bengal Infantry Regiment.

1881 (from). The Royal Sussex Regiment.

The Royal Sussex Regiment—*continued.*

PRINCIPAL CAMPAIGNS, BATTLES, &c.

* "Honours" on the Colours, the figures showing the Battalion concerned.

1702. Cadiz.
1704–5. Gibraltar.
1704–8. Spain.
1706. Barcelona.
1707. Almanza.
1757–60. Canada.
*1758. Louisbourg (1).
*1759. Quebec (1).
1760. Sillery.
1761. Martinique.
1762. Havannah.
1775–78. America.
1775. Bunker's Hill.

1776. Brooklyn.
1776. Brunx.
1778. St. Lucia.
1794. Martinique.
1794. St. Lucia.
1794. Guadaloupe.
1799. Bergen.
1799. Egmont-op-Zee.
1799. Crabbendam.
1799. Alkmaer.
1800. Malta.
*1806. Maida (1).
1807. Rosetta.

1807. Egypt.
1809. Naples.
1809. Flushing.
1810. Ionian Islands.
1814–15. Netherlands.
1814. Antwerp.
1857–58. Indian Mutiny.
*1882. Egypt (1).
*1884–85. Nile (1).
*1885. Abu Klea (1).
1900. South Africa.

UNIFORM.—1st Batt., Scarlet with Orange facings (1701–1832, the Orange being changed to Blue on proceeding to Ireland). 2nd Batt., Scarlet with White facings. Scarlet with Blue facings for both Batts. (present time).

REGIMENTAL AND OTHER BADGES.—"The United Red and White Rose." Also (though approved not in *Army List*) "A White Feather" (*see* Notes), "A Maltese Cross" (*see* Notes), and "The Centre of The Star of the Garter," combined.

NICKNAME.—"The Orange Lilies" (from its facings and white plume).

NOTES.—"The White Plume," worn till 1800, and now included in the regimental badge, was worn at Quebec, being taken from The Royal Roussillon French Grenadiers; while "The Maltese Cross" is in memory of the capture of Malta. The Regiment was also at one time known as "The Prince of Orange's Own," having received its facings as a mark of favour.

BIBLIOGRAPHY.—*Historical Memoir of The 35th Royal Sussex Regiment.* By Richard Trimen, late Captain 35th Foot. [Southampton. 1873.]

L 2

The Hampshire Regiment,

COMPRISING

1st Batt. (formerly) The 37th (North Hampshire) Regiment of Foot.

2nd Batt. („) The 67th (South Hampshire) Regiment of Foot; with Militia.

3rd Batt. The Hampshire Militia.

THE TIGER AND WREATH.
(As on Helmet-plate.)

THE HAMPSHIRE ROSE.
(As on Collar.)

TITLES.

1st Batt.

1702–51. Colonel Thomas Meredith's (or successive Colonels') Regiment of Foot.

1751–82. The 37th Regiment of Foot.

1782–1881. The 37th (North Hampshire) Regiment.

2nd Batt.

1758–82. The 67th Regiment of Foot.

1782–1881. The 67th (South Hampshire) Regiment of Foot.

1881 (from). The Hampshire Regiment.

The Hampshire Regiment—*continued.*

PRINCIPAL CAMPAIGNS, BATTLES, &c.

* "Honours" on the Colours, the figures showing the Battalion concerned.

1702–12. Germany.
1704. Schellenberg.
*1704. Blenheim (1).
1705. Helixem.
1705. Neer-Hespen.
*1706. Ramilies (1).
1707. Ath.
1708. Menin.
*1708. Oudenarde (1).
1709. Tournay.
*1709. Malplaquet (1).
1710. Douai.
1742–47. Flanders.
*1743. Dettingen (1).
1745. Jacobite rising.
1746. Culloden.
1747. Val.

1758–62. Germany.
1758. Cherbourg.
*1759. Minden (1).
1761. Kirk-Denkern.
1761. Belle Isle.
1762. Wilhelmstahl.
1776–80. America.
1776. Brooklyn.
1776. Long Island.
1793–95. Flanders.
1793. Famars.
1793. Dunkirk.
*1794. Tournay (1).
1794. Nimeguen.
1795. Guildermalsen.
*1805–26. India (2).
*1810–14. Peninsula (1 & 2).

*1811. Barrossa (2).
1814. Barcelona.
1814–15. Netherlands.
1814. Antwerp.
1814. Bergen-op-Zoom.
1819. Asseerghur.
1857–58. Indian Mutiny.
1860–62. China.
*1860. Taku Forts (2).
*1860. Pekin (2).
*1878–80. Afghanistan (2).
*1879. Charasiah (2).
*1879. Cabool (2).
*1885–87. Burma (2).
1885–87. Mandalay.
1900. South Africa.

UNIFORM.—Scarlet with Yellow facings (both Batts. till Territorialisation changed the facings, as in all non-"Royal" regiments, to White).

REGIMENTAL AND OTHER BADGES.—"The Royal Tiger in a Laurel-Wreath" (to the 67th for "India"). Also "The Hampshire Rose" on some appointments (Henry V., when *en route* to Agincourt, conferred the Lancastrian Rose on the City of Winchester).

BIBLIOGRAPHY.—*Annals of The 37th North Hampshire Regiment.* [Winchester: Warren. 1878.]

Historical Record of The 67th, or South Hampshire Regiment. 1758–1849. [London: Parker. 1849.]

Regimental Orders. By Lieutenant R. W. Barlow. [London: 1868.]

Colburn's United Service Magazine. January–February, 1874, and August 1882.

The South Staffordshire Regiment,

COMPRISING

1st Batt. (formerly) The 38th (1st Staffordshire) Regiment of Foot.

2nd Batt. („) The 80th (Staffordshire Volunteers) Regiment of Foot; with Militia Batts.

3rd & 4th Batts. The 1st (King's Own) Stafford Militia.

THE SPHINX.

THE STAFFORDSHIRE KNOT.

TITLES.

1st Batt.

1702–51. Colonel Luke Lillingstone's (or successive Colonels') Regiment of Foot.

1751–82. The 38th Regiment of Foot.

1782–1881. The 38th (1st Staffordshire) Regiment of Foot.

2nd Batt.

1758–64. The 80th (Light-armed) Regiment of Foot : disbanded.

1778–84. The 80th (Royal Edinburgh Volunteers) Regiment of Foot : disbanded.

1793–1881. The 80th (Staffordshire Volunteers) Regiment of Foot.

1881 (from). The South Staffordshire Regiment.

The South Staffordshire Regiment—*continued.*

PRINCIPAL CAMPAIGNS, BATTLES, &c.

* " Honours " on the Colours, the figures showing the Battalion concerned.

1759. Guadaloupe.
1762. Martinique.
1775–80. America.
1775. Bunker's Hill.
1776. Brooklyn.
1794–95. Flanders.
1794. Martinique.
1794. Guadaloupe.
*1801. Egypt (2).
1806. Cape of Good Hope.
1806. Buenos Ayres.
*1807. Monte Video (1).
*1808–14. Peninsula (1).
*1808. Roleia (1).
*1808. Vimiera (1).

*1809. Corunna (1).
1809. Flushing.
*1810. Busaco (1).
*1812. Badajos (1).
*1812. Salamanca (1).
1812. Burgos.
*1813. Vittoria (1).
*1813. St. Sebastian (1).
1813. Bidassoa.
*1813. Nive (1).
1813. Nivelle.
1814. Bayonne.
1819. Cape of Good Hope.
*1824–26. Ava (1).
*1845. Moodkee (2).

*1845. Ferozeshah (1).
*1846. Sobraon (2).
1852. Rangoon.
*1852–53. Pegu (2).
*1854. Alma (1).
*1854. Inkerman (1).
*1855. Sevastopol (1).
1857–58. Indian Mutiny.
1857. Cawnpore.
*1858. Lucknow (1).
*1858. Central India (2).
*1878–79. South Africa (2).
*1882. Egypt (1).
*1884–85. Nile (1).
*1885. Kirbecan (1).

UNIFORM.—Both Battalions Scarlet and Yellow facings (on formation) ; Scarlet with White facings (present time).

REGIMENTAL AND OTHER BADGES.—" The Sphinx," for " Egypt " (1801). Also " The Staffordshire Knot " (an ancient royal borough badge).

NICKNAMES.—" The Pump and Tortoise " (of the 38th). Also " The Staffordshire Knots " (of the 80th).

NOTES.—The late 80th captured a gun at Ferozeshah (1845).

The Dorsetshire Regiment,

COMPRISING

1st Batt. (formerly) The 39th (Dorsetshire) Regiment of Foot.

2nd Batt. („) The 54th (West Norfolk) Regiment of Foot; with Militia.

3rd Batt. The Dorset Militia.

" Primus in Indis."

THE CASTLE, KEY, AND MOTTO.

THE MARABOUT SPHINX.

TITLES.

1st Batt.

1702–51. Colonel Richard Coote's (or successive Colonels') Regiment of Foot.

1751–82. The 39th Regiment of Foot.

1782–1807. The 39th (East Middlesex) Regiment of Foot.

1807–81. The 39th (Dorsetshire) Regiment of Foot.

2nd Batt.

1755–57. The 56th Regiment of Foot; renumbered

1757–82. The 54th Regiment of Foot.

1782–1881. The 54th (West Norfolk) Regiment of Foot.

1881 (from). The Dorsetshire Regiment.

The Dorsetshire Regiment—*continued.*

PRINCIPAL CAMPAIGNS, BATTLES, &c.

* "Honours" on the Colours, the figures showing the Battalion concerned.

1707–12. Spain.	1800. Isle Houat.	*1813. Vittoria (1).
1707. Almanza (?).	1800. Cadiz.	*1813. Pyrenees (1).
1709. Caya.	1800. Minorca.	*1813. Nivelle (1).
1718. Messina.	1800. Malta.	*1813. Nive (1).
1727. Gibraltar.	1801. Egypt (2).	1814–15. Netherlands.
1757. Calcutta.	1801. Aboukir.	*1814. Orthes (1).
*1757. Plassey (1).	1801. Mandora.	1814. Tarbes.
1776–81. America.	1801. Alexandria.	1814. Bayonne.
1776. Brooklyn.	*1801. Marabout (2).	1814. Toulouse.
1778. Rhode Island.	1806. Buenos Ayres.	1814. Plattsburg.
1778. Connecticut.	1807. Monte Video.	1814. Antwerp.
*1779–84. Gibraltar (1).	*1809–14. Peninsula (1).	*1824–26. Ava (1).
1780. Charlestown.	1810. Busaco.	*1843. Maharajpore (1).
1794–95. Flanders.	*1811. Albuera (1).	*1855. Sevastopol (1).
1794. Martinique.	1811. Arroyo - dos -	*1858–59. Indian Mutiny.
1794. St. Lucia.	Molinos.	*1897–98. Tirah.
1794. Guadaloupe.	1812–14. Canada.	1900. South Africa.
1796. St. Vincent.	1812. Badajos.	

UNIFORM.—1st and 2nd Batts., Scarlet with Green facings (at formation); Scarlet with White facings (present time).

REGIMENTAL AND OTHER BADGES, &c.—The motto, "*Primus in Indis*" (the 39th Foot was the first King's Regiment to serve in India). Also "The Castle, Key, and Motto"—"*Mortis Insignia Calpe*" (for defence of Gibraltar—1779–83). Also the "Marabout Sphinx" for "Egypt" (1801)—at this battle a gun, now at Woolwich, was captured by the 54th.

NICKNAMES, &c.—"Sankey's Horse" (of the 39th, 1707, from its Colonel's name, and a tradition that to expedite its march to Almanza it was mounted on mules). Also (*circa* 1742) "The Green Linnets" (from its pea-green facings).

NOTES.—The 39th captured four guns and two standards at Maharajpore in 1843.

BIBLIOGRAPHY.—*Historical Record of the 39th, or Dorsetshire Regiment of Foot.* 1702–1853. Illustrated. [London : Parker. 1853.]
Records of the 54th West Norfolk Regiment. [Roorkee : Thomason. 1851.]

The Prince of Wales's Volunteers (South Lancashire Regiment),

COMPRISING

1st Batt. (formerly) The 40th (2nd Somersetshire) Regiment of Foot.

2nd Batt. („) The 82nd (Prince of Wales's Volunteers) Regiment of Foot; with Militia Battalion.

3rd Batt. The 4th Royal Lancashire Militia.

THE PRINCE OF WALES'S PLUME.

THE SPHINX.

TITLES.

1st Batt.

1717–51. Colonel Richard Philip's Regiment of Foot.

1751–82. The 40th Regiment of Foot.

1782–1881. The 40th (2nd Somersetshire) Regiment of Foot.

2nd Batt.

1793–1881. The 82nd (Prince of Wales's Volunteers) Regiment of Foot.

1881 (from). The Prince of Wales's Volunteers (South Lancashire Regiment).

PRINCIPAL CAMPAIGNS, BATTLES, &c.

* "Honours" on the Colours, the figures showing the Battalion concerned.

1757–60. Canada.	1776. Brooklyn.	1795. St. Vincent.
*1758. Louisbourg (1).	1776. Long Island.	1796. Grenada.
1759. Quebec.	1777. Brandywine.	1798. San Domingo.
1760. Montreal.	1777. Germantown.	1798. Leghorn.
1761. Guadaloupe.	1778. St. Lucia.	1798. Malta.
1762. Martinique.	1794–95. Flanders.	1799. Bergen.
1762. Havannah.	1794. Martinique.	1799. Egmont-op-Zee.
1776–78. America.	1794. Guadaloupe.	*1801. Egypt.

The Prince of Wales's Volunteers (South Lancashire Regiment)—*continued.*

PRINCIPAL CAMPAIGNS, BATTLES, &c.—*continued.*

1801. Aboukir.
1801. Mandora.
1801. Rosetta.
1801. Alexandria.
1806. Buenos Ayres.
*1807. Monte Video (1).
1807. Copenhagen.
*1808–14. Peninsula (1 & 2).
*1808. Roleia (1 & 2).
*1808. Vimiera (1 & 2).
1809. Corunna.
1809. Flushing.
*1809. Talavera (1).
1810. Busaco.
1811. Albuera.

1811. Barrossa.
1811. Tarifa.
*1812. Badajos (1).
1812. Burgos.
1812. Ciudad Rodrigo.
*1812. Salamanca (1).
1813. Maya.
*1813. Vittoria (1 & 2).
*1813. Pyrenees (1 & 2).
1813. St. Sebastian.
*1813. Nivelle (1 & 2).
1813. Nive.
*1814. Orthes (1 & 2).
*1814. Toulouse (1).
1814. Bordeaux.

*1814. Niagara (2).
*1815. Waterloo (1).
1815. Netherlands.
*1842. Candahar (1).
*1842. Ghuznee (1).
*1842. Cabool (1).
*1843. Maharajpore (1).
*1855. Sevastopol (2).
1857–58. Indian Mutiny.
*1857. Lucknow (2).
1857. Cawnpore.
*1860–65. New Zealand (1).
1900. South Africa.

UNIFORM.—1st Batt., Scarlet with Buff facings (1717). 2nd Batt., Scarlet and Yellow facings (1793). Both Batts., at present time, Scarlet with White facings.

REGIMENTAL AND OTHER BADGES.—"The Prince of Wales's Plume" (the Colonel of the 82nd when raised was attached to the household of the Prince of Wales). Also "The Sphinx" for "Egypt" (1801—to the 40th Foot).

NICKNAME.—"The Excellers" (of the 40th (XL.) Foot). "The Fighting Fortieth."

NOTES.—The 40th captured four standards at Maharajpore (1843).

BIBLIOGRAPHY.—*A Short Record of the 1st Battalion Prince of Wales's Volunteers, (South Lancashire Regiment), formerly the 40th (2nd Somersetshire) Regiment.* By Captain R. H. Raymond-Smithies, 1st Batt. Prince of Wales's Volunteers (South Lancashire Regiment). [Jersey: 1891.]

Historical Records of the 40th (2nd Somersetshire) Regiment, now 1st Battalion Prince of Wales's Volunteers (South Lancashire Regiment), from its formation in 1717 to 1893. With many coloured plates and other illustrations. By Captain R. H. Raymond-Smithies, 1st Batt. Prince of Wales's Volunteers (South Lancashire Regiment). [Devonport: Swiss. 1894.]

Historical Record of the 82nd Regiment (or Prince of Wales's Volunteers). By Major Jarvis, 82nd Regiment. [London: Mitchell. 1866.]

The Welsh Regiment,

COMPRISING

1st Batt. (formerly) The 41st (The Welsh) Regiment of Foot.
2nd Batt. („) The 69th (South Lincolnshire) Regiment of Foot; with Militia Battalion.
3rd Batt. The Royal Glamorgan Militia.

THE ROYAL CYPHER WITH THE
IMPERIAL CROWN.

CENTRE ORNAMENT ON
HELMET-PLATE.

THE DRAGON OF WALES.

TITLES.

1st Batt.

1719–87. Independent Companies of Invalids (at first); subsequently The 41st (Royal Invalids) Regiment.

1787–1822. The 41st Regiment of Foot.

1822–81. The 41st (The Welsh) Regiment of Foot.

2nd Batt.

1756–58. The 24th (2nd Batt.) Regiment of Foot; renumbered.

1758–82. The 69th Regiment of Foot.

1782–1881. The 69th (South Lincolnshire) Regiment of Foot.

1881 (from). The Welsh Regiment.

The Welsh Regiment—*continued.*

PRINCIPAL CAMPAIGNS, BATTLES, &c.

* "Honours" on the Colours, the figures showing the Battalion concerned.

1761. Belle Isle.	*1809. Bourbon (2).	*1815–26. India (2).
1778. St. Lucia.	1810. Mauritius.	*1824–26. Ava (1).
1793. Toulon.	*1811. Java (2).	*1842. Candahar (1).
1794. Corsica.	1812–14. Canada.	*1842. Ghuznee (1).
1794. San Domingo.	*1812. Detroit (1).	*1842. Cabool (1).
1795. Hyères.	*1812. Queenstown (1).	1842. Kohistan.
1796. Genoa.	*1813. Miami (1).	1842. Istuliff.
1796. Porto Ferrajo.	*1813. Niagara (1).	*1854. Alma (1).
*1797. St. Vincent (2).	1814–15. Netherlands.	*1854. Inkerman (1).
1799. Helder.	1814. Bergen-op-Zoom.	*1855. Sevastopol (1).
1799. Bergen.	1815. Quatre Bras.	1900. South Africa.
1806. Vellore.	*1815. Waterloo (2).	

UNIFORM.—1st Batt., Scarlet with Blue facings (1719–82); Scarlet with Scarlet facings (1782–1822); Scarlet with White facings (from 1822). 2nd Batt., Scarlet with Green facings (from 1758). 1st and 2nd Batts., Scarlet and White facings (present time).

REGIMENTAL AND OTHER BADGES.—"The Rose and Thistle on the same stalk within the Garter." Also "The Prince of Wales's Plume," with the motto, "*Gwell angua na Chywilydd*" (received with its title in 1822). Also "The Royal Cypher with the Imperial Crown." The foregoing are recognised in the *Army List*, but "The Dragon of Wales" also appears on some appointments.

NICKNAMES.—At St. Vincent (1797) Nelson dubbed the detachment of the 69th, serving as Marines, his "Old Agamemnons." "The Ups and Downs" (of the late 69th)—the number can be read either way. "Wardour's Horse."

NOTES.—Since its return from India in 1826 the 69th had been unfortunate enough to miss every chance of active service until sent to South Africa in 1900.

BIBLIOGRAPHY.—*A Narrative of the Historical Events connected with the 69th Regiment.* By W. F. Butler, 69th Regiment. [London: Mitchell. 1870.]

The Black Watch (Royal Highlanders),

COMPRISING

1st Batt. (formerly) The 42nd (Royal Highland—The Black Watch).
2nd Batt. („) The 73rd (Perthshire) Regiment of Foot; with Militia Battalion.
3rd Batt. The Royal Perth Militia.

THE COLLAR-BADGE.

THE ROYAL CYPHER
WITHIN THE GARTER.

THE WAIST BELT.

THE SPHINX.

TITLES.

1st Batt.

1725–39. The Black Watch (*see* Notes).
*c.*1739–51. The Highland Regiment.
*c.*1751–58. The 42nd Highland Regiment.
1758–1861. The 42nd Royal Highland
    Regiment of Foot.
1861–1881. The 42nd Royal Highland
    (The Black Watch) Regiment of Foot.

2nd Batt.

1758–86. The 2nd Batt. 42nd Royal
    Highlanders.
1786–1862. The 73rd Regiment of
    Foot.
1862–81. The 73rd (Perthshire) Regi-
    ment.

1881 (from). The Black Watch (Royal Highlanders).

PRINCIPAL CAMPAIGNS, BATTLES, &c.

* " Honours " on the Colours, the figures showing the Battalion concerned.

1743–47. Flanders.
1745. Fontenoy.
1745. Jacobite rising.
1757–60. Canada.

1758. Ticonderoga.
1759. Guadaloupe.
1762. Martinique.
1762. Havannah.

1762–67. Indian Frontier
    Service.
1763. Bushy Run.
1775–81. America.

1776. Long Island.
1776. White Plains.
1776. Brooklyn.
1776. Fort Washington.
1777. Pisquata.
1777. Brandywine.
1777. Germantown.
1778. Freehold.
1780. Charlestown.
*1783. Mysore (2).
*1783. Mangalore (2).
1793. Pondicherry.
1793-95. Flanders.
1793. Nieuport.
1794. Nimeguen.
1795. Ceylon.
1795. Guildermalsen.
1796. St. Lucia.
1797. St. Vincent.
1798. Minorca.
*1799. Seringapatam (2).
1799. Genoa.

1799. Cadiz.
1800. Malta.
*1801. Egypt (1).
1801. Alexandria.
1801. Aboukir.
1801. Mandora.
*1808-14. Peninsula (1).
1808. Roleia.
1808. Vimiera.
*1809. Corunna (1).
1810. Busaco.
*1811. Fuentes d'Onor (1).
1812. Ciudad Rodrigo.
1812. Salamanca.
1812. Burgos.
*1813. Pyrenees (1).
1813. Gohrde.
*1813. Nivelle (1).
*1813. Nive (1).
1814. Antwerp.
*1814. Orthes (1).
*1814. Toulouse (1).

1815. Quatre Bras.
*1815. Waterloo (1 & 2).
1815. Netherlands.
*1846-53. South Africa (2).
*1854. Alma (1).
1854. Balaclava.
1854. Kertch.
1855. Yenikale.
*1855. Sevastopol (1).
1857-58. Indian Mutiny.
1857. Cawnpore.
*1858. Lucknow (1).
*1874. Ashantee (1).
*1882-84. Egypt (1).
*1882. Tel-el-Kebir (1).
*1884-85. Nile (1).
1884. El-Teb.
1884. Tamai.
*1885. Kirbekan (1).
1900. South Africa.

UNIFORM.—1st Batt., 1725 to 1739, the Highland dress with the tartans of the respective captains ; 1739 to 1758, Red with Buff facings and "the 42nd tartan" ; 1758 to present time, Red with Dark Blue facings. 2nd Batt., as the 42nd, and also as the 73rd, the Highland garb and "42nd tartan" were long in wear. Subsequently (circa 1786) Scarlet, with Dark Green facings, was adopted.

REGIMENTAL BADGES.—"The Royal Cypher within the Garter." The badge and motto of the Order of the Thistle. Also (in each of the four corners) the Royal Cypher ensigned with the Imperial Crown. Also "The Sphinx" (for Egypt, 1801).

NOTES.—The 1st Battalion of this famous corps, the oldest Highland regiment in the British army, was raised (circa 1725-29) from six Independent companies of Highlanders. Its sombre dress of black, blue, and green tartan gave rise to its popular name. To enumerate its services is simply to narrate the military history of Great Britain since the early part of the last century. Hardly a campaign has been conducted, or a battle fought, in which the Black Watch—one battalion or the other, or both in company—has not participated ; always with bravery, and frequently with conspicuous gallantry. Thereto its record of services abundantly testifies. At Fontenoy, Ticonderoga, and at Bushy Run "extraordinary" and "unexampled" gallantry was shown. It received Royal distinction in its change of title in 1758, and was privileged to wear the red heckle in the bonnet, in recognition of its conduct at the battle of Guildermalsen in 1795. In Egypt (in 1801, for which it bears "The Sphinx"), before Alexandria, it captured the Standard of the French Invincible Legion. Since then it has heaped fame on fame, and added "honour" to "honour" to its Colours. Nor has the 2nd Battalion (raised in Perthshire in 1758 as the 2nd Battalion of the 42nd, but, renumbered, long known as the 73rd prior to the territorial restoration of the ancient status) failed to win fresh laurels as occasion arose. At Mangalore (1783) against Tippoo Sahib, and side by side with the senior battalion at Waterloo, in the Netherlands, in the Indian Mutiny, and in the Kaffir wars of 1846-53, it worthily sustained the undying fame of the regiment. Recent events in South Africa show that neither the officers nor the men of to-day have lost one iota of that traditional dash, determination, and bravery which have won for the Black Watch so glorious a place in British military annals.

BIBLIOGRAPHY.—*Historical Record of the 42nd, or Royal Highland Regiment of Foot.* 1729-1844. Illustrated. [London : Parker. 1845.]
Chronology and Book of Days of the 42nd Royal Highlanders, The Black Watch. 1729-1874. [Edinburgh : Elgin and Son. 1874.]
Historical Record of the 73rd Regiment. 1780-1851. Illustrated. [London : Parker. 1851.]

The Oxfordshire Light Infantry,

COMPRISING

1st Batt. (formerly) The 43rd (Monmouthshire Light Infantry) Regiment.

2nd Batt. („) The 52nd (Oxfordshire Light Infantry) Regiment ; with Militia Battalions.

3rd Batt. The Royal Bucks Militia.

4th Batt. The Oxford Militia.

THE UNITED RED AND WHITE ROSE.

THE BUTTON.

TITLES.

1st Batt.

1741–51. Colonel Thomas Fowkes' (or successive Colonels') Regiment of Foot.

1751–82. The 43rd Regiment of Foot.

1782–1803. The 43rd (Monmouthshire) Regiment of Foot.

1803–81. The 43rd (Monmouthshire Light Infantry) Regiment.

2nd Batt.

1755–57. The 54th Regiment of Foot.

1757–82. The 52nd Regiment of Foot.

1782–1803. The 52nd (Oxfordshire) Regiment of Foot.

1803–81. The 52nd (Oxfordshire Light Infantry) Regiment.

1881 (from). The Oxfordshire Light Infantry.

The Oxfordshire Light Infantry—*continued*.

PRINCIPAL CAMPAIGNS, BATTLES, &c.

* "Honours" on the Colours, the figures showing the Battalion concerned.

1759–60. Canada.
*1759. Quebec (1).
1760. Sillery.
1760. Montreal.
1762. Martinique.
1762. Havannah.
1775–82. America.
1775. Lexington.
1775. Bunker's Hill.
1776. Brooklyn.
1777. Brandywine.
1778. Freehold.
*1783. Mysore (2).
*1790–93. Hindoostan (2).
1791. Bangalore.
1791. Savendroog.
1792. Seringapatam.
1793. Pondicherry.

1794. Martinique.
1794. Guadaloupe.
1794. St. Lucia.
1807. Copenhagen.
*1808–14. Peninsula (1 & 2).
*1808. Vimiera (1 & 2).
*1809. Corunna (1 & 2).
1809. Flushing.
1809. Douro.
1809. Talavera.
*1810. Busaco (1 & 2).
1811. Sabugal.
*1811. Fuentes d'Onor (1 & 2).
*1812. Ciudad Rodrigo (1 & 2).

*1812. Badajos (1 & 2).
*1812. Salamanca (1 & 2).
1813. St. Sebastian.
*1813. Vittoria (1 & 2).
*1813. Nivelle (1 & 2).
*1813. Nive (1 & 2).
*1814. Orthes (2).
*1814. Toulouse (1 & 2).
1814–15. Netherlands.
*1815. Waterloo (2).
1815. New Orleans.
*1850–53. South Africa (1).
1857–58. Indian Mutiny.
*1857. Delhi (2).
*1864–66. New Zealand (1).
1900. South Africa.

UNIFORM.—1st Batt., Scarlet with White facings (from formation). 2nd Batt., Scarlet with Buff facings (till territorialised in 1881, when it came into line with all non-"Royal" regiments, and the facings were changed to White).

REGIMENTAL AND OTHER BADGES.—"The United Red and White Rose" (in *Army List*). A special badge on various appointments consists of a combination of "A Bugle with Strings," a "Laurel Wreath," and "A Crown" (*see* Button).

NICKNAME.—"The Light Bobs" (of the late 43rd).

NOTES.—It will be noticed that the two regiments now linked as The Oxfordshire Light Infantry have frequently fought side by side with distinction.

BIBLIOGRAPHY.—*Historical Records of The* 43rd *Regiment* (*Monmouthshire Light Infantry*). *To* 1867. By Sir Richard J. A. Levinge, Bart. [London: Clowes. 1868.]

Historical Record of The 52nd (*Oxfordshire Light Infantry*). By W. S. Moorsom, late Captain 52nd Light Infantry. [London: Bentley. 1860.]

M

The Essex Regiment,

COMPRISING

1st Batt. (formerly) The 44th (East Essex) Regiment of Foot.

2nd Batt. („) The 56th (West Essex) Regiment of Foot; with Militia Battalions.

3rd Batt. The Essex Rifles.

4th Batt. The West Essex Militia.

THE CASTLE AND KEY.

THE COUNTY ARMS.

THE SPHINX.

TITLES.

1st Batt.

1740–48. The 44th (or Wolfe's Marines) Regiment of Foot: disbanded.

1741–51. Colonel James Long's (or successive Colonels') Regiment of Foot.

1751–82. The 44th Regiment of Foot.

1782–1881. The 44th (East Essex) Regiment of Foot.

2nd Batt.

1741–48. The 56th (Sherwood Foresters) Regiment of Foot: renumbered as The 45th.

1755–57. The 58th Regiment of Foot.

1757–82. The 56th Regiment of Foot.

1782–1881. The 56th (West Essex) Regiment of Foot.

1881 (from). The Essex Regiment.

The Essex Regiment—*continued.*

PRINCIPAL CAMPAIGNS, BATTLES, &c.

* "Honours" on the Colours, the figures showing the Battalion concerned.

1741. Carthagena.
1745. Jacobite rising.
1746. Culloden.
1755–60. Canada.
1758. Ticonderoga.
1758. Louisbourg.
1760. Niagara.
*1762. Moro (2).
1762. Havannah.
1763. Montreal.
1775–80. America.
1776. Brooklyn.
1776. Long Island.
1777. Brandywine.
1777. Germantown.
1778. Freehold.
*1779–83. Gibraltar (2).
1794. Martinique.
1794. St. Lucia.

1794. Guadaloupe.
1794–95. Flanders.
1796. St. Lucia.
1796–98. San Domingo.
1799. Bergen.
1799. Egmont-op-Zee.
*1801. Egypt (1).
1801. Mandora.
1801. Alexandria.
1809. Ionian Islands.
1809. Bourbon.
1810. Mauritius.
*1810–13. Peninsula (1).
1810. Matagorda.
1811. Sabugal.
*1812. Badajos (1).
*1812. Salamanca (1).
1812. Burgos.
1814. Antwerp.

*1814. Bladensburg (1).
1814. Baltimore.
1814–15. Netherlands.
1814. Bergen-op-Zoom.
1815. New Orleans.
1815. Quatre Bras.
*1815. Waterloo (1).
*1824–26. Ava (1).
1841–42. Cabool.
*1854. Alma (1).
*1854. Inkerman (1).
*1855. Sevastopol (1 & 2).
1857–58. Indian Mutiny.
1860. China.
*1860. Taku Forts (1).
*1884–85. Nile (2).
1900. South Africa.

UNIFORM.—1st Batt., Scarlet with Yellow facings (from 1741 till territorialised, when White facings were substituted). 2nd Batt., Scarlet with Crimson facings (from 1741–64); Scarlet with Purple facings (from 1764 to 1881: see NICKNAMES).

REGIMENTAL AND OTHER BADGES.—"The Castle and Key" and Motto, "*Montis Insignia Calpe*" (for defence of Gibraltar by the 56th). Also "The Sphinx" for "Egypt" (1801 — by the 44th). Also, though not in *Army List*, "The County Arms."

NICKNAMES, &c.—"The Two Fours" (of the 44th). "The Little Fighting Fours" (the regiment saw hard service in the Peninsula, and its men were of small average stature). "The Pompadours" and "Saucy Pompeys." (Tradition relates that when the facings were changed in 1764 (the crimson not wearing well) the Colonel desired Blue, but, the authorities objecting, he chose Purple, a favourite colour of Madame de Pompadour, a mistress of Louis XV. of France.)

NOTES.—The 44th captured an Eagle of The 62nd French Infantry at Salamanca.

BIBLIOGRAPHY.—*Historical Record of The 44th, or East Essex Regiment of Foot.* Illustrated. [London: Mitchell. 1864.]
Historical Record of The 44th, or East Essex Regiment. By T. Carter. 2nd Edition. Illustrated. [Chatham: Gale and Polden. 1887.]
Historical Record of The 56th, or West Essex Regiment. 1755–1844. Illustrated. [London: Parker. 1844.]

The Sherwood Foresters (Derbyshire Regiment),

COMPRISING

1st Batt. (formerly) The 45th (Nottinghamshire—Sherwood Foresters) Regiment.

2nd Batt. („) The 95th (Derbyshire) Regiment of Foot; with Militia Battalions.

3rd Batt. The 1st and 2nd Derby Militia.

4th Batt. The Royal Sherwood Foresters Militia.

THE UNITED RED AND WHITE ROSE.

THE COLLAR BADGE.

TITLES.

1st Batt.

1741–48. The 45th Regiment of Foot; also Fraser's or The 2nd (Green) Marines; disbanded.

1741–51. Colonel D. Houghton's (or successive Colonels') Regiment of Foot; disbanded.

1751–82. The 45th Regiment of Foot.

1782–1866. The 45th (Nottinghamshire) Regiment of Foot.

1866–81. The 45th (Nottinghamshire—Sherwood Foresters) Regiment.

2nd Batt.

1760–63. The 95th Regiment of Foot; disbanded.

1780–83. The 95th Regiment of Foot; disbanded.

1794–96. The 95th Regiment of Foot; disbanded.

1802–16. The 95th (Rifles); re-named The Rifle Brigade.

1816–18—. The 95th Regiment of Foot; disbanded.

1824–5–1881. The 95th (Derbyshire) Regiment of Foot.

1881 (from). The Sherwood Foresters (Derbyshire Regiment).

The Sherwood Foresters (Derbyshire Regiment)—*continued.*

PRINCIPAL CAMPAIGNS, BATTLES, &c.

* " Honours " on the Colours, the figures showing the Battalions concerned.

1757–60. Canada.	*1808. Roleia (1).	*1824–26. Ava (1).
*1758. Louisbourg (1).	*1808. Vimiera (1).	*1846–47. South Africa (1).
1759. Quebec.	*1809. Talavera (1).	1852–53. South Africa.
1762. Martinique.	*1810. Busaco (1 & 2).	*1854. Alma (2).
1775–78. America.	*1811. Fuentes d'Onor (1).	*1854. Inkerman (2).
1776. Brooklyn.	*1812. Ciudad Rodrigo (1).	*1855. Sevastopol (2).
1776. Long Island.	*1812. Badajos (1).	1857–58. Indian Mutiny.
1776. Brunx.	*1812. Salamanca (1).	*1858–59. Central India(2).
1777. Brandywine.	1812. Burgos.	*1868. Abyssinia (2).
1777. Germantown.	*1813. Vittoria (1).	1868. Magdala.
1795. Cape of Good Hope.	*1813. Pyrenees (1).	*1882. Egypt (2).
1806. Buenos Ayres.	*1813. Nivelle (1).	*1897–98. Tirah.
1807. Monte Video.	*1814. Orthes (1).	1900. South Africa.
*1808–14. Peninsula (1).	*1814. Toulouse (1).	

UNIFORM.—Scarlet, with Green facings (1st Batt.), and Scarlet with Yellow facings (2nd Batt.), from formation in 1741 and 1823 respectively until territorialised. The facings are now White.

REGIMENTAL AND OTHER BADGES.—In the *Army List* "The United Red and White Rose." Also in various combinations, " A Maltese Cross surmounted by a Crown ; a White Stag (the municipal arms of Derby) within a Wreath."

NICKNAME.—"The Old Stubborns" (of the 45th Foot, during the Peninsular Campaigns).

NOTES.—The 45th captured a French flag at the storming of Badajos.

BIBLIOGRAPHY.—*The 95th (The Derbyshire) Regiment in the Crimea.* By Major H. C. Wylly. [London : Sonnenschein, 1900.]

The Loyal North Lancashire Regiment,

COMPRISING

1st Batt. (formerly)   The 47th (Lancashire) Regiment of Foot.

2nd Batt. („   )   The 81st (Loyal Lincoln Volunteers) Regiment of Foot; with
Militia Battalions.

3rd & 4th Batt.   The 3rd Royal Lancashire Militia.

THE RED ROSE.

THE ROYAL
CREST.

THE ARMS OF THE CITY OF
LINCOLN.

TITLES.

1st Batt.

1740–48. The 47th (4th Marines) Regiment of Foot; disbanded.

1741–51. Colonel John Mordaunt's (or Colonel's name) Regiment of Foot.

1751–82. The 47th Regiment of Foot.

1782–1881. The 47th (Lancashire) Regiment of Foot.

2nd Batt.

1759–63. The 81st (Invalids) Regiment; dispersed as Independent Companies.

1778–83. The 81st (Aberdeen Highlanders) Regiment of Foot; disbanded.

1793–94. The 81st (Loyal Lincoln Volunteers) Regiment.

1794–1833. The 81st Regiment of Foot.

1833–81. The 81st (Loyal Lincoln Volunteers) Regiment of Foot.

1881 (from).   The Loyal North Lancashire Regiment.

The Loyal North Lancashire Regiment—*continued.*

PRINCIPAL CAMPAIGNS, BATTLES, &c.

* " Honours" on the Colours, the figures showing the Battalion concerned.

1745. Jacobite rising.	1800. Kaffraria.	*1813. Vittoria (1).
1746. Falkirk.	*1806. Maida (2).	*1813. St. Sebastian (1).
1757–60. Canada.	1806. Buenos Ayres.	1814. Nive.
*1758. Louisbourg (1).	1807. Monte Video.	1814. Bayonne.
*1759. Quebec (1).	1809. Scylla Castle.	*1826. Ava (1).
1760. Sillery.	1809. Ionian Islands.	*1854. Alma (1).
1760. Montreal.	*1809. Corunna (2).	*1854. Inkerman (1).
1762. Martinique.	1809. Flushing.	*1855. Sevastopol (1).
1775–81. America.	*1810–14. Peninsula (1&2).	1857–58. Indian Mutiny.
1775. Lexington.	1811. Barrossa.	*1878–79. Afghanistan(2).
1775. Bunker's Hill.	*1811. Tarifa (1).	*1878. Ali Masjid (2).
1777. Stillwater.	1812. Burgos.	1900. South Africa.
1796. San Domingo.		

UNIFORM.—Scarlet and White facings (1st Batt.) and Scarlet with Buff facings (2nd Batt.) from formation ; both battalions have White facings at present time.

REGIMENTAL AND OTHER BADGES.—"The Red Rose of Lancaster." Also "The King's (or Royal) Crest of England" (which is also the badge of the Duchy of Lancaster, and is said to have been conferred on the 47th when raised in Scotland). Also on some appointments "The Arms of the City of Lincoln."

NICKNAMES, &c.—"Wolfe's Own" (of the 47th at Quebec—the black worm in the gold lace, as now worn, is in memory of the Hero of Quebec). "The Cauliflowers" (of the 47th, in allusion to its white facings, an unusual colour when the corps was raised). "The Lancashire Lads" (also of the 47th—from its county title).

NOTES.—This is the only regiment entitled " Loyal," but the term was originally applied, not to the Lancashire, but to the Lincoln battalion. When raised the Lincoln Militia volunteered in a body.

BIBLIOGRAPHY.—*Historical Record of The* 81st *Regiment, or Loyal Lincoln Volunteers.* 1793–1872. [Gibraltar, 1872.]

The Northamptonshire Regiment,

COMPRISING

1st Batt. (formerly) The 48th (Northamptonshire) Regiment of Foot.

2nd Batt. („) The 58th (Rutlandshire) Regiment of Foot; with Militia Battalions.

3rd Batt. The Northampton and Rutland Militia.

ORNAMENT ON HELMET PLATE.

THE SPHINX.

TITLES

1st Batt.

1740–48. The 48th (The 5th or Cochrane's Marines) Regiment; disbanded.

1740–51. Colonel James Cholmondeley's (or successive Colonels') Regiment of Foot.

1751–82. The 48th Regiment of Foot.

1782–1881. The 48th (Northamptonshire) Regiment of Foot.

2nd Batt.

1740–48. The 58th Regiment of Foot; renumbered the 47th, and now The 1st Batt. Loyal North Lancashire.

1756–57. The 58th Regiment of Foot; renumbered The 56th.

1755–57. The 60th Regiment of Foot; renumbered The 58th.

1757–82. The 58th Regiment of Foot.

1782–1881. The 58th (Rutlandshire) Regiment of Foot.

1881 (from). The Northamptonshire Regiment.

The Northamptonshire Regiment—*continued.*

PRINCIPAL CAMPAIGNS, BATTLES, &c.

* " Honours " on the Colours, the figures showing the Battalion concerned.

1744–47. Flanders.
1745. Fontenoy.
1745. Jacobite rising.
1746. Culloden.
1747. Val.
1758–62. Canada.
*1758. Louisbourg (1 & 2).
*1759. Quebec (1 & 2).
1760. Sillery.
1760. Montreal.
1762. Martinique.
1762. Havannah.
*1779–83. Gibraltar (2).
1794. Martinique.
1796. St. Lucia.
1798. Minorca.
1800. Malta.

*1801. Egypt (2).
1801. Aboukir.
1801. Mandora.
1801. Alexandria.
*1806. Maida (2).
1809. Scylla.
*1809–14. Peninsula (1 & 2).
*1809. Douro (1).
1809. Oporto.
*1809. Talavera (1).
1810. Busaco.
*1811. Albuera (1).
1812. Ciudad Rodrigo.
*1812. Badajos (1).
*1812. Salamanca (1 & 2).
1812. Burgos.

*1813. Vittoria (1 & 2).
*1813. Pyrenees (1 & 2).
*1813. Nivelle (1 & 2).
1813. Nive.
*1814. Orthes (1 & 2).
1814. Bordeaux.
*1814. Toulouse (1).
1814. Plattsburg.
1834. Coorg.
*1849–56. New Zealand (2).
*1855. Sevastopol (1).
*1879. South Africa (2).
1881. Transvaal.
*1897–98. Tirah.
1900. South Africa.

UNIFORM.—1st Batt., Red (afterwards Scarlet) with Buff facings (from 1741 to 1881). 2nd Batt., Scarlet with White (or Buff) facings (1755–1767); Scarlet with Black facings (1767–1881). The facings for both battalions are now White.

REGIMENTAL AND OTHER BADGES.—" The Castle and Key," with the motto, " *Montis Insignia Calpe* " (for the defence of Gibraltar by the 58th). Also " The Sphinx," for " Egypt " (1801—also an honour of the 58th).

NICKNAMES.—" The Black Cuffs " (from the facings of the 58th in 1767). Also " The Steel Backs."

NOTES.—It was declared of The 48th that they saved the day at Talavera by their " advance, position, and steadiness"—hence " Talavera " on the helmet and waist-plates.

Princess Charlotte of Wales's (Royal Berkshire Regiment),

COMPRISING

1st Batt. (formerly) The 49th (Hertfordshire—Princess Charlotte of Wales's) Regiment of Foot.

2nd Batt. („) The 66th (Berkshire) Regiment of Foot; with Militia Battalion.

3rd Batt. The Royal Berkshire Militia.

THE DRAGON OF CHINA.

TITLES.

1st Batt.

1742–48. The 49th (The 6th or Cotterell's Marines) Regiment; disbanded.
1743–51. Colonel Edward Trelawney's (or Colonel's name) Regiment of Foot.
1751–82. The 49th Regiment of Foot.
1782–1816. The 49th (Hertfordshire) Regiment of Foot.
1816–81. The 49th (Hertfordshire—The Princess of Wales's) Regiment.

2nd Batt.

1755–58. The 19th (2nd Batt.) Regiment of Foot; renumbered.

1758–82. The 66th Regiment of Foot.

1782–1881. The 66th (Berkshire) Regiment of Foot.

1881 (from). Princess Charlotte of Wales's (Royal Berkshire Regiment).

Princess Charlotte of Wales's (Royal Berkshire Regiment)—
continued.

PRINCIPAL CAMPAIGNS, BATTLES, &c.

* "Honours" on the Colours, the figures showing the Battalion concerned.

1775–78. America.	1812–14. America.	1842. Ningpoo.
1775. Bunker's Hill.	*1812. Queenstown (1).	*1854. Alma (1).
1776. Brooklyn.	1813. Chrystler's Farm.	*1854. Inkerman (1).
1776. Long Island.	*1813. Vittoria (2).	*1855. Sevastopol (1).
1776. Brunx.	*1813. Pyrenees (2).	*1879–80. Afghanistan (2).
1777. Brandywine.	*1813. Nivelle (2).	1880. Maiwand.
1778. St. Lucia.	*1813. Nive (2).	*1880. Kandahar (2).
1796. San Domingo.	*1814. Orthes (2).	*1882. Egypt (1).
*1799. Egmont-op-Zee (1).	1821. Cape of Good Hope.	*1885. Suakim (1).
*1801. Copenhagen (1).	*1840–42. China (1).	1885. Tamai.
*1809–14. Peninsula (2).	1842. Chusan.	1885. Nile.
*1809. Douro (2).	1842. Canton.	*1885. Tofrek (1).
*1809. Talavera (2).	1842. Amoy.	1900. South Africa.
*1811. Albuera (2).	1842. Shanghai.	

UNIFORM.—Scarlet (or Red) with Green facings (both Batts. when raised); Scarlet with Blue facings (present time).

REGIMENTAL AND OTHER BADGES.—"The Dragon" (for China). Also (on Helmet-plate, not mentioned in *Army List*) "A Stag under a Tree" (an old badge of the Militia Battalion).

NOTES.—Raised in Jamaica from Volunteer Companies left in the Island in 1714. For distinction in the American War (1776) the "Grenadier Company" wore a white feather with a black tip, and the "Light Company" a red heckle. Its title in 1816 was bestowed for services to the Princess at Weymouth. The 2nd Battalion (as the 66th Foot) was part of the St. Helena Garrison during the exile of the Emperor Napoleon I.

BIBLIOGRAPHY.—*The 66th Berkshire Regiment.* By J. Percy Groves. [Reading: Beecroft. 1887]

The Queen's Own (Royal West Kent) Regiment,

COMPRISING

1st Batt. (formerly) The 50th (Queen's Own) Regiment of Foot.
2nd Batt. („) The 97th (The Earl of Ulster's) Regiment of Foot; with Militia Battalions.
3rd Batt. The 1st West Kent Militia.

" Quo fas et gloria ducunt."

THE ROYAL CREST OF ENGLAND.

THE WHITE HORSE OF KENT.

THE WHITE HORSE AND MOTTO.

THE SPHINX.

TITLES.

1st Batt.

1740–48. The 58th (The 7th, or Cornwall's Marines) Regiment; disbanded.

1748–57. The 50th (Shirley's American Provincials) Regiment of Foot; disbanded.

1757–82. The 50th (raised in 1751 as the 52nd) Regiment of Foot.

1782–1827. The 50th (West Kent) Regiment of Foot.

1827–31. The 50th (The Duke of Clarence's) Regiment of Foot.

1831–81. The 50th (The Queen's Own) Regiment of Foot.

2nd Batt.

1759–63. The 97th Regiment of Foot; disbanded.

1779–83. The 97th Regiment of Foot; disbanded.

1794–95. The 97th (Strathspey Highlanders) Regiment; disbanded, the flank companies going to the Black Watch.

1798–1802. The 97th (Queen's Germans); renumbered The 96th.

1804–18. The 98th Regiment of Foot; renumbered and disbanded as The 97th.

1824–81. The 97th (The Earl of Ulster's) Regiment of Foot.

1881 (from). The Queen's Own (Royal West Kent) Regiment.

The Queen's Own (Royal West Kent) Regiment—*continued.*

PRINCIPAL CAMPAIGNS, BATTLES, &c.

* "Honours" on the Colours, the figures showing the Battalion concerned.

1759–62. Germany.	*1808–14. Peninsula (1).	*1845. Moodkee (1).
1760. Corbach.	1808. Roleia.	*1845. Ferozeshah (1).
1761. Belle Isle.	*1808. Vimiera (1).	*1846. Aliwal (1).
1761. Kirk Denkern.	*1809. Corunna (1).	*1846. Sobraon (1).
1762. Wilhelmstahl.	1809. Flushing.	*1854. Alma (1).
1783. Gibraltar.	*1812. Almaraj (1).	*1854. Inkerman (1).
1793. Toulon.	1812. Badajos.	*1855. Sevastopol (1 & 2).
1794. Corsica.	*1813. Vittoria (1).	1857–58. Indian Mutiny.
1797–99. Portugal.	1813. Maya.	*1858. Lucknow (2).
*1801. Egypt (1).	*1813. Pyrenees (1).	*1863–66. NewZealand(1).
1801. Mandora.	*1813. Nive (1).	1881. South Africa.
1801. Alexandria.	*1814. Orthes (1).	*1882. Egypt (1).
1807. Copenhagen.	1814. Plattsburg.	*1884–85. Nile (1).
1808. Cadiz.	*1843. Punniar (1).	1900. South Africa.

UNIFORM.—1st Batt., Scarlet with Scarlet facings (1755–67); Scarlet with Black facings (1767–1831); Scarlet with Blue facings (from 1831). 2nd Batt., Scarlet with Sky-blue facings (on formation in 1824).

REGIMENTAL AND OTHER BADGES.—"The Sphinx" for "Egypt" (1801). The Motto "*Quo fas et gloria ducunt*" ("Whither right and glory lead"), borne by the late 97th. Also, on appointments, "The Royal Crest"; "The White Horse of Kent" with "*Invicta*" (adopted since territorialisation). Also (formerly), "The White Horse of Hanover" (in common with many line Regiments).

NICKNAMES.—"The Blind Half-Hundred" (of the late 50th, many of its men suffering severely from ophthalmia in Egypt, 1801). "The Dirty Half-Hundred" (at Vimiera, where the 50th fought with much distinction; Major Napier wrote their faces were "begrimed with powder as black as their own lapels"). "The Devil's Royals" (also of the 50th). "The Gallant Fiftieth" (this sobriquet was likewise bestowed for gallantry at Vimiera, 900 "tumbling down on Laborde's division of French [5,300 strong] amidst a fearful war-cry, and with a shock that nothing could withstand"—so also wrote Major Napier. "The Celestials" (from the Sky-blue facings of the 97th raised by the Earl of Ulster, the colour being that of the ribbon of the Order of St. Patrick).

NOTES.—Its county connection apparently dates from the time of the American War, when its Colonel was one of the distinguished Kentish Wilson family, who also have been intimately connected with the Kentish Militia.

BIBLIOGRAPHY.—*The History of The 50th (The Queen's Own) Regiment.* From the earliest date to the year 1881. By Colonel Fyler. Coloured illustrations, maps, and plans. [London: Chapman and Hall. 1895.]

The King's Own (Yorkshire Light Infantry),

COMPRISING

1st Batt. (formerly) The 51st (2nd Yorkshire West Riding) Regiment.

2nd Batt. („   ) The 105th (Madras Light Infantry) Regiment; with Militia Battalion.

3rd Batt. The 1st West York Militia.

" Cede Nullis."

THE WHITE ROSE (OF YORK).

TITLES.

1st Batt.

1740–48. The 51st (The 8th or Sir Thomas Hanmer's Marines) Regiment; disbanded.

1745–57. The 51st (raised in 1745 as Pepperil's American Provincials) Regiment of Foot; disbanded.

1755–57. The 53rd Regiment of Foot; renumbered.

1757–82. The 51st Regiment of Foot.

1782–1809. The 51st (2nd Yorkshire, West Riding) Regiment of Foot.

1809–21. The 51st (2nd Yorkshire, West Riding, Light Infantry) Regiment.

1821–81. The 51st (2nd Yorkshire, West Riding, The King's Own Light Infantry) Regiment.

2nd Batt.

1761–63. The 105th (Queen's Own Royal Highlanders) Regiment; raised as a wedding escort to Queen Charlotte; disbanded.

1781–83. The 105th (Volunteers of Ireland) Regiment.

1794–96. The 105th Regiment of Foot.

1839–58. The Hon. East India Company's 2nd Madras (European Light Infantry) Regiment.

1858–61. The 2nd Madras (Light Infantry) Regiment.

1861–81. The 105th (Madras Light Infantry) Regiment.

1881 (from). The King's Own Yorkshire Light Infantry.

The King's Own (Yorkshire Light Infantry)—*continued.*

PRINCIPAL CAMPAIGNS, BATTLES, &c.

* " Honours " on the Colours, the figures showing the Battalion concerned.

1758–62. Germany.	1809. Flushing.	*1814. Orthes (1).
*1759. Minden (1).	*1811. Fuentes d'Onor (1).	*1815. Waterloo (1).
1760. Corbach.	1812. Badajos.	1815. Netherlands.
1760. Warbourg.	*1812. Salamanca (1).	*1852–3. Pegu (1).
1782. Minorca.	1812. Burgos.	*1878–80. Afghanistan (1).
1793. Toulon.	*1813. Vittoria (1).	*1878. Ali Masjid (1).
1794. Corsica.	*1813. Pyrenees (1).	*1885–7. Burma (1).
*1808–14. Peninsula (1).	*1813. Nivelle (1).	1900. South Africa.
*1809. Corunna (1).		

UNIFORM.—1st Batt., Scarlet with Sea-Green (and latterly " full " Green) facings (1755–1821) ; Scarlet with Blue facings (from 1821). 2nd Batt., Scarlet with Buff facings (1839–1881) ; Scarlet with Blue facings (from 1881).

REGIMENTAL BADGE.—" The White Rose " (of York). The Motto, " *Cede Nullis* " (" Yield to None "—brought by the late 105th. It appears first in the Indian Army List for 1841). On most of the appointments " A French Horn " appears in combination with " The White Rose."

NICKNAME.—" The Kolis " (from the title received in 1821—K[ing's] O[wn] L[ight] I[nfantry]).

BIBLIOGRAPHY.—*A Record of the Services of The* 51st (*2nd West York*) *The King's Own Light Infantry Regiment.* By W. Wheater. [London : Longmans. 1870.]

The King's (Shropshire Light Infantry),

COMPRISING

1st Batt. (formerly) The 53rd (Shropshire) Regiment of Foot.

2nd Batt. („) The 85th (Bucks Volunteers) (King's Light Infantry) Regiment; with Militia Battalions.

3rd Batt. The Shropshire Militia.

4th Batt. The Hereford Militia.

"Aucto splendore resurgo."

THE UNITED RED AND WHITE ROSE.

TITLES.

1st Batt.

1741–48. The 53rd (The 10th or Jeffrey's, afterwards Agnew's Marines) Regiment; disbanded.

1755–57. The 55th Regiment of Foot; renumbered.

1757–82. The 53rd Regiment of Foot.

1782–1881. The 53rd (Shropshire) Regiment of Foot.

2nd Batt.

1759–63. The 85th (Royal Volunteers Light Infantry) Regiment; disbanded.

1778–83. The 85th (Westminster Volunteers) Regiment; mostly lost at sea returning from Jamaica; rest disbanded.

1794–1808. The 85th (Bucks Volunteers) Regiment of Foot.

1808–15. The 85th (Bucks Volunteers Light Infantry) Regiment.

1815–21. The 85th (Bucks Volunteers) (Duke of York's Own Light Infantry) Regiment.

1821–81. The 85th (Bucks Volunteers) (King's Light Infantry) Regiment.

1881 (from). The King's (Shropshire Light Infantry).

The King's (Shropshire Light Infantry)—*continued.*

PRINCIPAL CAMPAIGNS, BATTLES, &c.

* " Honours " on the Colours, the figures showing the Battalion concerned.

1761. Belle Isle.	1809. Burdelkund.	1814. Washington.
1762. Portugal.	*1809–14. Peninsula(1&2).	1815. New Orleans.
1776–81. America.	*1809. Talavera (1).	1817–19. Pindarree War.
1793–95. Flanders.	*1811. Fuentes d'Onor (2).	18—. Copal Droog.
1793. Famars.	1812. Badajos.	1838–39. Canada.
*1793. Nieuport (1).	*1812. Salamanca (1).	*1846. Aliwal (1).
1793. Valenciennes.	1812. Mahratta War.	184–. Buddiwal.
*1794. Tournay (1).	1814–15. Nepaul.	*1846. Sobraon (1).
1794. Nimeguen.	1814–15. Kalunga.	*1848–49. Punjaub (1).
1795. Guildermalsen.	*1813. Vittoria (1).	*1849. Goojerat. (1)
*1796. St. Lucia (1).	*1813. Pyrenees (1).	1856–57. South Africa.
1797. St. Vincent.	1813. St. Sebastian.	1857–58. Indian Mutiny.
1797. Port-au-Prince.	1813. Bidassoa.	*1857. Lucknow (1).
1797. Trinidad.	*1813. Nive (1).	1857. Cawnpore.
1799. Helder.	*1813. Nivelle (1).	*1879–80. Afghanistan (2).
1799. Bergen.	1814. Bayonne.	*1882. Egypt (1).
1799. Egmont-op-Zee.	*1814. Toulouse (1).	*1885. Suakim (1).
1809. Flushing.	*1814. Bladensburg (2).	1900. South Africa.

UNIFORM.—1st Batt., Scarlet with Scarlet facings (1755 till 1881); Scarlet with Blue facings (present time). 2nd Batt., Scarlet with Yellow facings (1794–1821); Scarlet with Blue facings (since 1821).

REGIMENTAL BADGE.—" The United Red and White Rose." Motto : " *Aucto splendore resurgo* " (from 1821). " A Bugle with Strings " is also worn on various appointments.

NICKNAMES.—" The Brickdusts " (from the facings of the 53rd). " The Old Five and Threepennies " (from its number, and the daily pay of an ensign). " The Elegant Extracts " (dissensions amongst the staff of the 85th were [*circa* 1811] so frequent that the Duke of York dispersed the lot, substituting officers from other corps). " The Young Bucks " (in distinction to The 16th—" The Old Bucks ").

NOTES.—The 1st 85th was the first Light Infantry Regiment in the service.

BIBLIOGRAPHY.—*Historical Record of The* 53*rd, or Shropshire Regiment of Foot.* 1755–1848. Illustrated. [London : Parker. 1849.]

Historical Records of The 53*rd (Shropshire) Regiment, now* 1*st Batt. King's (Shropshire) Light Infantry.* 1755–1889. By Colonel W. Rogerson. [Devonport : Swiss. 1890.]

The Duke of Cambridge's Own (Middlesex Regiment),

COMPRISING

1st Batt. (formerly) The 57th (West Middlesex) Regiment of Foot.

2nd Batt. („) The 77th (East Middlesex) Regiment of Foot; the 3rd and 4th Batts. are authorised; with Militia Batts.

5th Batt. The Royal Elthorne Militia.

6th Batt. The Royal East Middlesex Militia.

THE PLUME OF THE PRINCE OF WALES.

THE HELMET BADGE.

TITLES.

1st Batt.

1741–48. The 57th Regiment of Foot; renumbered The 46th.

1755–57. The 57th Regiment of Foot; renumbered The 55th.

1755–57. The 59th Regiment of Foot; renumbered The 57th.

1757–82. The 57th Regiment of Foot.

1782–1881. The 57th (West Middlesex) Regiment of Foot.

2nd Batt.

1756–63. The 77th (Montgomery Highlanders) Regiment; disbanded.

1775–83. The 77th (Atholl Highlanders) Regiment; disbanded.

1787–1807. The 77th Regiment of Foot.

1807–76. The 77th (East Middlesex) Regiment of Foot.

1876–81. The 77th (East Middlesex) (Duke of Cambridge's Own) Regiment of Foot.

1881 (from). The Duke of Cambridge's Own (Middlesex Regiment).

The Duke of Cambridge's Own (Middlesex Regiment)—*continued.*

PRINCIPAL CAMPAIGNS, BATTLES, &c.

* " Honours " on the Colours, the figures showing the Battalion concerned.

1758–60. Canada.	*1799. Seringapatam (2).	1814–15. Canada.
1762. Havannah.	*1809–1814. Peninsula	1814. Bayonne.
1776–82. America.	(1 & 2).	1819. Asseerghur.
1776. Brooklyn.	1809. Flushing.	1854. Balaclava.
1781. York Town.	*1811. Albuera (2).	*1854. Alma (1).
1793–95. Flanders.	1811. El-Bodon.	*1854. Inkerman (1 & 2).
1793. Nieuport.	*1812. Ciudad Rodrigo (2).	*1855. Sevastopol (1 & 2).
1793. Dunkirk.	*1812. Badajos (2).	1858. Indian Mutiny.
1794. Nimeguen.	*1813. Vittoria (1).	*1861–66. New Zealand (1).
1790–1807. Hindoostan.	*1813. Pyrenees (1).	*1879. South Africa (1).
1796. St. Lucia.	*1813. Nivelle (1).	1900. South Africa.
*1799. Mysore (2).	*1813. Nive (1).	

UNIFORM.—1st Batt., Scarlet (or Red) with Green facings (1755–67); Scarlet with Yellow facings (1767–1881); Scarlet with White facings (from 1881). 2nd Batt., Scarlet with Yellow facings (from 1787 to territorialisation, when White facings were adopted).

REGIMENTAL AND OTHER BADGES.—" The Plume of the Prince of Wales " (the 77th badge). Also " The Duke of Cambridge's Cypher and Coronet." Amongst other badges not specified in official lists are (1) " A Laurel Wreath, with Albuera " (an old 57th badge for gallantry at that battle); (2) " The County Arms."

NICKNAMES.—" The Die-Hards," for stubborn valour at Albuera, by which the 57th practically insured victory; at the finish the Colours were riddled by thirty bullets, and the survivors numbered one officer in twenty-four, and 168 men out of 584. Colonel Inglis rallied his men again and again by " Die hard, my men, die hard ! " The 57th had previously been known as " The Steelbacks," from the frequency with which its men, largely recruited by militiamen from London, were flogged. " The Pothooks " (the 77th), from the two sevens in its number.

NOTES.—The 77th at El-Bodon was specially commended by Lord Wellington for " steadiness, discipline and confidence " when largely outnumbered.

BIBLIOGRAPHY.—*Historical Records of The 57th (or West Middlesex Regiment).* 1755–1878. By General H. J. Warre, C.B. [London : Mitchell. 1878.]
Some Reminiscences of the " Die-Hards " (57th West Middlesex). By Sergeant-Major E. Bezar. [Dunedin : Dick & Co. 1891.]
A History of The 57th (West Middlesex Regiment) from 1755–1881. Including a record of the services of the " Die-Hards " in the American War of Independence, Flanders, the West Indies, the Peninsula, France, the Crimea, New Zealand, Zululand, etc. By Captain Henry H. Woolwright, Middlesex Regiment. With coloured plates and other illustrations and maps. Demy 8vo. 406 pp.

N 2

The King's Royal Rifle Corps,

1st to 4th Batts. (formerly) The 60th (The King's Royal Rifle Corps); with Militia Batts.

5th Batt. The Huntingdon Militia.
7th Batt. The 2nd Royal Middlesex Militia.
8th Batt. The Carlow Militia.
9th Batt. The North Cork Militia.

" Celer et audax."

THE ROYAL CYPHER
WITHIN GARTER.
WITH THE IMPERIAL CROWN.

THE WHITE HORSE.

TITLES.

1741–48. The 60th Regiment of Foot.

1755–57. The 62nd (Royal American) Regiment of Foot; renumbered.

1757–1824. The 60th (Royal American) Regiment of Foot.

1824. The 60th (Duke of York's Rifle Corps and Light Infantry).

1824–30. The 60th (The Duke of York's Own Rifle Corps).

1830–81. The 60th (The King's Royal Rifle Corps).

1881 (from). The King's Royal Rifle Corps.

The King's Royal Rifle Corps—*continued.*

PRINCIPAL CAMPAIGNS, BATTLES, &c.

* "Honours," the figures showing the Battalion concerned.

1757-60. Canada.
1758. Ticonderoga.
*1758. Louisbourg (2 & 3).
*1759. Quebec (2 & 3).
1760. Sillery.
1762. Martinique.
1762. Havannah.
1796. Grenada.
1799. Surinam.
*1808–14. Peninsula (5).†
*1808. Roleia (5).
*1808. Vimiera (5).
1809. Corunna.
1809. Douro.
*1809. Martinique (3).
*1809. Talavera (5).
1810. Guadaloupe.
*1810. Busaco (5).

*1811. Fuentes d'Onor (5).
*1811. Albuera (5).
*1812. Ciudad Rodrigo (5).
*1812. Badajos (5).
*1812. Salamanca (5).
*1813. Vittoria (5).
*1813. Pyrenees (5).
*1813. Nivelle (5).
*1813. Nive (5).
*1814. Orthes (5).
*1814. Toulouse (5).
1814. Bayonne.
*1848–49. Punjaub (1).
*1849. Mooltan (1).
*1849. Goojerat (1).
*1850–53. South Africa (2).
1857–58. Indian Mutiny.
*1857. Delhi (1).

1860. China.
*1860. Taku Forts (2).
*1860. Pekin (2).
*1878–80. Afghanistan (2).
*1879. Ahmed Khel (2).
*1880. Kandahar (2).
*1879–81. South Africa (3).
*1882–84. Egypt (3).
*1882. Tel-el-Kebir (3).
1884–85. Nile.
1884. El Teb.
1884. Tamai.
1885. Abu Klea.
1890–92. Burma.
*1895. Chitral.
1900. South Africa.

UNIFORM.—Scarlet, with Blue facings (1755 to 1814); Green, with Scarlet facings (present time).

REGIMENTAL AND OTHER BADGES.—Among those appearing on the appointments but not in the *Army List* are "The Royal Cypher within the Garter, surmounted by a Crown," and "A Maltese Cross." Also formerly "The White Horse" (of Hanover). Motto, "*Celer et Audax*" ("Swift and Bold," bestowed, according to tradition, by General Wolfe in recognition of its conduct before Quebec)

NOTES.—This regiment, though possessing no "Colours," bears more honours than any other regiment, the Highland Light Infantry coming next with twenty-nine.

BIBLIOGRAPHY.—*A Regimental Chronicle and List of Officers of The 60th, or The King's Royal Rifle Corps, formerly The 62nd, or The Royal American Regiment of Foot.* By Captain Nesbit Willoughby Wallace, 60th Royal Rifles. [London : Harrison. 1879.]

"*Celer et Audax,*" or *The Services of The 5th Battalion, 60th Regiment (Rifles).* By Major-General Gibbes Rigaud, late Lieutenant-Colonel, 60th Rifles. [Oxford : Hall & Stacy. 1879.]

† The 5th Battalion here mentioned is, of course, one of the former regular battalions, and *not* the present militia battalion.

The Duke of Edinburgh's (Wiltshire Regiment),

COMPRISING

1st Batt. (formerly) The 62nd (Wiltshire) Regiment of Foot.
2nd Batt. („) The 99th (Duke of Edinburgh's) Regiment of Foot; with Militia Batt.
3rd Batt. The Royal Wiltshire Militia.

THE DUKE OF EDINBURGH'S CORONET AND CYPHER.

TITLES.

1st Batt.

1743–48. The 62nd Regiment of Foot: disbanded.

1755–57. The 62nd (Royal American) Regiment of Foot: renumbered The 60th.

1756–57. The 62nd Regiment of Foot: renumbered The 77th.

1756–58. The 4th King's Own (2nd Batt.): separately regimented as The 62nd Foot.

1758–82. The 62nd Regiment of Foot.

1782–1881. The 62nd (Wiltshire) Regiment of Foot.

2nd Batt.

1760–63. The 99th Regiment of Foot: disbanded.

1780–83. The 99th (Jamaica) Regiment of Foot: disbanded.

1794–98. The 99th Regiment of Foot: disbanded.

1804–11. The 99th Regiment of Foot: renumbered The 98th (or Prince of Wales' Tipperary) Regiment of Foot: disbanded in 1818.

1805–15. The 100th Regiment of Foot: renumbered in

1815–18. The 99th (H.R.H. The Prince Regent's County of Dublin) Regiment of Foot: disbanded.

1824–74. The 99th (Lanarkshire) Regiment of Foot.

1874–81. The 99th (The Duke of Edinburgh's) Regiment of Foot.

1881 (from). The Duke of Edinburgh's (Wiltshire Regiment).

The Duke of Edinburgh's (Wiltshire Regiment)—*continued.*

PRINCIPAL CAMPAIGNS, BATTLES, &c.

* " Honours " on the Colours, the figures showing the Battalion concerned.

1743. Dettingen.	1795. Essequebo.	*1845–47. New Zealand (2).
1745. Fontenoy.	1795. Berbice.	*1845. Ferozeshah (1).
1745. Jacobite rising.	1809. Scylla.	*1846. Sobraon (1).
1746. Culloden.	1813. Niagara.	*1855. Sevastopol (1).
1758. Carrickfergus.	*1813–14. Peninsula (1).	1860. China.
1776–80. America.	1813. Bidassoa.	*1860. Pekin (2).
1777. Stillwater.	*1813. Nive (1).	*1878–80. South Africa (2).
1793–8. San Domingo.	1814. Bayonne.	1900. South Africa.
1795. Demerara.	1814–15. America.	

UNIFORM.—Scarlet with Buff facings (1st Batt. from 1758–1881), and Scarlet with Yellow facings (2nd Batt. from 1824–1881). Now Scarlet with White facings for both batts.

REGIMENTAL AND OTHER BADGES.—" The Duke of Edinburgh's Coronet and Cypher " (this in combination with a Maltese Cross, adopted by the 62nd in 1806, and the Regulation Star and Wreath).

NICKNAME.—" The Springers " (tradition says that the 62nd was so called from its employment as a light battalion during the American War in 1777).

NOTES.—For its defence, in 1760, against the French, of the Castle of Carrickfergus it at one time wore a " splash " on the buttons. After the ammunition was expended bricks and stones were thrown, and, so the story runs, their buttons were used as bullets. The 99th were raised in Lanarkshire—hence its former county title.

BIBLIOGRAPHY.—" *The Springers.*" *The 62nd Regiment.* By H. M. C. [Dublin : Carson. 1891.]

The Manchester Regiment,

COMPRISING

1st Batt. (formerly)   The 63rd (West Suffolk) Regiment of Foot.
2nd Batt. („   )   The 96th Regiment of Foot ; with Militia Batts.
3rd & 4th Batts.   The 6th Royal Lancashire Militia.

THE ARMS OF THE CITY OF
MANCHESTER.

THE SPHINX.

TITLES.

1st Batt.

1744–48. The 63rd (American) Regiment of Foot : renumbered The 49th.

1757–58. The 8th King's (2nd Batt.) Regiment ; regimented in

1758–82. The 63rd Regiment of Foot.

1782–81. The 63rd (West Suffolk) Regiment of Foot.

2nd Batt.

1760–63. The 96th Regiment of Foot (raised for service in the Carnatic) : disbanded.

1780–83. The 96th (British Musketeers) Regiment : disbanded.

1793–98. The 96th (The Queen's Royal Irish) Regiment ; dispersed.

1803–16. The 96th Regiment of Foot (raised as 2nd Batt. 52nd Foot : renumbered The 95th, and as such disbanded in 1818).

1815–18. The 96th (Queen's Own) Regiment of Foot (raised in 1798 as The Queen's Germans : numbered The 97th in 1802 : renumbered, in 1815, the 96th : disbanded in 1818—the Egyptian and Peninsular honours of this corps were assumed by the late 96th).

1824–81. The 96th Regiment of Foot.

1881 (from). The Manchester Regiment.

The Manchester Regiment—*continued.*

PRINCIPAL CAMPAIGNS, BATTLES, &c.

* " Honours" on the Colours, the figures showing the Battalion concerned.

1759. Guadaloupe.	1794. Guadaloupe.	1809. Flushing.
1775–81. America.	1796. Grenada.	*1810. Guadaloupe (1).
1775. Bunker's Hill.	1796. St. Vincent.	1814. Bergen-op-Zoom.
1776. Long Island.	1796. St. Lucia.	1815. Guadaloupe.
1776. Brooklyn.	1799. Bergen.	*1845–47. New Zealand(2).
1777. Brandywine.	*1799. Egmont-op-Zee (1).	*1854. Alma (1).
1777. Germantown.	1799. Alkmaer.	*1854. Inkerman (1).
1781. Entaw Springs.	*1801. Egypt (2).	*1855. Sevastopol (1).
1794–95. Flanders.	1801. Alexandria.	*1879–80. Afghanistan (1).
1794. Nimeguen.	*1808–11. Peninsula (2).	*1882. Egypt (1 & 2).
1794. Martinique.	*1809. Martinique (1).	1900. South Africa.

UNIFORM.—Scarlet with White facings (before territorialisation the facings of the 1st and 2nd Batts. were Green and Yellow respectively).

REGIMENTAL AND OTHER BADGES.—"The Sphinx" for Egypt (1801) by descent from the 96th Regiment of 1798–1818. Also (since 1881) The Arms of the City of Manchester.

NICKNAME.—"The Bloodsuckers" (of the 63rd).

BIBLIOGRAPHY.—*The History of the late 63rd (West Suffolk) Regiment.* By Major James Slack, late 63rd Regiment. [London: Army and Navy Co-operative Society. 1884.]

The Prince of Wales's (North Staffordshire Regiment),

COMPRISING

1st Batt. (formerly) The 64th (2nd Staffordshire) Regiment of Foot.

2nd Batt. („) The 98th (Prince of Wales's) Regiment of Foot; with Militia Batts.

3rd Batt. The 2nd King's Own Stafford Militia.

4th Batt. The 3rd King's Own Stafford Militia.

THE DRAGON OF CHINA.

THE PLUME OF
THE PRINCE
OF WALES.

THE STAFFORDSHIRE KNOT.

TITLES.

1st Batt.

1740–48. The 64th (Irish) Regiment of Foot: disbanded.

1756–58. The 11th (2nd Patt.) Regiment of Foot: regimented in

1758–82. The 64th Regiment of Foot.

1782–1881. The 64th (2nd Staffordshire) Regiment of Foot.

2nd Batt.

1760–63. The 98th Regiment of Foot: disbanded.

1779–84. The 98th Regiment of Foot: disbanded.

1793–1802. The 98th (Highland) Regiment of Foot: renumbered the 91st.

1805–15. The 98th Regiment of Foot: renumbered and disbanded in 1818.

1805–18. The 99th (Prince of Wales's Tipperary) Regiment of Foot: renumbered The 98th in 1815, and afterwards disbanded.

1824–76. The 98th Regiment of Foot.

1876–81. The 98th (The Prince of Wales's) Regiment of Foot.

1881 (from). The Prince of Wales's (North Staffordshire Regiment).

The Prince of Wales's (North Staffordshire Regiment)—*continued*.

PRINCIPAL CAMPAIGNS, BATTLES, &c.

* " Honours " on the Colours, the figures showing the Battalion concerned.

1759. Guadaloupe.	1780. Charlestown.	*1856–57. Persia (1).
1761. Belle Isle.	1780–84. Carnatic.	*1856. Reshire (1).
1762. Martinique.	1781. Entaw Springs.	*1856. Bushire (1).
1762. Havannah.	1794. Guadaloupe.	*1857. Koosh-ab (1).
1776–81. America.	1794. Martinique.	1857–58. Indian Mutiny.
1775. Lexington.	*1803. St. Lucia (1).	1857. Cawnpore.
1775. Bunker's Hill.	*1804. Surinam (1).	*1857. Lucknow (1).
1776. Brooklyn.	*1842. China (2).	*1896. Hafir.
1777. Brandywine.	*1848–49. Punjaub (2).	1900. South Africa.

UNIFORM.—Scarlet with White facings (when raised the 64th had Black, and the 98th White facings respectively).

REGIMENTAL AND OTHER BADGES.—" The Prince of Wales's Plume " (in memory of the visit to Malta in 1875). " The Dragon," for " China " (1842). Also (since territorially organised) " The Staffordshire Knot."

BIBLIOGRAPHY.—*Memoirs of the Services of The 64th Regiment (2nd Staffordshire). 1758–1881.* By H. G. Purdon, 64th Regiment. [Stafford : Halden. 1882.]

The York and Lancaster Regiment,

COMPRISING

1st Batt. (formerly) The 65th (2nd Yorkshire, North Riding) Regiment of Foot.

2nd Batt. („   ) The 84th (York and Lancaster) Regiment of Foot; with Militia Batt.

3rd Batt. The 3rd West York Militia.

THE ROYAL TIGER.

THE UNION ROSE.

TITLES.

1st Batt.

1756–58. The 12th (2nd Batt.) Regiment of Foot; renumbered in

1758–82. The 65th Regiment of Foot.

1782–1881. The 65th (2nd Yorkshire, North Riding) Regiment of Foot.

2nd Batt.

1758–64. The 84th Regiment of Foot: disbanded.

1775–78. The 84th Royal Highland Emigrants Corps: renamed

1778–84. The 84th (Royal Highland Emigrants) Regiment of Foot: disbanded.

1793–1809. The 84th Regiment of Foot.

1809–81. The 84th (York and Lancaster) Regiment of Foot.

1881 (from). The York and Lancaster Regiment.

The York and Lancaster Regiment—*continued.*

PRINCIPAL CAMPAIGNS, BATTLES, &c.

* " Honours " on the Colours, the figures showing the Battalion concerned.

1759–62. India
1759. Guadaloupe.
1760. Wyndewash.
1760. Arcot.
1760. Villanova.
1761. Martinique.
1761. Pondicherry.
1762. Havannah.
1775–81. America.
1775. Bunker's Hill.
1782. Gibraltar.
1794–95. Flanders.
1794. Martinique.
1794. Guadaloupe.

1795. Cape of Good Hope.
*1796–1822. India (1).
1803. Gujerat.
1804. Malwa.
1805. Bhurtpore.
1807. Goa.
1809. Flushing.
1809. Arabia.
1810–11. Mauritius.
*1813–14. Peninsula (2).
1813. Bidassoa.
*1813. Nive (2).
1814. Bayonne.

1817. Kirkee.
*1821. Arabia (1).
*1821. Beni-Boo-Ally.
1857–58. Indian Mutiny.
1857. Cawnpore.
*1857. Lucknow (2).
*1861–65. New Zealand (1).
*1882–84. Egypt (1 & 2).
1882. Kassassin.
*1882. Tel-el-Kebir (2).
1884. El Teb.
1884. Tamai.
1900. South Africa.

UNIFORMS.—Scarlet and White facings (in the 65th from formation in 1758 ; the 84th had Yellow facings from 1793 to 1831).

REGIMENTAL AND OTHER BADGES.—" The Royal Tiger " with " India " (for lengthy and distinguished services by the 65th). " The Union Rose " (from 1809). The 65th was also entitled to " Arabia " under the regimental figure.

NICKNAME.—" The Tigers."

BIBLIOGRAPHY.—*The Roll of Officers of The York and Lancaster Regiment.* By Major G. A. Raikes, F.S.A. Demy 8vo. Vol. I.—The 1st Battalion, late 65th Foot. Vol. II.—The 2nd Battalion, late 84th Foot.

The Durham Light Infantry,

COMPRISING

1st Batt. (formerly)   The 68th (Durham—Light Infantry) Regiment of Foot.

2nd Batt. („   )   The 106th (Bombay Light Infantry) Regiment; with Militia Batts.

3rd Batt.   The 1st Durham Militia.

4th Batt.   The 2nd Durham Militia.

THE UNITED RED AND WHITE ROSE.

TITLES.

1st Batt.

1756–58. The 23rd (2nd Batt.) Royal Welsh Fusiliers: regimented in

1758–82. The 68th Regiment of Foot.

1782–1812. The 68th (Durham) Regiment of Foot.

1812–81. The 68th (Durham Light Infantry) Regiment.

2nd Batt.

1826–58. The Hon. East India Co.'s 2nd Bombay European Light Infantry.

1858–61. The 2nd Bombay Light Infantry Regiment.

1861–81. The 106th Bombay Light Infantry Regiment.

1881 (from). The Durham Light Infantry.

The Durham Light Infantry—*continued.*

PRINCIPAL CAMPAIGNS, BATTLES, &c.

* " Honours" on the Colours, the figures showing the Battalion concerned.

1758. Cherbourg.
1795. St. Lucia.
1796. St. Vincent.
1796. Grenada.
1803. St. Lucia.
1809. Flushing.
*1811–14. Peninsula (1).
*1812. Salamanca (1).

1812. Burgos.
1813. Adour.
*1813. Vittoria (1).
*1813. Pyrenees (1).
*1813. Nivelle (1).
*1814. Orthes (1).
1814. Bordeaux.
*1854. Alma (1).

*1854. Inkerman (1).
*1855. Sevastopol (1).
*1856–57. Persia (2).
*1856. Reshire (2).
*1856. Bushire (2).
*1857. Kooshab (2).
*1864–66. New Zealand (1).
1900. South Africa.

UNIFORM.—Scarlet, with White facings (present time: the 68th wore Green facings from 1758 to 188–, and the 106th Buff from 1839–42).

REGIMENTAL BADGE.—" The United Red and White Rose."

NICKNAME.—" The Faithful Durhams."

BIBLIOGRAPHY.—*A Short Record of The Durham Light Infantry, from 1758 to 1894.* Compiled by Lieutenant-Colonel W. Gordon, Commanding 1st Batt. [Devonport: Swiss. 1894.]

The Highland Light Infantry,

COMPRISING

1st Batt. (formerly) The 71st (Highland Light Infantry) Regiment.

2nd Batt. („) The 74th (Highlanders) Regiment; with Militia Batts.

3rd & 4th Batts. The 1st Royal Lanark Royal Militia.

THE ELEPHANT.

SPECIAL DEVICE, AS ON COLLAR BADGE.

TITLES.

1st Batt.

1758–63. The 71st Regiment of Foot (raised as 2nd Batt. 32nd Foot, but separately regimented the same year : disbanded in 1763.

1764–65. The 71st (Invalids) Regiment of Foot (previously the 81st (Invalids); reduced to Independent Garrison Companies in 1769).

1775–83. The 71st (Highland) Regiment of Foot : also Fraser's Highlanders (chiefly engaged in American Rebellion and afterwards disbanded).

1777–86. The 1st Batt. 73rd (Highland) Regiment of Foot.

1786–1808. The 71st (Highland) Regiment of Foot.

1808–9. The 71st (Glasgow Highland) Regiment of Foot.

1809–10. The 71st (Glasgow Highland Light Infantry) Regiment.

1810–81. The 71st (Highland) Light Infantry.

2nd Batt.

1758–63. The 74th Regiment of Foot (raised as 2nd Batt. of 36th Foot in 1756 ; separately regimented in 1758 ; disbanded in 1764).

1763–65. The 74th (Invalids) Regiment of Foot ; formerly the 117th Invalids : dispersed as Independent Garrison Companies.

1777–83. The 74th (Highland) Regiment of Foot : also The Argyll Highlanders : disbanded in 1783.

1787–1816. The 74th (Highland) Regiment of Foot : also "The Assaye Regiment" (1803).

1816–45. The 74th Regiment of Foot.

1845–81. The 74th (Highlanders) Regiment of Foot.

1881 (from). The Highland Light Infantry.

PRINCIPAL CAMPAIGNS, BATTLES, &c.

* "Honours" on the Colours, the figures showing the Battalion concerned.

1780–83. Gibraltar.
*1780–97. Hindoostan (1).
*1780. Carnatic (1).
1780. Arcot.
1781. Porto-Novo.
*1781. Sholingur (1).
1782. Arnee.
*1783. Mysore (1).
1783. Cuddalore.
1791. Bangalore.
1791. Nundy-Droog.
1791. Savendroog.
1792. Seringapatam.
1793. Pondicherry.
1795. Ceylon.
*1799. Seringapatam (2).
1800. Polygar.
1802. Ahmednuggar.
1803. Argaum.
*1803. Assaye (2).

*1806. Cape of Good Hope (1).
1806. Buenos Ayres.
1807. Monte Video.
*1808–14. Peninsula (1 & 2).
*1808. Roleia (1).
*1808. Vimiera (1).
*1809. Corunna (1).
1809. Flushing.
*1810. Busaco (2).
*1811. Fuentes d'Onor (1 & 2).
1811. Arroyo dos Molinos.
*1812. Almaraj (1).
*1812. Ciudad Rodrigo (2).
*1812. Badajos (2).
*1812. Salamanca (2).
*1813. Nivelle (2).

*1813. Vittoria (1 & 2).
1813. Maya.
*1813. Pyrenees (1 & 2).
*1813. Nive (1).
*1814. Orthes (1 & 2).
*1814. Toulouse (2).
1815. Quatre Bras.
*1815. Waterloo (1).
1815. Netherlands.
*1851–53. South Africa (2)
1854–56. Crimea.
1854. Balaclava.
1855. Kertch.
1855. Yenikale.
*1855. Sevastopol (1).
*1858. Central India (1).
1858. Indian Mutiny.
*1882. Egypt (2).
*1882. Tel-el-Kebir (2).
1900. South Africa.

UNIFORM.—1st Batt., Scarlet, Buff facings, and the Mackenzie tartan, with chako instead of feather bonnet (from 1777). 2nd Batt., Scarlet and grass Green facings (from 1758 till 1881).

REGIMENTAL BADGES.—That in the *Army List* is "The Elephant" with "Assaye"; but on the chako-plate and collar a special design is worn, combining "The Star of the Order of the Thistle" with "The Crown" as on the collar of the Order of the Star of India (for distinction gained by each battalion in India); a Horn on the Star with monogram H.L.I. surmounting a scroll with "Assaye" and "The Elephant" (without howdah or trappings) below.

NICKNAME.—"The Pig and Whistle Light Infantry."

NOTES.—The two veteran regiments now known as the 1st and 2nd Highland Light Infantry possess the longest "honour" record (twenty-nine in all) of any British regiment whatsoever, save the King's Royal Rifle Corps, which have thirty-two all told. The roll commences with "Carnatic," won by the 1st Batt. in the Hyder Ali campaign, seconded by the laurels of the 2nd Batt. at the Siege of Seringapatam, in which on several occasions it particularly distinguished itself. The same battalion contributed "Assaye" (with "The Elephant"). It is recorded that in this battle "Every officer present, save one, was killed or wounded, and the battalion reduced to a mere wreck." "Assaye" is an honour shared only with The Seaforths and The 19th Hussars. For its services in India the Honourable East India Company presented it (1803) with a complimentary Colour. Henceforward honours fell thick and fast on both battalions—at the Cape, particularly so throughout the Peninsula campaign, in the Kaffir wars of 1851–53 (a large draft of its men went down in the ill-fated *Birkenhead*), at the Crimea, in the Indian Mutiny, and more latterly in the Egyptian campaigns of the eighties.

BIBLIOGRAPHY.—*Historical Record of The 71st Regiment Highland Light Infantry.* 1777–1852. Illustrated. [London: Parker. 1852.]
    Historical Record of The 71st Regiment Highland Light Infantry. 1777–1876. By Lieut. Henry J. T. Hildyard, 71st Highland Light Infantry. [London: Harrison. 1876.]
    Historical Record of The 74th Highlanders. 1787–1850. Illustrated. [London: Parker. 1850.]
    Historical Records of The 74th Highlanders (now 2nd Battalion Highland Light Infantry). 1787–1887. Illustrated. [Dumfries: Macveigh. 1887.]

The Seaforth Highlanders (Ross=shire Buffs, The Duke of Albany's Own Regiment of Foot).

(3 Batts.)

1st Batt. (formerly) The 72nd (Duke of Albany's Own Highlanders) Regiment of Foot.

2nd Batt. („) The 78th (Highlanders—Ross-shire Buffs) Regiment of Foot; with Militia Battalion.

3rd Batt. The Highland Rifle Militia.

THE ELEPHANT WITH "ASSAYE." THE CORONET AND CYPHER OF THE DUKE OF ALBANY. THE SEAFORTH CREST.

TITLES.

1st Batt.

1756–63. The 2nd Highland Batt.: afterwards regimented as The 78th (Highland) Regiment of Foot; also Fraser's Highlanders; disbanded 1763. (See TITLES, 2nd Batt.)

1778–86. The Seaforth (Highland) Regiment of Foot; after establishment regimented as The 78th (Highland) Regiment of Foot. (See 2nd Batt.)

1786–1823. The 72nd (Highland) Regiment of Foot. (At the peace of 1783 many regiments were disbanded.) There had previously been three 72nds—(a) The 72nd Foot (1756–63); (b) The 72nd (Invalids) Foot (1764–65); and (c) The 72nd (Royal Manchester Volunteers) Regiment of Foot (1777–84).

1823–1881. The 72nd (Duke of Albany's Own Highlanders) Regiment of Foot.

1881 (from). The Seaforth Highlanders (Ross-shire Buffs, The Duke of Albany's).

2nd Batt.

1756–63. The 2nd Highland Batt.: afterwards regimented as The 78th (Highland) Regiment of Foot; also Fraser's Highlanders; disbanded.

1793–18——. The 78th (Highlanders) Regiment of Foot; also Ross-shire Buffs; between 1777–86 The 78th was represented in the 1st Batt. by the Seaforth Highlanders.

PRINCIPAL CAMPAIGNS, BATTLES, &c.

* "Honours" on the Colours, the figures showing the Battalion concerned.

1758. Louisbourg.
1758. Montmorenci.
1759. Quebec.
*1780–97. Hindoostan (1).
*1780. Carnatic (1).
1782. Arnee.
*1783. Mysore (1).
1783. Cuddalore.
1791. Bangalore.
1791. Savendroog.
1792. Seringapatam.
1793. Pondicherry.
1794–95. Flanders.
1794. Nimeguen.
1795. Guildermalsen.
1795. Quiberon.
1803. Ahmednuggar.

*1803. Assaye (2).
1803. Argaum.
*1806. Maida (2).
*1806. Cape of Good Hope (1).
1807. Egypt.
1807. Rosetta.
*1811. Java (2).
1814–15. Netherlands.
1814. Antwerp.
*1835. South Africa (1).
1854. Kertch.
*1855. Sevastopol (1).
*1856–57. Persia (2).
1857–58. Indian Mutiny.
*1857. Koosh-ab (2).
1857. Cawnpore.

*1857. Lucknow (2).
*1858. Central India (1).
*1878. Peiwar Kotal (1).
*1879. Charasiah (1).
*1878–80. Afghanistan (1 & 2).
*1879. Kabul (1).
*1880. Kandahar (1).
*1882. Egypt (1).
1882. Kassassin.
*1882. Tel-el-Kebir (1).
*1895. Chitral.
*1898. Atbara.
*1899. Khartoum.
1900. South Africa.

UNIFORM.—1st Batt., Scarlet with Buff facings, and the "Mackenzie" tartan (from 1778, but in 1823 the tartan was changed to "Stuart," as directed by the Commander-in-Chief, Duke of York and Albany; subsequently the "Mackenzie" tartan was revived). The hackle is white. 2nd Batt., Scarlet with Buff facings and the "Mackenzie" tartan; from date of "linking" the facings have matched those of the 1st Batt.

REGIMENTAL BADGES, MOTTOES, &C.—The Coronet and Cypher of the late Duke of York (who was also Duke of Albany); also, subsequently, the Cypher of the late Prince Leopold, Duke of Albany; also a Stag's Head (the cognisance of the Earls of Seaforth); also an Elephant (without howdah and trappings) with "Assaye" on scroll underneath; also a Thistle bearing the Star of the Order of the Thistle, with circle superimposed, within which is the Cypher (F) of the late Duke of York, surmounted by the Ducal Coronet. *Mottoes.*—(1) *Cuidich'n Righ* (Help, to the King): this, with the Stag's Head, appertains to the Mackenzies, and, according to tradition, was bestowed through the founder of the clan having saved the life of King Alexander II. of Scotland when attacked by a wounded stag. Borne by the Ross-shire Buffs from the first: officially recognised in 1825. (2) *Caber Feidh* (The Antlers of the Deer), the Seaforth slogan; and (3) *Tulloch ard* (The High Hill), the old gathering-ground of the Mackenzies on Loch Duich in Ross-shire.

NICKNAMES.—(1) "The Regiment of the Macraes" (from the large proportion of men of this name in the 72nd when raised); also (2) "The Wild Macraes" (when in Edinburgh their doings seriously frightened the inhabitants; (3) "The King's Men" (from the ancient motto of the 78th, "Help, to the King").

NOTES, &C. — Both Batts. are successors of the old 78th (Highland) Regiment of Foot—Fraser's Highlanders—which saw much service under General Wolfe; disbanded in 1763. The second 78th was raised in 1778 by Kenneth Mackenzie, Earl of Seaforth, was renumbered as the 72nd in 1786, and is the direct ancestor of the present 1st Seaforth Highlanders. Seven years later the present 2nd Seaforth Highlanders were raised as The 78th (Highland) Regiment of Foot, being also known, shortly afterwards, as the Ross-shire Buffs. The combined battle-roll of honour is much the same as that of the Black Watch and the Argyll and Sutherland Highlanders. "Assaye" (in 1803) was specially recognised by the Honourable East India Company presenting honorary colours to the late 78th (2nd Batt.). Half a century later, during the Mutiny, it rendered unparalleled service under Havelock, Outram, and Clive, adding "Lucknow" to the Colours, while its achievements in "Central India," "Afghanistan," "Kabul," "Kandahar," "Egypt," and "Tel-el-Kebir" are well within living memory.

BIBLIOGRAPHY.—*Historical Records of The 72nd Regiment, or Duke of Albany's Own Highlanders.* 1778–1848. [London: Parker. 1848.]
    Historical Records of The 72nd Highlanders, now 1st Batt. Seaforth Highlanders. 1777–1886. [Edinburgh: Blackwood. 1886.]

O 2

The Gordon Highlanders.

(3 Batts.)

1st Batt. (formerly)   The 75th (Stirlingshire) Regiment of Foot.

2nd Batt. („)   The 92nd (Gordon Highlanders) Regiment of Foot; with

3rd Batt.   The Royal Aberdeenshire Militia.

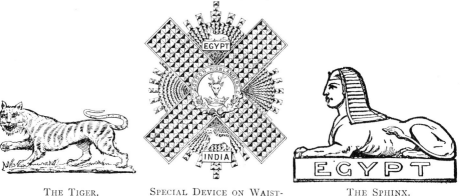

THE TIGER.   SPECIAL DEVICE ON WAIST-   THE SPHINX.
PLATE AND BUTTONS.

TITLES.

1st Batt.

1758–63. The 75th Regiment of Foot; raised in 1756 as 2nd Batt. 37th Foot, separately regimented as 75th in 1758, and disbanded in 1765.

1764–65. The 75th (Invalids) Regiment of Foot; formerly (1760) the 118th Invalids; dispersed for garrison service.

1778–83. The 75th (Prince of Wales's) Regiment of Foot; disbanded at the close of the American War.

1787–1809. The 75th (Highland) Regiment of Foot; also "Abercrombie's Highlanders."

1809–62. The 75th Regiment of Foot.

1862–81. The 75th (Stirlingshire) Regiment of Foot.

2nd Batt.

1794–98. The 100th (Gordon Highlanders) Regiment of Foot.

1798–1861. The 92nd (Highland) Regiment of Foot; there had previously been three other regiments bearing this number, but none incorporated for more than four years.

1861–81. The 92nd (Gordon Highlanders) Regiment of Foot.

1881 (from). The Gordon Highlanders.

The Gordon Highlanders—*continued*.

PRINCIPAL CAMPAIGNS, BATTLES, &c.

* "Honours" on the Colours, the figures showing the Battalion concerned.

1761. Belle Isle.
1762. Portugal.
1778–83. America.
*1791–1806. India (1).
1792. Seringapatam.
1795–97. Malabar and Goa.
*1799. Mysore (1).
1799. Sedaseer.
*1799. Seringapatam (1).
1799. Helder.
1799. Crabbendam.
1799. Bergen.
*1799. Egmont-op-Zee (2).
1799. Quiberon.
1800. Ferrol.
*1801. Mandora (2).
*1801. Egypt (2).
1801. Alexandria.
1803. Gujerat.

1804. Malwa.
1805. Bhurtpore.
1807. Copenhagen.
1808–14. Peninsula (2).
*1809. Corunna (2).
1809. Flushing.
*1811. Fuentes d'Onor (2).
1811. Arroyo dos Molinos.
*1812. Almaraj (2).
*1813. Vittoria (2).
1813. Maya.
*1813. Pyrenees (2).
*1813. Nive (2).
1814. Gâve.
*1814. Orthes (2).
1815. Quatre Bras.
*1815. Waterloo (2).
1815. Netherlands.
*1835. South Africa (1).

1857–58. Indian Mutiny.
*1857. Delhi (1).
1857. Bulundshuhur.
1857. Agra.
1857. Cawnpore.
*1858. Lucknow (1).
*1878–80. Afghanistan (2).
*1879. Charasiah (2).
*1879. Kabool (2).
*1880. Kandahar (2).
1881. Transvaal.
*1882–84. Egypt (1).
*1882. Tel-el-Kebir (1).
*1884–85. Nile (1).
1884. El Teb.
1884. Tamai.
*1895. Chitral.
*1897–98. Tirah.
1900. South Africa.

UNIFORM.—Red, with deep Yellow facings, and the Gordon tartan bearing a yellow distinguishing stripe (the Marquis of Huntly, who raised the late 92nd, 2nd Batt., became the fifth Duke of Gordon). The hackle is white.

REGIMENTAL BADGES, &c.—"The Sphinx" (for Egypt), and "The Royal Tiger" (for India). In the device on buttons and waist-plate these are shown in the upper and lower divisions of the St. Andrew Cross, with "Egypt" and "India" underneath, respectively; also within a scroll, inscribed "Gordon Highlanders," on the centre of the cross, and resting on a thistle wreath, is worn the crest (a stag's head issuing from the ducal coronet) of the Marquis of Huntly.

NICKNAME.—"The Gay Gordons."

NOTES, &c.—Both regiments were raised in Scotland, the 75th specially for service in India at the instance and cost of the late Honourable East India Company, receiving on its return "The Royal Tiger" in recognition of nineteen years of eventful and arduous service. Fifty years later it again fought in India through the Mutiny. During this period the 2nd Batt., as the late 92nd, was distinguishing itself in Holland, in Egypt (with special distinction at Mandora), and particularly in the Peninsula Campaigns of 1809–14, no less that seven "honours" falling to its share. Fresh laurels were won at Quatre Bras in company with the Black Watch and the Royal Scots. Of its later exploits only the barest mention can be made—of its services in the Indian Mutiny, in Afghanistan (1878–80), including Kabul and the march to Kandahar and the rest—the emblazonments on the "Colours" tell a sufficiently emphatic story.

BIBLIOGRAPHY.—*Historical Record of the 92nd Regiment (Gordon Highlanders).* 1794–1850. Illustrated. [London : Parker. 1851.]

The Queen's Own Cameron Highlanders,

COMPRISING

1st Batt. (formerly) The 79th (Queen's Own Cameron Highlanders) Regiment.

2nd Batt. Authorised; with Militia Battalion.

3rd Batt. The Highland Light Infantry Militia.

THE THISTLE AND CROWN.   THE SPHINX.

TITLES.

1759–64. The 79th Regiment of Foot.

1778–84. The 79th (Royal Liverpool Volunteers) Regiment of Foot; also The Liverpool Blues; disbanded.

1793–1804. The 79th (Highland—Cameronian Volunteers) Regiment.

1804–73. The 79th (Cameron Highlanders) Regiment of Foot.

1873–81. The 79th (Queen's Own Cameron Highlanders) Regiment.

1881 (from). The Queen's Own Cameron Highlanders.

The Queen Own Cameron Highlanders—*continued*.

PRINCIPAL CAMPAIGNS, BATTLES, &c.

* " Honours " on the Colours.

1762. Manilla.
1783. Carnatic.
1794–95. Flanders.
1794. Nimeguen.
*1799. Egmont-op-Zee.
1800. Quiberon.
1800. Ferrol.
1800. Vigo.
1800. Cadiz.
1801. Mandora.
1801. Egypt.
1801. Alexandria.
1807. Copenhagen.
*1808–14. Peninsula.
1809. Corunna.
1809. Flushing.
1810. Cadiz.
1810. Busaco.
*1811. Fuentes d'Onor.
*1812. Salamanca.

1812. Burgos.
*1813. Pyrenees.
*1813. Nivelle.
*1813. Nive.
*1814. Toulouse.
1815. Quatre Bras.
*1815. Waterloo.
1815. Netherlands.
*1854. Alma.
1854. Balaclava.
*1855. Sevastopol.
1858. Indian Mutiny.
*1858. Lucknow.
1874 Ashantee.
*1882. Egypt.
*1882. Tel-el-Kebir.
*1884–85. Nile.
*1898. Atbara.
*1899. Khartoum.

UNIFORM.—Scarlet with Green facings (1793–1873) ; Scarlet with Blue facings (from 1873).

REGIMENTAL AND OTHER BADGES.—" The Thistle ensigned with the Imperial Crown " (with the change of title in 1873). " The Sphinx " for " Egypt," (1801).

NOTES.—This is the sole Territorial Regiment having one line battalion only.

BIBLIOGRAPHY.—*Historical Records of the 79th Queen's Own Cameron Highlanders.* By Captain Mackenzie, Lieutenant Ewart, and Lieutenant Findlay. [Devonport : Swiss. 1887.]

Some Account of the Part Taken by the 79th Regiment, or Cameron Highlanders, in the Indian Mutiny, 1858. By Captain D. Dunberley. [Inverness, 1891.]

The Royal Irish Rifles,

COMPRISING

1st Batt. (formerly) The 83rd (County Dublin) Regiment of Foot.
2nd Batt. („) The 86th (Royal County Down) Regiment of Foot; with Militia Battalions.
3rd Batt. The Royal North Down Militia.
4th Batt. The Royal Antrim Militia.
5th Batt. The Royal South Down Militia.
6th Batt. The Royal Louth Militia.

THE HARP AND CROWN.

THE SPHINX.

TITLES.

1st Batt.

1758–63. The 83rd Regiment of Foot; disbanded.

1778–83. The 83rd (Royal Glasgow Volunteers) Regiment of Foot; disbanded.

1793–1859. The 83rd Regiment of Foot.

1859–81. The 83rd (County of Dublin) Regiment of Foot.

2nd Batt.

1759–63. The 86th Regiment of Foot; formerly 2nd Batt. 76th Foot; disbanded.

1779–83. The 86th Regiment of Foot; disbanded.

1793–1806. The 86th (The Shropshire Volunteers) Regiment of Foot.

1806–12. The 86th (The Leinster) Regiment of Foot.

1812–81. The 86th (Royal County Down) Regiment of Foot.

1881 (from). The Royal Irish Rifles.

The Royal Irish Rifles—*continued*.

PRINCIPAL CAMPAIGNS, BATTLES, &c.

* " Honours," the figures showing the Battalion concerned.

1795. Jamaica.
1797–8. San Domingo.
*1799–1819. India (2).
*1801. Egypt (2).
1805. Bhurtpore.
*1806. Cape of Good Hope (1).
*1809–14. Peninsula (1).
*1809. Talavera (1).
*1810. Bourbon (2).

*1810. Busaco (1).
*1811. Fuentes d'Onor (1).
1811. El Bodon.
*1812. Ciudad Rodrigo (1).
*1812. Badajos (1).
*1812. Salamanca (1).
*1813. Vittoria (1).
*1813. Nivelle (1).
*1814. Orthes (1).
*1814. Toulouse (1).

1817–19. Kandy.
1838–39. Canada.
*1842–59. Central India (1 & 2).
1857–58. Indian Mutiny.
1858. Jhansi.
1858. Golowlee.
1858. Calpe.
1858. Gwalior.
1900. South Africa.

UNIFORM.—1st Batt., Scarlet with Yellow facings (1793–1881). 2nd Batt., Scarlet with Yellow facings (1793–1812); Scarlet with Blue facings (1812–1881). 1st and 2nd Batts., Green with Dark Green facings (at present time).

REGIMENTAL AND OTHER BADGES.—"The Harp and Crown," with Motto, " *Quis separabit.*" Also "The Sphinx" for "Egypt" (1801), won by the 86th. The "Honours" formerly on the "Colours" have, since the conversion of the regiments into a Rifle Corps, been placed on the special pattern helmet-plate.

NICKNAMES.—"Fitch's Grenadiers" (of the 83rd when raised in 1793, on account of smallness of stature). "The Irish Giants" (in India, 1842, of the 86th).

NOTES.—The 86th captured several standards at Jhansi (1858).

BIBLIOGRAPHY.—*Historical Record of The 86th, or Royal County Down Regiment.* 1793–1842. [London: Parker. 1842.]
   Memoirs and Services of the 83rd Regiment. [Bray. 1863.]

𝔓rincess 𝔙ictoria's (𝔕oyal 𝔍rish 𝔉usiliers),

COMPRISING

1st Batt. (formerly)   The 87th (Royal Irish Fusiliers) Regiment of Foot.
2nd Batt. („   )   The 89th (Princess Victoria's) Regiment of Foot; with Militia
   Battalions.
3rd Batt.   The Armagh Militia.
4th Batt.   The Cavan Militia.
5th Batt.   The Monaghan Militia.

THE PLUME OF THE PRINCE
OF WALES.

THE HARP AND
CROWN.

THE SPHINX.

THE PRINCESS VICTORIA'S
CYPHER AND CORONET.

THE EAGLE.

TITLES.

1st Batt.

1759–63. The 87th (Highland Volunteers) Regiment of Foot; also "Keith's Highlanders"; disbanded.

1779–83. The 87th Regiment of Foot; disbanded.

1793–1811. The 87th (The Prince of Wales's Irish) Regiment of Foot.

1811–27. The 87th (The Prince of Wales's Own Irish) Regiment of Foot.

1827–81. The 87th (The Royal Irish Fusiliers) Regiment of Foot (for a short period The Prince of Wales's Own Irish Fusiliers).

2nd Batt.

1759–65. The 89th (Gordon Highlanders) Regiment of Foot; disbanded.

1779–83. The 89th Regiment of Foot; disbanded.

1793–1866. The 89th Regiment of Foot.

1866–81. The 89th (The Princess Victoria's) Regiment of Foot.

1881 (from). The Princess Victoria's (Royal Irish Fusiliers).

Princess Victoria's (Royal Irish Fusiliers)—*continued.*

PRINCIPAL CAMPAIGNS, BATTLES, &c.

* " Honours" on the Colours, the figures showing the Battalion concerned.

1760. Zierenberg.	1801. Alexandria.	1814–15. Netherlands.
1760. Warbourg.	1806. Buenos Ayres.	*1814. Orthes (1).
1760. Campen.	*1807. Monte Video (1).	*1814. Toulouse (1).
1761. Fellinghausen.	*1809–14. Peninsula (1).	1814. Bergen-op-Zoom.
1761. Johannisberg.	*1809. Talavera (1).	1815–16. Nepaul.
1762. Wilhemstahl.	1810. Mauritius.	*1824–26. Ava (2).
1764. Buxar.	*1811. Barrossa (1).	*1855. Sevastopol (2).
1780. St. Lucia.	*1811. Tarifa (1).	1857–58. Indian Mutiny.
1780. Antigua.	*1811. Java (2).	1860. China.
1793. Alost.	*1813. Vittoria (1).	*1882. Egypt (1).
1794–5. Flanders.	1813. Bidassoa.	*1882. Tel-el-Kebir (1).
1794. Boxtel.	*1813. Nivelle (1).	*1884. Egypt (2).
1794. Nimeguen.	1813–14. Canada.	1884. El Teb.
1795. Tuyl.	1813. Chrystler's Farm.	1884. Tamai.
1800. Malta.	*1813. Niagara (2).	1900. South Africa.
*1801. Egypt (2).		

UNIFORM.—1st Batt., Scarlet with Green facings (1793–1823, when the facings were changed to Blue) ; 2nd Batt., Scarlet with Black facings (1793 to 1881, when the latter gave place to the present Blue facings).

REGIMENTAL AND OTHER BADGES.—" The Princess Victoria's Coronet " (received with its title in 1866, when Her Majesty exchanged the colours presented by her in 1833, as Princess Victoria, for new ones). " The Sphinx" for " Egypt " (1801). " An Eagle with a Wreath of Laurel " in addition to " The Plume of the Prince of Wales " (for distinction at Barrossa in 1811, where it captured the Eagle [the first taken in the Peninsular War] of the 8th French Light Infantry— *cf.* the figure " 8 " below the Eagle—whence also its title " The Prince of Wales's Own Irish." " The Harp and Crown " (the badge of the 87th, when raised in 1793).

NICKNAMES, &c.—" The Old Togs," or " The Faugh-a-Ballagh Boys " (from the war cry of the 87th at Barrossa—" Fag an Bealac " = " Clear the Way "). " The Eagle Takers " (also a sobriquet of the 87th—see above). " Blayney's Bloodhounds " (for skill in tracing rebels in the Irish Rebellion of 1798). " The Rollickers."

NOTES.—The Royal Fusiliers wear two collar badges, a distinction shared only with the Seaforth Highlanders.

BIBLIOGRAPHY.—*Historical Record of The* 89*th, or Royal Irish Fusiliers.* 1793-1853. [London : Parker. 1842.]

Historical Record of The 89*th Princess Victoria's Regiment.* By Captain R. Brinckman, 2nd Royal Inniskilling Fusiliers. Illustrated. [Gale and Polden. 1888.]

The Connaught Rangers,

COMPRISING

1st Batt. (formerly) The 88th (Connaught Rangers) Regiment of Foot.

2nd Batt. („) The 94th Regiment of Foot ; with Militia Battalions.

3rd Batt. The South and North Mayo Militia.

4th Batt. The Galway Militia.

5th Batt. The Roscommon Militia.

THE ELEPHANT (CAPARISONED).   THE HARP AND CROWN.   THE SPHINX.

TITLES.

1st Batt.

1760–63. The 88th (Royal Highland Volunteers) Regiment of Foot; disbanded.

1779–83. The 88th Regiment of Foot; disbanded.

1793–1881. The 88th (Connaught Rangers) Regiment.

2nd Batt.

1760–63. The 94th (Royal Welsh Volunteers) Regiment of Foot; disbanded.

1779–83. The 94th Regiment of Foot; disbanded.

1794–95. The 94th (Irish) Regiment of Foot; disbanded.

1803–1818. The 94th (Scots Brigade) Regiment of Foot; disbanded.

1823–81. The 94th Regiment of Foot.

1881 (from). The Connaught Rangers.

The Connaught Rangers—*continued.*

PRINCIPAL CAMPAIGNS, BATTLES, &c.

* " Honours " on the Colours, the figures showing the Battalion concerned.

1760–62. Germany.
1760. Warbourg.
1760. Campen.
1762. Wilhelmstahl.
1794–95. Flanders.
1794. Nimeguen.
1793. Alost.
1796. Grenada.
1796. St. Lucia.
1799. Bergen.
*1799. Seringapatam (2)
*1801. Egypt (1).
1803. Argaum.
1806. Buenos Ayres.

1807. Monte Video.
*1809-14. Peninsula (1 & 2).
*1809. Talavera (1).
1810. Matagorda.
*1810. Busaco (1).
1811. Sabugal.
*1811. Fuentes d'Onor (1).
*1812. Ciudad Rodrigo (1 & 2).
*1812. Badajos (1 & 2).
*1812. Salamanca (1 & 2).
1812. Burgos.
*1813. Vittoria (1 & 2).
*1813. Nivelle (1 & 2).

1813. Pyrenees.
*1814. Orthes (1 & 2).
*1814. Toulouse (1 & 2).
1814. Plattsburg.
*1854. Alma (1).
*1854. Inkerman (1).
*1855. Sevastopol (1).
1857–58. Indian Mutiny.
*1858. Central India (1).
*1877–79. South Africa (1 & 2).
1880–81. Transvaal.
1900. South Africa.

UNIFORM.—1st Batt., in 1793, Scarlet with Yellow facings ; now (1900) Scarlet and Deep Green.   2nd Batt., in 1823, Scarlet with Buff facings ; at present the same as 1st Batt.

REGIMENTAL AND OTHER BADGES.—" The Harp and Crown," with the Motto, " *Quis separabit*" (the badge of the 88th from formation).   " The Sphinx " for " Egypt " (1801 ; also an 88th distinction).   " The Elephant " (without the howdah, but caparisoned : this with " Seringapatam " on the honours has descended to the Connaughts through its 2nd Batt. from the 94th of 1803–1818.   *See* Notes).

NICKNAMES.—" The Devil's Own " (88th), " The Gawies " (94th).

NOTES.—The 94th of 1803-18 was a Scots Brigade in the service of Holland from 1586–1793, save one interregnum of three years from 1688–91.   In 1804 it was taken into the English service, earning much distinction in India and in the Peninsular campaigns, the " honours " of which were revived in the 94th of 1823.

BIBLIOGRAPHY.—*Historical Record of The 88th, or Connaught Rangers.*   1793–1837. [London : Clowes.   1838.]

The Princess Louise's (Argyll & Sutherland Highlanders).

(4 Batts.)

1st Batt. (formerly) The 91st (Princess Louise's Argyllshire Highlanders).

2nd Batt. („) The 93rd (Sutherland Highlanders) Regiment of Foot; with Militia Battalions.

3rd Batt. The Highland Borderers Militia.

4th Batt. The Royal Renfrew (Prince of Wales's) Militia.

THE PRINCESS LOUISE'S CYPHER AND CORONET. A CAT: THE BOAR'S HEAD.

TITLES.

1st Batt.

1794–96. The 98th (Argyllshire Highlanders) Regiment of Foot; re-numbered.

1796–1809. The 91st (Argyllshire Highlanders) Regiment of Foot. Three other corps had previously borne this number; neither had been retained longer than four years.

1809–21. The 91st Regiment of Foot; its distinctive title was probably dropped for the same reason that the Highland dress was for a time discarded, because of its supposed impediment to recruiting.

1821–64. The 91st (Argyllshire) Regiment of Foot.

1864–72. The 91st (Argyllshire) Highlanders.

1872–1881. The 91st (Princess Louise's Argyllshire) Highlanders.

2nd Batt.

1760–96. The 93rd Regiment of Foot; during this period three 93rds were raised and disbanded — 1760–63; 1779–83 (American War); and 1793–96 (served in Demerara, Essequibo, and Berbice, and then was drafted into the 39th).

1800–61. The 93rd Highlanders.

1861–81. The 93rd (Sutherland Highlanders).

1881 (from). The Princess Louise's (Argyll and Sutherland Highlanders).

The Princess Louise's (Argyll & Sutherland Highlanders)—*continued.*

PRINCIPAL CAMPAIGNS, BATTLES, &c.

* " Honours " on the Colours, the figures showing the Battalion concerned.

1779–83. America.

1796. Guiana.

*1806. Cape of Good Hope (2).

*1808–14. Peninsula (1).

*1808. Roleia (1).

*1808. Vimiera (1).

*1809. Corunna (1).

1809. Flushing.

1809. Talavera.

*1813. Pyrenees (1).

*1813. Nivelle (1).

1813. Bidassoa.

*1813. Nive (1).

*1814. Orthes (1).

*1814. Toulouse (1).

1814. Bayonne.

1814–15. Netherlands.

1814. Bergen-op-Zoom.

1814. Antwerp.

1815. New Orleans.

1838. Canada.

*1846–47. South Africa (1).

*1851–53. South Africa (1).

*1854. Alma (2).

*1854. Balaclava (2).

1855. Kertch.

1855. Yenikale.

*1855. Sevastopol (2).

1857–58. Indian Mutiny.

*1857. Lucknow (2).

1858. Rohilcund.

*1879. South Africa (1).

1900. South Africa.

UNIFORM, &c.—Scarlet, with bright Yellow facings, and the Sutherland tartan.

REGIMENTAL BADGES, &c.—" The Princess Louise's Cypher and Coronet," " The Boar's Head " (the Campbell crest), and " *Ne obliviscaris.*" Also " A Cat " and " *Sans peur* " (the Sutherland cognisance).

NICKNAME.—" The Rory's."

NOTES.—The old 91st was raised at Stirling by the Duke of Argyll : hence its title, crest, and motto. The Cape was the scene of its first campaign, since which it, with its companion battalion, has seen much service—a forty-one years' combined record—in South Africa. Its " honours " were, however, chiefly won in the Peninsular campaigns at the beginning of the century. The 2nd Batt. was also raised in Scotland from the Sutherland Fencible Highlanders, and has had a most distinguished career from then till now. Little need to dwell on its prowess. Who amongst us does not remember, or who has not read of that " thin red line " drawn up by Colin Campbell to resist the onslaught of the Russian Horse at Balaclava ; how the 93rd stood their ground, successfully stemming and finally repulsing that memorable charge ; how it alone of all regiments of foot enjoys the proud distinction of " Balaclava " on its " colours " ? And surely there is still less need to tell how a few months later, in the Mutiny, and especially at Lucknow, this famous corps added new and undying laurels to its regimental record—a record which is in the memory or ken of all.

BIBLIOGRAPHY.—*Historical Records of The 91st Argyllshire Highlanders* (*now the 1st Battalion Argyll and Sutherland Highlanders*). From the formation of the Regiment in 1794 to 1881. By G. L. Goff, 91st Highlanders. With full-page coloured and other illustrations. [London : Bentley. 1891.]

Historical Record of The 93rd Sutherland Highlanders, now 2nd Battalion Princess Louise's Argyll and Sutherland Highlanders. By Roderick H. Burgoyne. [London : Bentley. 1883.]

History of the 1st Battalion Princess Louise's Argyll and Sutherland Highlanders. By Lieut.-Colonel H. G. Robley and P. J. Aubin. [Cape Town : Murray and S. Zeyer. 1883.]

The Prince of Wales's Leinster Regiment (Royal Canadians),

COMPRISING

1st Batt. (formerly) The 100th (Prince of Wales's Royal Canadian) Regiment.
2nd Batt. („) The 109th (Bombay Infantry) Regiment; with Militia Battalions.
3rd Batt. The King's County Militia.
4th Batt. The Queen's County Militia.
5th Batt. The Meath Militia.

THE PLUME OF THE PRINCE OF WALES.

A MAPLE LEAF.

TITLES.

1st Batt.

1761–63. The 100th (Highland) Regiment of Foot; disbanded.

1780–84. The 100th Regiment of Foot; disbanded.

1794–18[?]. The 100th (Gordon Highlanders) Regiment of Foot; the late 92nd, now 2nd Gordon Highlanders.

1805–19. The 100th (Prince Regent's County of Dublin) Regiment of Foot; disbanded as the 99th.

1816–18. The 100th (Duke of York's Irish) Regiment of Foot; raised as the 101st.

1858–1881. The 100th (Prince of Wales's Royal Canadian) Regiment of Foot.

2nd Batt.

1761–63. The 109th Regiment of Foot; disbanded.

1794–95. The 109th (Aberdeenshire) Regiment of Foot; disbanded.

1854–58. The Hon. East India Company's 3rd (Bombay European) Regiment.

1858–61. The 3rd (Bombay) Regiment.

1861–81. The 109th (Bombay Infantry) Regiment.

1881 (from). The Prince of Wales's Leinster Regiment (Royal Canadians).

The Prince of Wales's Leinster Regiment (Royal Canadians)—
continued.

PRINCIPAL CAMPAIGNS, BATTLES, &c.

* " Honours " on the Colours, the figures showing the Battalion concerned.

1761–62. Martinique.	1858. Ratgur.	1858. Koouch.
1761. Belle Isle.	1858. Barodia.	1858. Calpe.
1783. Carnatic.	1858. Sangor.	1858. Morar.
1812–14. Canada.	1858. Garrakota.	1858. Gwalior.
*1813. Niagara (1).	1858. Muddenpore.	1900. South Africa.
1857–58. Indian Mutiny.	1858. Betura.	
*1858. Central India (2).	1858. Jhansi.	

UNIFORM.—Scarlet with Blue facings (from formation with 1st Batt.: the 2nd Batt. wore White facings till 1881).

REGIMENTAL AND OTHER BADGES.—" The Plume of the Prince of Wales," " A Maple Leaf" (the late 100th was raised in Canada).

NICKNAMES.—" The German Mob " (of the 109th, from the number of Germans in the regiment when taken over from the Hon. East India Company). " The Brass Heads " (also of the 109th because, physique being good, they suffered little from the sun).

NOTES.—The 100th Foot was an expression of Canadian loyalty at the time of the Mutiny.

The Royal Munster Fusiliers,

COMPRISING

1st Batt. (formerly)   The 101st (Royal Bengal Fusiliers) Regiment.

2nd Batt. („   )   The 104th (Bengal Fusiliers) Regiment; with Militia Battalions.

3rd Batt.   The South Cork Militia.

4th Batt.   The Kerry Militia.

5th Batt.   The Royal Limerick County Militia.

" *Spectamur Agendo.*"

THE ROYAL TIGER. THE ARMS OF MUNSTER.

TITLES.

1st Batt.

1760–63. The 101st (Highland) Regiment of Foot; also Johnstone's Highlanders; disbanded.

1780–83. The 101st Regiment of Foot; disbanded.

1794–95. The 101st (Irish) Regiment of Foot; drafted.

1806–17. The 101st (Duke of York's Irish) Regiment of Foot; disbanded.

1759–1840. The Hon. East India Company's Bengal (European) Regiment.

1840–41. The Hon. East India Company's 1st Bengal (European) Regiment.

1841–46. The Hon. East India Company's 1st (Bengal European) Light Infantry.

1846–58. The Hon. East India Company's 1st (Bengal European) Fusiliers.

1858–61. The 1st Bengal Fusiliers.

1861–81. The 101st Royal Bengal Fusiliers.

2nd Batt.

1761–63. The 104th (King's Volunteers) Regiment of Foot; disbanded.

1780–83. The 104th Regiment of Foot; disbanded.

1794–95. The 104th (Royal Manchester Volunteers) Regiment of Foot; drafted.

1806–16. The 104th Regiment of Foot; disbanded.

1839–50. The Hon. East India Company's 2nd Bengal (European) Regiment.

1850–58. The Hon. East India Company's 2nd (Bengal European) Fusiliers.

1858–61. The 2nd Bengal Fusiliers.

1861–81. The 104th Bengal Fusiliers.

1881 (from). The Royal Munster Fusiliers.

The Royal Munster Fusiliers—*continued*

PRINCIPAL CAMPAIGNS, BATTLES, &c.

* " Honours" on the Colours, the figures showing the Battalion concerned.

1757. Chandernagore.
*1757. Plassey (1).
*1758. Condore (1).
*1759. Masulipatam (1).
*1759. Badara (1).
1760–61. Delhi.
1760. Wyndewash.
*1763–65. Gujerat (1).
*1764. Buxar (1).
*1774–94. Rohilcund (1).
1781. Porto Novo.
*1781. Sholingur.
1782. Arnee.

*1783. Carnatic (1).
1783. Cuddalore.
*1804. Deig.
1805. Bhurtpore.
1808. Macao.
1810. Amboyna.
1813–14. Canada.
1814–15. Nepaul.
1815. Java.
*1826. Bhurtpore (1).
*1839–40. Afghanistan (1).
*1839. Ghuznee (1).
*1845. Ferozeshah (1).

*1846. Sobraon (1).
*1848–49. Punjaub (2).
*1849. Chillianwallah (2).
*1849. Goojerat (2).
1851–53. Burma.
*1852–53. Pegu (1 & 2).
1857–58. Indian Mutiny.
*1857. Delhi (1 & 2).
*1858. Lucknow (1).
*1885–87. Burma (1).
1900. South Africa.

UNIFORM.—The 101st (when raised) wore Scarlet with Sky-blue facings, the latter being changed to Blue in 1846; the 104th have worn Scarlet with Blue facings throughout.

REGIMENTAL AND OTHER BADGES.—" A Shamrock." " The Royal Tiger." Also (since territorialisation) " The Arms of Munster." Motto, " *Spectamur agendo.*

NICKNAMES.—" The Dirty Shirts" (the 101st fought without the tunic at Delhi in 1857).

NOTES.—The two battalions received their titles in 1846 and 1850, for distinction in the Sutlej and Punjaub Campaigns respectively; the officers of the 104th being allowed to wear also a scarlet band in the forage cap for services in India.

BIBLIOGRAPHY.—*History of the Royal European Regiment, now the Royal Munster Fusiliers.* By Lieutenant-Colonel P. R. Innes. Illustrated. [London : Simpkin. 1885.]

The Royal Dublin Fusiliers,

COMPRISING

1st Batt. (formerly) The 102nd (Royal Madras Fusiliers).
2nd Batt. („) The 103rd (Royal Bombay Fusiliers) ; with Militia Battalions.
3rd Batt. The Kildare Militia.
4th Batt. The Royal Dublin City Militia.
5th Batt. The Dublin County Militia.

" *Spectamur Agendo.* "

THE ELEPHANT.   THE ARMS OF THE CITY OF DUBLIN.   THE ROYAL TIGER.

TITLES.

1st Batt.

1760–63. The 102nd (Queen's Own Royal Volunteers) Regiment of Foot ; disbanded.

1780–83. The 102nd Regiment of Foot ; disbanded.

1793–94. The 102nd (Irish) Regiment of Foot ; drafted.

1809–16. The 102nd Regiment of Foot ; raised in 1798 as the New South Wales Corps ; disbanded in 1818 as the 100th Foot.

1746–1830. The Hon. East India Company's European Regiment.

1830–39. The Hon. East India Company's Madras (European) Regiment.

1839–43. The Hon. East India Company's 1st Madras (European) Regiment.

1843–58. The Hon. East India Company's 1st Madras (European) Fusiliers.

1858–61. The 1st Madras Fusiliers.

1861–81. The 102nd (Royal Madras) Fusiliers.

2nd Batt.

1761–63. The 103rd (Volunteer Hunters) Regiment of Foot ; disbanded.

1781–83. The 103rd (King's Irish Infantry) Regiment of Foot ; disbanded.

1794–95. The 103rd (Loyal Bristol Volunteers) Regiment of Foot ; drafted.

1809–17. The 103rd Regiment of Foot.

1661–68. The Bombay Regiment.

1668–1839. The Hon. East India Company's Bombay (European) Regiment.

1839–44. The Hon. East India Company's 1st Bombay (European) Regiment.

1844–58. The Hon. East India Company's 1st Bombay (European) Fusiliers.

1858–61. The 1st Bombay Fusiliers.

1861–81. The 103rd Royal Bombay Fusiliers.

1881 (from). The Royal Dublin Fusiliers.

The Royal Dublin Fusiliers—*continued.*

PRINCIPAL CAMPAIGNS, BATTLES, &c.

* " Honours" on the Colours, the figures showing the Battalion concerned.

*1747–83. Carnatic (2).
*1747–83. Mysore (2).
*1751. Arcot (1).
*1757. Plassey (1 & 2).
*1758. Condore (1).
*1760. Wyndewash (1).
*1764. Buxar (2).
1764. Madras.
1764. Pondicherry.
1767–69. Mysore.
1778–80. Pondicherry.
*1780. Gujerat (1).
1780. Ahmedabad.

*1781. Sholingur (1).
1782. Arnee.
1783. Cuddalore.
1791. Bangalore.
*1791. Nundy-Droog (2).
*1792. Seringapatam (2).
*1793. Pondicherry (1).
*1810. Amboyna (1).
*1810. Ternate (1).
*1810. Banda (1).
*1817. Kirkee (2).
*1817. Maheidpore (1).
1819. Asseerghur.

*1821. Beni-Boo-Ally (2).
*1824. Ava (1).
*1839. Aden (2).
*1848–49. Punjaub (2).
*1849. Mooltan (2).
*1849. Gujerat (2).
*1852–53. Pegu (2).
1857–58. Indian Mutiny.
1857. Cawnpore.
*1857. Lucknow (1).
1900. South Africa.

UNIFORM.—1st Batt., Scarlet with Buff facings when raised, but the facings frequently changed—Blue, French Grey, White, and Blue; they are now (1900) Blue. 2nd Batt., when raised in 1661, the Sea-Green facings to the Scarlet uniform were adopted in compliment to Catherine of Braganza (Queen of Charles II.), Bombay being part of her dowry, and sea-green her favourite colour. The uniform and facings are now Scarlet and Blue.

REGIMENTAL AND OTHER BADGES.—" The Royal Tiger" (for Nundy-Droog in 1791), " The Elephant" (for Mysore), also (since 1881) " The Arms of the City of Dublin." Motto, " *Spectamur agendo*" (this for services under Lord Clive).

NICKNAMES.—" The Lambs" (of the 102nd Foot), " The Old Toughs" (for long and arduous service of the 103rd in India).

The Rifle Brigade (Prince Consort's Own),

COMPRISING

4 Batts., with Militia Battalions.

5th Batt. The Queen's Own Royal Tower Hamlets Militia.

6th Batt. The Royal Longford and West Meath Militia.

7th Batt. The King's Own Royal Tower Hamlets Militia.

SPECIAL DEVICE ON THE POUCH.

TITLES.

1800–2. The Corps of Riflemen; also Manningham's Sharpshooters.

1802–16. The 95th (Rifle Corps) Regiment of Foot.

1816–62. The Rifle Brigade.

1862–81. The Prince Consort's Own Rifle Brigade.

1881 (from). The Rifle Brigade (Prince Consort's Own).

The Rifle Brigade (Prince Consort's Own)—*continued.*

PRINCIPAL CAMPAIGNS, BATTLES, &c.

* "Honours" inscribed on the Pouch, &c.

*1801. Copenhagen.
1806. Buenos Ayres.
*1807. Monte Video.
1807. Copenhagen.
*1808–14. Peninsula.
*1808. Roleia.
*1808. Vimiera.
*1809. Corunna.
1809. Flushing.
*1810. Busaco.
*1811. Barrossa.
1811. Sabugal.
*1811. Fuentes d'Onor.
1811. Tarifa.

*1812. Ciudad Rodrigo.
*1812. Badajos.
*1812. Salamanca.
*1813. Vittoria.
1813. St. Sebastian.
*1813. Nivelle.
*1813. Nive.
*1814. Orthes.
1814. Tarbes.
*1814. Toulouse.
1814. Antwerp.
1814–15. Netherlands.
1815. New Orleans.
1815. Quatre Bras.

*1815. Waterloo.
*1846–53. South Africa (2 Honours).
*1854. Alma.
*1854. Inkerman.
*1855. Sevastopol.
1857–58. Indian Mutiny.
*1858. Lucknow.
*1874. Ashantee.
*1878–79. Afghanistan.
*1878. Ali Masjid.
*1885–87. Burma.
*1899. Khartoum.
1900. South Africa.

UNIFORM.—Green faced with Black (from formation).

REGIMENTAL AND OTHER BADGES.—None given in *Army List.* On appointments appear "A Maltese Cross," surmounted by "A Crown." Previous to 1830 a figure of "Fame" surmounted the Cross. At one time the badge was "A Bugle Horn."

NICKNAME.—"The Sweeps" (from its facings).

NOTES.—Formed in 1800 by detachments from various regiments. As King William IV. remarked, "What more can be said of you, Riflemen, than that wherever there has been fighting there you have been, and wherever you have been you have distinguished yourselves?"

BIBLIOGRAPHY.—*History of The Rifle Brigade (The Prince Consort's Own). Formerly The 95th.* By Sir William H. Cope, Bart. Illustrated. [London : Chatto and Windus. 1877.]

The West India Regiment,

COMPRISING

1st Batt. (formerly) Malcolm's Black Rangers: originally The Carolina Black Corps.

2nd Batt. („) The St. Vincent's Black Rangers.

3rd Batt. Authorised.

PRINCIPAL CAMPAIGNS, BATTLES, &c.

* "Honours" on the Colours.

1779. Savannah.	*1805. Dominica.	1853–55. Sabbajee.
1780. Charlestown.	*1809. Martinique.	1864. Ashantee.
1781. Hobkirk's Hill.	1809. San Domingo.	1865. Jamaica.
1781. Entaw Springs.	*1810. Guadaloupe.	1872. Orange Walk.
1794. Martinique.	1815. New Orleans.	*1873–74. Ashantee.
1794. Guadaloupe.	1815. Mobile.	*1887, 1892–4. West
1795. St. Lucia.	1823. Mahaica.	Africa.
1795. St. Vincent.	1848. Coomassie.	
1796. St. Lucia.	1853–54. Christenbourg.	

UNIFORM.—Zouave dress, Scarlet with White facings.

BIBLIOGRAPHY.—*A History of The 1st West India Regiment.* By Major A. B. Ellis. [London. 1885.]

The Royal Marines,

COMPRISING

Royal Marine Artillery; and Royal Marine Light Infantry.

THE GLOBE AND LAUREL WREATH.

TITLES.

1664–89. The Lord Admiral's (H.R.H. The Duke of York and Albany's) Maritime Regiment; also ranked as The 3rd Foot: drafted into The Coldstreams.

1694–97. Maritime Regiments: several raised and disbanded.

1702–13. Maritime Regiments: six raised, of which three were disbanded, the rest being now represented by The 1st Batt. East Lancashire, The 1st East Surrey, and The 1st Duke of Cornwall's Light Infantry; at the same time other regiments were placed on the Marine Establishment for sea-service—these regiments are now represented by The 2nd Gloucester Regiment, The Yorkshire, The Lancashire Fusiliers, The 1st Border, The 1st Royal Sussex, and The 2nd Worcester.

1740–48. Marine Regiments: ten raised and disbanded.

1755–1802. Marines: 50 Companies permanently established.

1802 (from). Royal Marines.

The Royal Marines—*continued.*

PRINCIPAL CAMPAIGNS, BATTLES, &c.

[It is impossible to instance more than the most distinguished of the varied services of this branch of the Army. Reference should also be made to the Regimental Records of Corps specially mentioned as having at one time served as Marines.]

1705. Gibraltar.	1775. America.	1840–1. Egypt.
1706. Spain.	1775. Bunker's Hill.	1840–2. China.
1708. Minorca.	1783. Gibraltar.	1845–9. New Zealand.
1708. Nice.	1797. St. Vincent.	1851–3. Burma.
1708. Ostend.	1797. Camperdown.	1855. Baltic.
1708. Sardinia.	1801. Copenhagen.	1855. Sevastopol.
1709. Nova Scotia.	1801. Egypt.	1858. Lucknow.
1709. West Indies.	1801. Teneriffe.	1860. China.
1709. Dunkirk.	1801. Acre.	1868. Abyssinia.
1741. Carthagena.	1801. Elba.	1874. Ashantee.
1746. Culloden.	1805. Trafalgar.	1882. Egypt.
1747–8. Aria-Coupang.	1807. Copenhagen.	1884. Nile.
1747–8. Pondicherry.	1807. Dardanelles.	1884–5. Egypt.
1747–8. Coromandel Coast.	1808–14. Peninsula.	1884–90. Zululand.
	1809. Flushing.	1887, 1892–4. West Africa.
1758. Louisbourg.	1811. Cape Lissa.	1900. South Africa.
1761. Belle Isle.	1812–15. America.	&c., &c., &c.
1762. Manilla.	1836–38. Spain.	
1762. Havannah.	1840. Syria.	

UNIFORM.—Scarlet with Yellow facings (1664); Red Waterman's Frocks with bright Yellow facings (1702); the 1740–48 contingents wore the usual red Waterman's frock with different facings and cloth caps for each regiment:—1st Regiment, Yellow; 2nd, Green; 3rd, Yellow; 4th, White; 5th, Yellow; 6th, Green; 7th, White; 8th, Yellow; 9th, Buff; 10th, Yellow. From 1755 to 1802 a Scarlet Uniform with White facings was worn, the facings being changed to Blue in 1802. At the present time the Royal Marine Artillery wear Blue with Scarlet facings, and the Royal Marine Light Infantry Scarlet with Blue facings.

The Royal Marines—*continued.*

REGIMENTAL AND OTHER BADGES.—"The Globe" with the Motto, "*Per Mare, per Terram.*" "The Crown—the Anchor and Laurel"—Her Majesty's Cypher, with the word "Gibraltar" (the latter for services at the various sieges).

NICKNAMES.—"The Little Grenadiers" (at Belle Isle the Corps wore the old-fashioned Grenadier caps of the earlier maritime regiments). "The Jollies." "The Globe Rangers." "Neptune's Bodyguard." "The Admiral's Regiment."

NOTES.—The Royal Marines rank next to The Berkshire Regiment.

BIBLIOGRAPHY.—*Historical Records of The Royal Marines.* Compiled and edited by Major L. Edye, R.M.L.I., Barrister-at-Law. Vol. I. 1664–1701. [London: Harrison. 1893.]

Historical Review of the Royal Marine Corps. By Captain Gillespie. [London: 1803.]

Historical Record of the Royal Marine Forces. By Colonel Nichols. [London: 1845.]

The Army Service Corps.

THE BADGE OF THE ARMY SERVICE CORPS.

TITLES.

1794.   Corps of Royal Waggoners ; disbanded shortly after.

1801–33.   The Royal Waggon Train ; disbanded.

1855–57.   Land Transport Corps ; disbanded.

1857–70.   The Military Train.

1870–75.   The Control Department.

1875–80.   The Commissariat and Transport Department.

1880–88.   The Commissariat and Transport Staff.

1888 (from).   The Army Service Corps.

SERVICES.—These are obviously to be found in English Military History *passim*.

UNIFORM.—Blue with White facings.

BADGE.—*See* above.

NICKNAMES.—" The London Thieving Corps " (*i.e.*, the initials of the Land Transport Corps of 1855–57).   " The Moke (or Muck) Train," or " The Murdering Thieves " (the initials of The Military Train of 1857–70) ; the first of the two because horses were exchanged for Spanish mules.

The Chaplain's Department.

MALTESE CROSS.

Motto : " In This Conquer."

UNIFORM.—As per *Regulations*, but seldom worn except on active service.

NOTES.—Chaplains first received commissions in 1662. The present Chaplain's Department was formed in 1858. The "relative rank" is—

Chaplain General to the Forces, as Major-General.
Chaplains of the First Class, as Colonels.
Chaplains of the Second Class, as Lieutenant-Colonels.
Chaplains of the Third Class, as Majors.
Chaplains of the Fourth Class, as Captains.

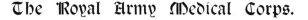

The Royal Army Medical Corps.

UNIFORM.—Blue with dull cherry facings.

BADGE.—See above.

NICKNAMES.—" The Licensed Lancers," " The Poultice Wollopers," " The Linseed Lancers," " The Pills."

NOTES.—The Army Medical Staff was organised in 1873.

The Ordnance Store Department and Ordnance Store Corps.

TITLES.

The Military Store Staff Corps.

The Ordnance Store Corps.

UNIFORM. —Blue with Scarlet facings and edgings.

BADGE.—The Royal Crest within a Garter, bearing the word " Ordnance."

NICKNAME.—" The Sugar Stick Brigade " (from the trimming on uniform).

NOTES.—The present department dates from 1875.

The Army Pay Department.

THE ROYAL CYPHER AND CROWN.

UNIFORM.—Blue with Yellow facings

BADGE.—On the pouches appears "The Royal Cypher and Crown."

NOTES.—Instituted in 1878.

The Army Veterinary Department.

UNIFORM.—Blue with Maroon velvet facings.

BADGE.—*See* above.

NOTES.—Instituted in 1881.

APPENDIX I.

A Table giving the Former Numbers and Territorial Titles of the Foot Regiments.

APPENDIX II.

BIBLIOGRAPHY OF REGIMENTAL HISTORY

Although each section, dealing with individual regiments, contains a bibliography it covers only those histories published prior to 1901. Since that date there have been many books published on the subject the majority of which are catalogued below. The list, however, concentrates on the regiments' history and does not include individual memoirs, pamphlets or small private printings commemorating anniversaries etc.

The Story of the Household Cavalry, by SIR GEORGE ARTHUR, 2 vols., Constable, 1909. 3rd vol., Heinemann, 1926

The Story of the First Life Guards, by C. W. BELL, Harrap, 1922

His Majesty's Royal Regiment of Horse Guards (The Blues), Gale & Polden, 1947

A History of the 1st Kings Dragoon Guards 1685–1929, Gale & Polden, 1929

A History of the King's Dragoon Guards 1938–1945, by D. McCORQUODALE, 1950

A History of the Queen's Bays (2nd Dragoon Guards) 1685–1929, by F. WHYTE & A. HILLIARD, Cape, 1930

A History of the Queen's Bays (2nd Dragoon Guards) 1929–1945, by W. R. BEDDINGTON, Warren & Son, 1954

The Story of a Regiment of Horse (5th Princess Charlotte of Wales' Dragoon Guards) 1685–1922, by R. I. POMEROY, 2 vols., Blackwood, 1924

The Inniskilling Dragoons, by E. S. JACKSON, Humphreys, 1909

History of the Royal Dragoons 1661–1934, by C. T. ATKINSON, Hale, 1934

The History of the Second Dragoons "Royal Scots Greys", by EDWARD ALMACK, Moring, 1908

Second to None, The Royal Scots Greys 1919–1945, by R. M. P. CARVER, McCorquodale

The Galloping Third: The Story of the 3rd. Kings Own Hussars, by HECTOR BOLITHO, Murray, 1963

4th Hussar: the Story of the 4th Queen's Own Hussars 1685–1958, by D. SCOTT DANIELL, Gale & Polden, 1959

The 7th. (Queen's Own) Hussars, by C. R. B. BARRETT, 2 vols. R.U.S. Institute, 1914

The History of the VIII King's Royal Irish Hussars 1693–1927, by R. H. MURREY, 2 vols., Heffer & Sons, 1928

Men of Valour (the third volume of the 8th's history) 1927–1958, by OLIVIA FITZROY, Tinling & Co., 1961

The Ninth Queen's Royal Lancers 1715–1936, by E. W. SHEPPARD, Gale & Polden, 1939

The Ninth Queen's Royal Lancers 1936–1945, Gale & Polden, 1951

The Historical Records of the Eleventh Hussars Prince Albert's Own, by T. WILLIAMS, Newnes, 1908

History of the Eleventh Hussars (Prince Albert's Own) 1908–1934, by L. R. LUMLEY, R.U.S. Institute, 1936

The History of the XII Royal Lancers (Prince of Wales's), by P. T. STEWART, OUP, 1950

History of the XIII Hussars, by C. R. B. BARRETT, 2 vols., Blackwood, 1911

Historical Record of the 14th. (King's) Hussars 1715–1900, by H. B. HAMILTON, Longmans, 1901

Historical Record of the 14th. (King's) Hussars 1900–1922, by BROWNE & BRIDGES, R.U.S. Institute, 1932

XVth. (The King's) Hussars 1759–1913, by H. C. WYLLY, Caxton, 1914

The History of the 15th. The King's Hussars 1914–1922, by LORD CARNOCK, Crypt House Press, 1932

History of the 16th/5th Queen's Royal Lancers, 1925–1961, by C. N. BARCJ Gale & Polden, 1963

A History of the 17th Lancers, by G. MICHOLLS, vol. 2, MacMillan, 1931

A History of the 17th/21st Lancers, 1922–1959, by R. L. V. FFRENCH-BLAKE, MacMillan, 1962

The Historical Memoirs of the XVIIIth. Hussars, by H. MALET, Simpkin, 1907

The Memoirs of the 18th (Queen Mary's Own) Royal Hussars, 1906–1922, by C. BURNETT, Warren & Son, 1926

History of the 13th/18th Royal Hussars, 1922–1947, by C. H. MILLER, Chisman & Bradshaw, 1949

The History of 15/19 The King's Royal Hussars, 1939–1945, by G. COURAGE, Gale & Polden, 1949

The History of the Royal Artillery, by J. R. JOCELYN, Murray, 1911

History of the Corps of Royal Engineers, 9 vols., Longmans/Royal Eng. Inst.

A History of the Foot Guards to 1856, by H. L. AUBREY-FLETCHER, Constable, 1927

The Grenadier Guards in the Great War of 1914–18, by SIR FREDERICK PONSONBY, MacMillan, 1920

The Grenadier Guards in the War of 1939–1945, by N. NICOLSON, 2 vols., Gale & Polden, 1949

The Coldstream Guards 1885–1946, 4 vols., OUP, 1928–1951

The History of the Scots Guards, by SIR F. MAURICE, 2 vols., Chatto & Windus, 1921

The Scots Guards in the Great War, by PETRE, EWART & LOWTHER, Murray, 1925

The Scots Guards 1919–1945, Clowes & Sons, 1956

The Irish Guards in the Great War, ed. RUDYARD KIPLING, 2 vols., MacMillan, 1923

History of the Irish Guards 1939–1945, by D. J. L. FITZGERALD, Gale & Polden, 1949

History of the Welsh Guards, by C. H. DUDLEY WARD, Murray, 1920

The First of Foot; the History of the Royal Scots, by A. MUIR, Edinburgh, 1961

The History of the Second, Queen's Royal Regiment, by J. DAVIS, vols. 1–3, Bentley & Sons, 1887–1895. Vols. 4–6, Eyre & Spottiswoode, 1902–1906. Vols. 7–9, Gale & Polden, 1925–1961

Historical Records of the Buffs, East Kent Regiment (3rd Foot) by C. R. KNIGHT & R. S. MOODY, 4 vols. Vol. 1, Gale & Polden, 1905. Vols. 2–4, Medici Society, 1922–1951

The King's Own: The Story of a Royal Regiment, 3 vols. Vol. 1–2, OUP, 1939. Vol. 3, Gale & Polden, 1957

A History of the Northumberland Fusiliers, 1674–1902, by H. M. WATTS, Murray, 1919

The Story of the Royal Warwickshire Regiment, by C. L. KINGSFORD, Country Life, 1921

History of the Royal Warwickshire Regiment, 1919–1955, by M. CUNLIFFE, Clowes, 1956

The Story of the King's (Liverpool Regiment) by R. THRELFALL, Country Life, 1917

A History of the King's Regiment, 1914–1919, by E. WYRALL, 3 vols., Arnold, 1928–1935

The Story of the King's Regiment, 1914–1948, by J. J. BURKE GAFFNEY, Sharpe & Kellet, 1954

The History of the Norfolk Regiment, 1685–1918, by F. LORAINE PETRE, 2 vols., Jarrold, 1924

The History of the Norfolk Regiment, 1919–1951, by P. K. KEMP, Regimental Assoc., 1953

The History of the Tenth Foot (Lincolnshire Regiment) by A. LEE, 2 vols., Gale & Polden

The History of the Lincolnshire Regiment, 1914–1918, ed. C. R. SIMPSON, Medici Soc., 1931

The Devons. A History of the Devonshire Regiment, 1685–1945, by J. TAYLOR, White Swan, 1951

The Devonshire Regiment, 1914–1918, by C. T. ATKINSON, Eland Bros., 1926

History of the 12th (The Suffolk) Regiment, 1685–1913, by E. A. H. WEBB, Spottiswoode, 1914

A History of the Suffolk Regiment, 1914–1927, by C. C. R. MURPHY, Hutchinson, 1928

The Suffolk Regiment, 1928–1946, by W. N. NICHOLSON, The Anglian Magazine, 1948

The History of the Somerset Light Infantry, 1685–1914, by SIR HENRY EVERETT, Methuen, 1934

The History of the Somerset Light Infantry, 1914–1919, by E. WYRALL, Methuen, 1927

1919–1945, by G. MOLESWORTH, SLI Reg. Comm. 1951

1946–1960, by K. WHITEHEAD, SLI Reg. Comm. 1961

The West Yorkshire Regiment, 1914–1918, by E.WYRALL, Bodley Head, 2 vols., 1924–1927

The East Yorkshire Regiment, 1914–1918, by E. WYRALL, Harrison & Sons, 1928

The 16th Foot. A History of the Bedfordshire & Hertfordshire Regiment by SIR F. MAURICE, Constable, 1931

A History of the 17th (The Leicestershire) Regiment, by E. A. H. WEBB, Vacher & Sons, 1911

The Campaigns and History of the Royal Irish Regiment, vol. 1, by G. LE M. GRETTON, Blackwood, 1911, vol. 2, by S. GEOGHEGAN, Blackwood, 1927

A History of 19th Yorkshire Regiment, 1688–1911, by M. L. FERRAR, Eden Fisher, 1911

The Green Howards in the Great War, 1914–1919, by H. C. WYLLY, 1926

The Story of the Green Howards, 1939–1945, by W. A. T. SYNGE, 1953

Regiment of the Line, The Story of the XXth the Lancashire Fusiliers, by C. RAY, Batsford, 1963

The History of the Royal Scots Fusiliers (1678–1918), by J. BUCHAN, Nelson, 1925

The History of the Royal Scots Fusiliers, 1919–1939, by J. C. KEMP, Maclehose, 1963

The History of the Twenty-Second Cheshire Regiment, 1689–1849, by W. H. ANDERSON, Hugh Rees, 1920

Twenty-Second Footstops, 1849–1914, by A. CROOKENDEN, Evans, 1956

The History of the Cheshire Regiment, 1914–1918 & 1939–1945, 2 vols., A. CROOKENDEN, Evans, 1948/49

The Story of the Royal Welsh Fusiliers, by H. AVRAY, Tipping, Country Life, 1915

Regimental Records of the Royal Welsh Fusiliers, 4 vols., Forster, Groom & Co., 1921/29

The Red Dragon; Royal Welsh Fusiliers, 1919–1945, by P. K. KEMP & J. GRAVES, Gale and Polden, 1960

History of the South Wales Borderers, 1937–1952, 5 vols., Hughes & Son, 1953/56

The King's Own Scottish Borderers, 1914–1918, by S. GILLON, Nelson, 1930

Borderers in Battle, 1939–1949, by H. CUNNING, Martin's Printing, 1948

The History of the Cameronians, 1689–1968, 4 vols., by S. H. F. JOHNSTON, H. H. STORY, C. N. BARCLAY, J. BAYNESS

The Royal Inniskilling Fusiliers, 1688–1914, Constable, 1928

The Gloucestershire Regiment in War, 1914–1918, by E. WYRALL, Methuen, 1931

Cap of Honour; the Story of the Glosters, 1694–1950, by D. SCOTT DANIELL, Harrap, 1951

The Worcestershire Regiment in the Great War, by H. FITZ-M. STACKE, Cheshire & Sons, 1929

The Worcestershire Regiment, 1922–1950, by LORD BIRDWOOD, Gale & Polden, 1952

History of the Thirtieth Regiment, 1689–1881, by N. BANNATYNE, Littlebury Bros., 1923

History of the East Lancashire Regiment, 1914–1918, by NICHOLSON & Mc-MULLEN, Littlebury Bros., 1936

History of the East Lancashire Regiment, 1939–1945, ed. G. W. P. N. BURDEN, Rawson, 1953

History of the 31st/70th Foot, East Surrey Regt. 1702–1952, 4 vols., by H. W. PEARSE, H. S. SLOMAN, D. SCOTT DANIELL

The History of the Duke of Cornwall's Light Infantry, 1914–1919, by E. WYRALL, Methuen, 1932

History of the Duke of Wellington's Regt., 1881–1923, by C. D. BRUCE, Medici Soc., 1927

A History of the Royal Sussex Regiment, 1701–1953, by G. D. MARTINEAU, Moore & Tillyer, 1955

Regimental History of the Royal Hampshire Regiment, 1702–1953, 3 vols. Vol. 1 & 2 by C. T. ATKINSON, vol. 3 by SCOTT DANIELL, Gale & Polden, 1955

A History of the South Staffordshire Regiment (1705–1923) by J. P. JONES, Whitehead, 1923

The Dorset Regiment, vol. 1 The 39th, vol. 2 The 54th, by C. T. ATKINSON, OUP, 1947

The South Lancs. Regiment (The Prince of Wales Volunteers) by B. R. MULLALY, White Swan, 1905

The History of the Welsh Regiment, 1719–1951, 3 vols., by A. C. WHITEHORN, T. O. MARDEN, J. DE COURCEY, C. E. N. LOMAX, 1952

The Black Watch, Cassell, 1903

A Short History of the Black Watch, 1725–1907, by A. G. WAUCHOPE, Constable, 1912

The Story of the Oxfordshire & Buckinghamshire Light Infantry, by HENRY NEWBOLT, Country Life, 1915

The Essex Regiment, 1741–1919, by J. W. BURROWS, 2 vols. (1923–1937)

The Essex Regiment, 1929–1950, by T. A. MARTIN, Essex Regt. Assoc. 1952

History of the 1st & 2nd Battalions The Sherwood Foresters, 1740–1914, 2 vols., by H. C. WYLLY (1929)

The Sherwood Foresters in the Great War, by H. C. WYLLY, Gale & Polden, 1924

The History of the Sherwood Foresters, 1919–1957, by G. N. BARCLAY, Clowes & Sons, 1959

The Loyal North Lancashire Regiment, by H. C. WYLLY, R.U.S. Institute, 2 vols., 1933

The Loyal Regiment (North Lancashire) 1919–1953, by C. G. T. PRESTON, Regt. H.Q., 1955

History of the Northamptonshire Regiment, 1742–1934, by R. GURNEY, Gale & Polden, 1935

The Royal Berkshire Regiment, by F. LORAINE PETRE, 2 vols., The Barracks, 1925

The History of the Royal Berkshire Regiment, 1920–1947, by G. BLIGHT, Staples Press, 1953

The Queen's Own Royal West Kent Regiment, 1881–1961, 4 vols., by H. D. CHAPLIN & C. T. ATKINSON

History of the King's Own Yorkshire Light Infantry, 1755–1948, 6 vols., by H. C. WYLLY, R. C. BOND, W. HINGSTON, G. R. ELLENBERGER (1926–1961)

The Eighty-Fifth King's Light Infantry, ed. C. R. B. BARRETT, Spottiswoode, 1913

The History of the King's Shropshire Light Infantry 1914–1918, ed. W. DE B. WOOD, Medici Society, 1925

The Story of the Duke of Cambridge's Own, by C. L. KINGSFORD, Country Life, 1916

The Annals of the King's Royal Rifle Corps, 5 vols., Smith, Elder & Co./Murray, 1913–1932

The Story of the Wiltshire Regiment (1756–1959), by N. C. E. KENRICK, Gale & Polden, 1963

History of the Manchester Regiment, by H. C. WYLLY, 2 vols., Forster, Groom & Co., 1923–1925

The York and Lancaster Regiment, 1758–1919, by H. C. WYLLY, 2 vols., Butler & Tanner, vol. 3, 1919–1953, by O. F. SHEFFIELD, Gale & Polden, 1956

The Durham Light Infantry, by W. L. VANE, Gale & Polden, 1914

Faithful; The Story of the Durham Light Infantry, by S. G. P. WARD, Nelson, 1963

Proud Heritage, The Story of the Highland Light Infantry, by L. OATTS, 4 vols. Vols. 1 & 2, Nelson 1953–1959, vols. 3 & 4, House of Grant 1961–1963

Seaforth Highlanders, ed. J. M. SYM, Gale & Polden, 1962

The Life of a Regiment; The History of the Gordon Highlanders, 5 vols. (1794–1945), by C. GREENHILL GARDYNE, C. FALLS, W. MILES. Vol. 1, Douglas, 1901, vols. 2 & 3, Medici Society, 1929–1939, vols. 4 & 5, Aberdeen U.P. 1958–1961

History of the Royal Irish Rifles, 3 vols. (1793–1948), by G. BRENTON ALURIE, C. FALLS, C. GRAVES. Vols. 1 & 2, Gale & Polden 1914–1925, vol. 3, Times Printing, 1950

The Royal Irish Fusilliers, 1793–1950, by M. CUNLIFFE, OUP, 1952.

The Connaught Rangers, 3 vols., by H. F. N. JOURDAIN & E. FRASER, R.U.S. Institute, 1924–1928

Crown and Company, The Historical Records of the 2nd Batt. Royal Dublin Fusiliers, 1666–1911, by A. E. MAINWARING, Humphreys, 1911

History and Campaigns of the Rifle Brigade, 2 vols., by W. VERNER, Bale Sons, 1912

The History of the Rifle Brigade, 1914–1919, 2 vols., by R. BERKELEY, W. W. SEYMOUR, Rifle Brigade Club, 1927–1936

The Rifle Brigade, 1939–1945, by R. H. W. S. HASTINGS, Gale & Polden, 1950

Britain's Sea Soldiers: a History of the Royal Marines, 3 vols., by C. FIELD, Lycean Press, 1924, Swiss & Co., 1927

The Royal Marines, 1939–1943, H.M.S.O., 1944

The Royal Army Service Corps. 2 vols., by J. FORTESCUE, R. H. BEADON, Cambridge U.P., 1930

A History of the Army Ordnance Services, 3 vols., by A. FORBES, Medici Society, 1929

A History of the Royal Army Veterinary Corps, 2 vols. Vol. 1 (1796–1919) by SIR FREDERICK SMITH, Bailliere, Tindall & Cox, 1927. Vol. 2 (1919–1961) by J. CLABBY, Allen, 1963